The
Becoming *a memoir*

The Becoming *a memoir*

Nicole Luongo

Memoir Series

Copyright © 2021 Nicole Luongo

Except for the use of short passages for review purposes, no part of this book may be reproduced, in part or in whole, or transmitted in any form or by any means, electronically or mechanically, including photocopying, recording, or any information or storage retrieval system, without prior permission in writing from the publisher.

The publisher gratefully acknowledges the support of the Canada Council for the Arts and the Ontario Arts Council. The publisher is also grateful for the financial assistance received from the Government of Canada.

Cover design: Val Fullard

Library and Archives Canada Cataloguing in Publication

Title: The becoming : a memoir / Nicole Luongo.
Names: Luongo, Nicole (Nicole M.), author.
Series: Inanna memoir series.
Description: Series statement: Inanna memoir series | Includes bibliographical references.
Identifiers: Canadiana (print) 2021024626X | Canadiana (ebook) 20210258969 | ISBN 9781771338134
  (softcover) | ISBN 9781771338141 (EPUB) | ISBN 9781771338158 (PDF)
Subjects: LCSH: Luongo, Nicole (Nicole M.)—Mental health. | LCSH: Mentally ill—Biography. | LCSH:
  Addicts—Biography. | LCSH: Eating disorders—Patients—Biography. | LCSH: Psychic trauma—Patients—
  Biography. | LCSH: Mental illness—Philosophy. | LCSH: Psychiatry—Philosophy. | LCGFT: Autobiographies.
Classification: LCC RC464.L86 A3 2021 | DDC 616.890092—dc23

Printed and bound in Canada

Inanna Publications and Education Inc.
210 Founders College, York University
4700 Keele Street, Toronto, Ontario M3J 1P3 Canada
Telephone: (416) 736—5356   Fax (416) 736—5765
Email: inanna.publications@inanna.ca Website: www.inanna.ca

"Mea Culpa, mea culpa, mea maxima culpa"

Parrhesia: The frankness, freedom, and openness that leads one to say what one has to say, as one wishes to say it, when one wishes to say it, and in the form one thinks is necessary for saying it…[Parrhesia] is linked to courage in the face of danger: it demands the courage to speak the truth in spite of some danger. And in its extreme form, telling the truth takes place in the "game" of life or death.

– Michel Foucault
The Meaning and Evolution of the Word Parrhesia
in *Discourse & Truth: The Problematization of Parrhesia*, 1999.

For those who may never have access to the words. Speak anyway.

Contents

1	INTRODUCTION
7	THE LETTER
15	PART SIX
51	PART FIVE
81	PART FOUR
113	PART THREE
163	PART TWO
207	PART ONE
253	And, Then…
261	*Acknowledgements*
263	*Notes*

Introduction

INTRODUCTION

To my knowledge, the following account is completely factual. But facts are tricky things. They twist, morph, and change over time. They transform before us as we unearth them from their burial sites and expose them to the light of day, realizing, once visible, they were safer underground. There are reasons why we run from facts.

I considered calling this *Too Pissed Off to Die: The Nicole Luongo Story*, but that implies my story will have ended, and I'm not sure I'm content with that. Whatever the case, this is all I have. I am thirty-two years old but going on one thousand. I am stretching my fingers through barbed-wire fences and pleading for someone, anyone, to stop for a moment and listen. I have not survived this long for my existence to die on a publisher's desk.[1] Nor have I survived to have others describe it for me. I would like to collapse, but I am standing. I am crooked, sure, and a little dizzy, but I am standing, nonetheless. I may need someone to prop me up.

My life has amounted to a series of unfortunate events. At times, it feels all I have known is pain. I have shuffled (been shuffled – passive tense is appropriate here) from institution to institution, all of which have promised to fix my eating disorder, my substance abuse, my Madness. When I began writing, I considered incorporating my medical records into my narrative. But imagining the thousands of documents I would have to wade through was debilitating, and I see now they would have undermined the purpose(s) of this – whatever this is. I am only just developing a sense of self. To do so, I cannot indulge what psychiatrist A at institution X has said about me. Their perception has differed from that of psychiatrist B at institution Y, whose perception has differed from that of psychiatrist C at institution Z, and so on. Over time, I have received virtually every diagnosis in the *Diagnostic and Statistical Manual of Mental Disorders*, fifth edition (DSM-5).[2] Depending on who you ask, I could be schizophrenic; I could be bipolar with psychotic symptoms; I could have borderline personality disorder; I could have a dissociative disorder; I could have obsessive compulsive disorder; I could have anorexia, bulimia, alcoholism, stimulant use disorder, ad infinitum. I could be or have any of these conditions, but ultimately, I am a person who is maybe strange, who is definitely hurt and, as a result, I behave as such – often.

The Becoming

What follows then is neither a justification for my actions nor an apology. Rather, it is a battle cry – an analysis of disordered eating, substance abuse, mental illness, and trauma that is informed somewhat by scholarship but is far from academic. I do not claim scientific objectivity and I do not wish to. I am emotional. I am irrational. I am nothing more and nothing less than someone who is in pain. I now want to understand why – on my own terms. Emotions, memories, and hope; each is fickle, unreliable, and un-generalizable, yet they are the closest I have to truth. What I say may resonate with some, may confuse or disgust others, and will invariably hurt a few. I accept this – I welcome this – because for over three decades, others have done the storytelling for me. Now it is my turn.

The one consistency in my writing is that time and space are rarely linear. I used to wonder why I wrote about one event, then digressed to another, then another, only to eventually return to the first. This is not an easy text, and while I feel the urge to explain this now, I should trust you (I am trying to trust you) to take from it what you need. You are invited to transpose your own meaning onto more ambiguous segments. All of – this – is purposeful, I think. I will note that my lack of written linearity reflects my inner world. Those of us who are devastated may not wish to remember (we may sometimes *need* to forget) and so memories become fragmented; fractured. So, too, do our subjectivities. There is nothing inherently wrong with this, and there are advantages to being a ghost, but in a society governed by time discipline and clock-watchers, shapeshifting can be difficult.

All that I ask is that you follow in earnestness. Have patience. What may originally seem obscure, out of place, or anecdotal will eventually make more sense. At least this is what I have told myself as I have written – as I have remembered. I have at times been frustrated with myself and been rife with self-doubt and criticism. Is this logical? Intelligible? Important? Or, as I so often feel, am I just a lunatic, a crazy person who is too cruelly optimistic to admit defeat?[3] That is for me to decide, but your opinion also matters. All of us wield power.

Madness is rarely politicized. The homeless person screaming, the disoriented junkie with crack pipe in hand, begging for change from passersby, and the emaciated teen hospitalized, tube-fed, still doing crutches when the nurses' backs are turned – I have been all of them, and I have been considered a leech on society, my loose morals and looser clothing indicative of pathology, nothing more. I have been insanity unencumbered, different people whose one commonality is her lack of autonomy. But health and normalcy are myths. And, with this text, I hope to play a small but meaningful role in changing how you too think about healthy and normal. Ideally, I would like to ameliorate the stigma associated with Madness, not by reifying it through a biomedical gaze but by meeting this gaze head on and calling it on its bluff. This is a tall order, and lest you think I am being selfless, know that irrespective of impact, I also need to speak for myself. For so long I have been bursting.

Throughout, I would like you to consider the transformative potential of survivor narratives. Rather than reduce us to symptoms, why not offer us a chance to tell you who we are? Our testimonies are invaluable but sorely lacking amid the knowledge produced by well-intentioned researchers and clinicians. And like the survivors themselves, these narratives are disorganized. Mad studies and antipsychiatry projects have subverted common-sense assumptions about mental illness by theorizing extreme, altered states; feminists have made admirable gains in de-mystifying eating disorders, while those leading body politics movements have contextualized our societal fear of fatness in anti-Black racism, colonialism, and capitalism; drug user activists have elbowed our way into policy and lay discussions about what addiction is, what it isn't, and what it could be, and we have arrived at much the same conclusions about the roots of the drug war as have fat activists and Mad people. We know that ignorance is structural, systemic, and interpersonal. Yet regardless of whether we approach these phenomena through neuroscience, constructionism, poststructuralism, or from the frontlines, these groups and our written output too rarely communicate. I yearn for cross-disciplinary solidarities because, as someone with all and none of these labels, who embodies all and none of these identities, I am tired of being incomplete.

For now, I will say this: When I began writing, I was separate. I contained multiple, competing parts that were strangers inhabiting a foreign not-quite home. This is the nature of trauma. As I reflect on everything that transpired before, during, and after writing, I am slightly more integrated. This is the nature of healing. I do not believe in healing as you may, but I have done something, and as I have done it, the urge to kill myself has ebbed. Before I die, I have things to tell you. I am still pissed off. To write has been arduous. To write has been painful. To write has been deeply cathartic and viscerally necessary.

And it all began with a letter.

The Letter

THE LETTER

Nov. 9, 2015

Meris,

There is a very calm, very definitive voice assuring me – the Real me, whatever that means – that things will be fine. It speaks for (the Real) me. This voice, however calm and definitive, though, is not soothing. It frightens me because it silences (the Real) me. I believe that it may be my mother's voice, or one of the many manifestations of my mother's voice that live inside me. These voices – the ones we began to visit on Friday, that emerged during my teenage years as my mother mocked me for my bulimia – are what have kept me marginally alive since getting sober. They have prohibited me from seeking help for my depression ("Stop being so ungrateful," they say, "look at all you have!"); they have berated me for having an eating disorder ("You're twenty-six and you're still doing this?," they say, "Come on, Nic"); and lately I believe they may have talked me through a series of psychotic breaks ("Enough with the attention seeking!" they say. I hear this even as I am in my apartment, alone and frightened, which signifies an internal incongruence of sorts).

(Here I hesitate to use a medicalized term like "psychotic break." Am I having a psychotic break, or am I beginning to respond very sanely to what feels like an impossible realization? Of course, "impossible realization" implies that I've arrived at some sort of Truth, when all I've done is filter and aggregate my lived experience [including the knowledge I've acquired through institutional engagement, which is always suspect] to produce a story that is intelligible. I could return to AA and six months from now I would believe that I'm merely being ungrateful [a 10-item gratitude list before bed each night is the solution to that, said treatment centres two and three; four agreed but offered a bit more intensive support, which is probably why I stuck around and allowed myself to be indoctrinated. Plus, Mom was being nice to me again, and that was always a goal when I agreed to this treatment shit]. Or is my brain so pliable that I am instead absorbing your anger toward my mother [and responding to the prompts you have been using to encourage my own anger] and constructing a logical narrative to explain my condition? Is anything real?)

When I say I feel like I am lying it is not because the details that I've shared are factually inaccurate. We both understand that I am hyperaware of my

Badness, and that I am fastidious about sharing only the Truth with you. But despite this, I often sense that you are misreading my Wellness. You are fond of me (I have endeared myself toward you; I have done this intentionally) and you believe me (I am not technically lying), so you logically conclude, based on what you know to be True, that I am reasonably okay. I am not reasonably okay.

Do you remember the other day when you said that you felt a bit hysterical? You weren't quite sure what to say, and I suggested that I show you a picture of Sean, instead? I believe the hysteria you experienced (the hysteria I live with constantly) is the feeling of having run out of options. I believe very deeply that I have run out of options, and I may have been so persuasive that I destabilized your own world view momentarily, even as you believe that I have not yet run out of options.

(Am I having delusions of grandeur? Am I still right?)

Due to this (very understandable – don't blame yourself for this) miscommunication, I fear I may have "tricked you" even as I have explained that I'm fearful of accidentally tricking you. This is really some meta mental illness shit we're dealing with (levity – levity is good right now) and I can't help but think that perhaps something else is going on (this could, of course, also be my mental illness not wanting to accept that I have mental illness).

Something that I have yet to mention (it's unfortunate we only have one hour because there is always so much to talk about) is that I've feeling myself getting into that taxi over and over ("that taxi" being the car that took me from the psych ward in Burnaby to the Downtown Eastside when I became homeless). I sense that something inside of me may have broken that day, and that experiencing that degree of rejection killed whatever it was that made me, Me. I come to see you and speak about feeling Bad and Broken and maybe even Evil, and this may be because I have no real identity. This sensation – that I have no baseline identity – is one I have brought up often. When I do, you reassure me that "Nicole" appears to be mostly stable, and yet I feel there may be other "Nicoles" who are not. These versions are as much Nicole as Nicole is Nicole, but discrete versions emerge based on her (my) environment. Each version seems reasonably cohesive, and thus no one else is aware of what is happening because each experiences his or her own consistent version of Nicole. Thus, I (Nicole?) am the only one who is aware of it.

Paradoxically, I believe that as I begin to Live again (that is, to let people in, whether that be through school or friendship or you or Sean), my lack of identity is killing me. It is not psychologically possible to maintain so many "truths" without breaking. Further, my multiple identities are beginning to collide. Through each of the social roles I now embody (former homeless youth, social scientist, daughter, friend, partner) I must navigate vastly different language, mannerisms, and epistemologies. Thus, I feel a sort of internal fracturing due to my inability to amalgamate widely disparate social role obligations. I don't yet know whether this fracturing is a manifestation of trauma – it requires multiple selves to endure that type of suffering – or whether a latent mental illness has emerged (they likely have a bidirectional relationship, but right now I am too angry and too confused to arrive at any sort of conclusion around that).

My uncertainty is further complicated by many of the theoretical approaches to mental illness that I endorse. How am I to know if I am normal? All each of us has to communicate our normalcy (or lack thereof) is language, and to date I have received little other than praise for my use of language. I am therefore led to conclude that I am at least Well, if not totally normal. And yet…

The irony here is that I am mostly concerned for my mother; concerned that if and when she reads this, it will break her. Despite all of this – and perhaps because of it – I believe my parents love me. I believe them when they tell me this, and to some extent, I return and am desperate for their love (you know this). Some things, however, may be more important than love.

I believe that I am having an extremely eloquent nervous breakdown. I believe this may be my only way to communicate (typically this is the conversation we have around behaviours such as biting, or hair-pulling) because I have so diligently trained myself to Hold it Together.

I am still Holding it Together.

(Later, when I try to explain this, all I will be able to say is that the words have a rhythm and I intuitively understand what must happen next; it is the same trance-like state I fall into while completing an assignment, but now it has taken on the urgency of life and death).

I believe that once I stop smoking pot, I will talk myself out of this. I believe I will convince myself that I was confused.

I am not confused.

I also believe that I am capable of convincing most people I am confused. Meris (and now Mark, who is currently reading this – Hi Mark) you both know that I am not confused. Please help me.

I believe that with the support of Sean (and you, [Meris], and you, [Mark]) I have managed to hold it together. I am still Well enough to seek help voluntarily, and to have a startling degree of lucidity around what is happening to me (previously, I had always been too distracted by external conflict – how can you discern whether your insanity is a product of mental illness when you live in a fucking war zone?). I have upwards of 95% in all my classes; I am stably housed; I have yet to hurt myself too badly.

One thing is very apparent: Bulimia is a tool I have used to stay alive. My primary diagnosis is not an eating disorder. Last night, after Sean left, I was extremely disoriented (I have been extremely disoriented for days). I wasn't able to follow him around like a lap dog and pretend to be okay, so I binged and purged at the airport and on the train home in order to hold onto my brain. This was a very conscious, very intentional decision. I do have willpower. I am now shaking very badly, and I feel very angry.

I start to explain things to you and it begins to hurt, but then something else comes up and this something else is also very urgent and this leads to another something that is of equal importance (because all of the things are connected) so by the time I have returned to my original point I have complicated things to such a degree that while I am very aware of what is happening (I am leading the conversation, after all) you are a bit dizzy and I become frustrated. I believe that you only experience one version of me (the version of me that is pre- and post-hurt), but I must do an enormous amount of invisible work to navigate between my selves.

I have now written this thing, and I have done so excitedly and frenetically, and it has all been Fast and Urgent and Good. As soon as I have finished, however, I am exhausted. I find this all quite silly, and just as quickly as I began, now the words have left me. This is a pattern within me. I need to describe it as it is happening because so much is happening – so much is happening, all at once – that I often forget to relay important things (things that would otherwise seem major, but, because there are so many things to keep track of, I cannot possibly remember each of). I am only human, after all. This is all so lonely.

I can no longer do the mental gymnastics required to make life tolerable. I am too tired. Every interaction feels like a performance and thus every interaction becomes a performance and I am getting so goddamn old.

Part Six

ONE

At twenty-six years old, I came undone.

It was late at night, the day after my partner, Sean, left for a six-month work trip to Australia. I had been high as a kite for weeks, when suddenly something went wrong.

Without my consent (or so it felt), I began to write. Midway through my suicide letter I texted Mark. I told him I was writing something important and asked him to read it *immediately*. Mark had once been employed by the homeless shelter I stayed at for nearly three years as a young person. He now lives back East, and our lives are antithetical. Still, Mark remains a trusted confidant. He was (is) one of the few people with whom I can be honest, even when my honesty is, for all intents and purposes, bat-shit crazy.

I'm not sure who called the cops first – Mark, myself, or my academic advisor who was the unfortunate recipient of the letter (Meris, the therapist to whom the letter is addressed, eventually saw it, though it's taken years to understand why I didn't send it to her directly). I know that after I realized what was happening – that is, after I realized the world was rolling backwards, voices rising into a violent crescendo and threatening to carry me away – I became intensely frightened. In the weeks prior I had been uncharacteristically drawn to Sylvia Plath, and in that moment the thought of being found dead of carbon monoxide poisoning seemed like a real possibility. Rather than turn on the oven, I dialed 9-1-1.

Before the cops arrived, I combed my hair, applied mascara, and calmly descended five flights of stairs. I waited – again, very calmly – to greet them. I knew the voices I referenced in the letter – the ones that, when I am particularly terrified and confronted with power imbalances, refuse to let me say or do anything to reveal my vulnerability – were in charge. I had the foresight to bring my laptop.

Understandably, the cops were confused. When they asked if I was Nicole I smiled, nodded, and told them cheerfully I was at once myself but also not *quite* myself. At some point during our conversation Mark called and asked to speak with the cops. "Nicole is very intelligent," he said, "Nicole will seem okay. Nicole must not be left alone."

By then I had spent several months working with Meris. Initially I had been hesitant to contact her, hesitant to destabilize the delicate equilibria I had maintained with relative ease since attending eating disorder and addiction treatment some five years prior. However, I sensed that while I was doing remarkably well behaviourally, the wounds I sustained in the first years of life had not fully healed. This was evident in a number of ways: My inability to eat in public; the obsessive weighing, measuring, and calorie counting that had started, once more, to consume me; the flashbacks; the nightmares. I had also spent nearly two years in a tremendous amount of physical pain. The severity of this pain defies language, but after months of dietary changes, emergency room visits, and puzzled stares from gastroenterologists, hematologists, and internal medicine specialists, each of whom told me that my test results were normal, one doctor suggested the pain could be somatoform. I had never heard the word, I did not like the idea, and I wished instead for ulcers, cancer, anything that could be detected through bloodwork and masked with medical marijuana. There is a lack of understanding within the medical community about somatoform disorders, particularly somatoform disorders that feel as though two fists have been inserted into your abdomen and are clawing at your ribcage while a third, knife-wielding hand stabs your spleen and a fourth pours acid over your pubic bone. The marijuana, along with the cocktail of anti-psychotics I was eventually prescribed, did not work. They did, however, induce sheer terror.

The younger cop, who was lean, bald, and tall, went outside to greet the paramedics as they arrived. I sat on the short, two-person bench in my lobby and spoke with the other as he did so. I have no idea what either of us said, but I remember feeling a combination of horror (*Oh my god, you are going to have to trust a cop*) and cautious optimism (*Oh my god, this interaction could be your first positive one with a cop.*) As a homeless teenager on Vancouver's Downtown Eastside I had learned that cops will handcuff you, steal your shit, and beat your friends. Later, as a sociology student, I learned that cops play an integral role in settler-colonialism, and that their primary role under capitalism is protecting private property. Needless to say, I did not like cops.

PART SIX

After reading Meris's dissertation and deciding I could trust her, I began telling her about my past. At first, I did so carefully (after many years of repression, the things one must do to support multiple addictions feel unspeakable). Before long, though, I started to share parts of myself I had forgotten existed. The details are not yet relevant, but you should know I spent weeks telling Meris I wished I could cry; I spent weeks telling Meris I wished I could scream. The night I sent the letter, I finally did both.

Two

When I came to, I was on all fours, back arched, *howling*, roughly twenty feet from where the cop still sat. I don't know how I got there or what the cop might have said to trigger such a violent reaction. I've concluded the guttural screams I heard, which were mine but sounded far away, were inevitable. I had been suppressing my emotions for so many years, in so many ways, that I had to erupt eventually. The older cop seemed disturbed and tried to shush me while the younger one, who held my laptop and had read the letter at my insistence, said nothing.

My next memory is of arriving at the hospital and being asked if I wanted to be committed voluntarily or involuntarily. At the time, to be given the option of voluntary commitment seemed ludicrous. I was utterly Mad. Still, after (calmly) inquiring about the long-term implications of voluntary versus involuntary commitment, I heard myself say that voluntary commitment seemed like the rational choice. I was sent to the waiting room, laptop in hand, and I was told to relax.

Next, I began to type field notes. I was in the first term of a two-year master's degree, and, though I had months to pick a topic, I was already fixated on my thesis. It would not be – it could not be – just a means to an end. It had to be remarkable. My life until then had been difficult, and, though I was not fully conscious of this, I saw writing a thesis as a chance for redemption. Doing so would channel my pain and fear into something useful.

That evening, the goings-on of the emergency room seemed rife with sociological significance. Racism, sexism, classism, ableism – all the "isms" – were everywhere, all at once, and, in preparation for my thesis, I felt I had to document them. My notetaking went unnoticed until a disgruntled man entered the waiting room some minutes or hours later. The man was Indigenous, rough around the edges, and flanked by security guards. I got incredibly agitated – security guards are, after all, rent-a-cops – and I intervened. This man, I realized, could be my first study participant. It was imperative that I interview him.

The video footage from that night has remained on my cell phone unwatched for over two years. When I review it now, I am instantly transported back, and I am reminded once more of the panic and helplessness I felt not just for myself but for the man, who explained he needed morphine for multiple sclerosis.[i] He was as distraught as I was, and after I obtained verbal consent to record him (I didn't fully know who I was or where I was or what I was doing, but I remained cognizant of research ethics, nonetheless), he told me about assaulting a man who was, in his words, "beating the shit out of his old lady." "She was bloody and crying," he told me. "I protect females," and then, after clenching his fists, stuttering, and beginning to murmur incoherently, "I keep slipping into... I keep slipping... I can't... " Here he puts his head in his hands and begins to rock back and forth, cradling his abdomen – "I just... can't."

I could relate.

After my laptop and cell phone were confiscated because recording strangers in the emergency room is illegal, I broke again. The guttural screams returned, only this time they were accompanied by a voice that begged someone – anyone – to tell me *what the fuck* was wrong with me. I was escorted out of the waiting room, and after a conversation that appears on my medical records, the on-call psychiatrist told me he "strongly suspected" I have borderline personality disorder. He told me this as I was being discharged, as, again, the world rolled backwards and the oven felt like a viable option. I said nothing, sobbed, and staggered toward the exit and into the frigid night wearing a t-shirt and pyjama bottoms but no shoes.

I didn't know it at the time – I wouldn't know it until I unravelled again, exactly two years later, this time thousands of miles away from home and far more catastrophically – but I was trying to heal.

---

[i] Racism in the Canadian-occupied territories' healthcare system is pervasive. On November 20, 2020, the government of British Columbia's Minister of Health Adrian Dix issued a statement of apology to Indigenous, Métis, and Inuit people following a months-long investigation by former judge and children's commissioner Hon. Dr. Mary-Ellen Turpel-Lafond. As per her report, healthcare in Canadian-occupied territories lacks cultural safety, non-Indigenous employees of the system regularly profile Indigenous patients, and many Indigenous people fear having to access care due to widespread racial and cultural prejudice.[1]

Three

Two years after writing the letter, I realize why I sent it to my academic advisor. To offer some context: I had entered university four years prior while still in extended care at an addiction treatment facility. I quickly realized that I was good at academics – very good at it – and I began to replace spiritual homework (e.g. prayer, meditation, asking for help) with literal homework. The latter was easier to excel at, and with it came the external markers of validation that I craved so deeply. After being homeless for nearly three years and self-destructing in horrific ways throughout, to receive A+ after A+ was concrete evidence that my life was salvageable. My parents also began to say they were proud of me, which felt more revelatory than anything a twelve-step program offered. I left treatment and gradually, imperceptibly, my dedication to recovery declined, while my dedication to academia took on a life of its own.

In my second term of university, I enrolled in an introductory sociology course. On day one, our professor greeted us and asked if we knew about Rat Park. When we shook our heads, he explained that experimental psychologists once researched addiction by keeping rats in stark, windowless cages made of sheet metal. Needles were surgically implanted into the rats' jugular veins, and they were provided with an infinite supply of heroin, morphine, amphetamines, or cocaine. Because the rats had to press a lever to release the substances, they had agency over how much or little they consumed. And, more often than not, they dosed themselves to death.

While the results of these experiments implied that some drugs are inherently addictive, Bruce Alexander recognized that animals become substance-dependent for reasons more nuanced than pharmacology. He designed his own cage, Rat Park, which was roughly two hundred times the size of the others and housed dozens of rats together. The cage also permitted the rats to eat, play, and socialize. Alexander conducted a variety of experiments over several years, but his main conclusion, that rats who are stimulated, comfortable, and purposeful are less likely to abuse substances than those who are not, can be applied to addiction in humans.[2]

I was stunned. The notion that changing a rat's behaviour could be accomplished by changing its cage was at once incredibly obvious and wholly profound. By describing Rat Park, my professor's intention was to demonstrate that negative mental and physical health outcomes may originate outside of and before the individual. For instance, there aren't higher rates of crack cocaine use in poor neighbourhoods because residents there are innately drawn to it. Rather, those born into poverty must contend with multiple external factors, such as stigma, racism, difficulty securing meaningful employment, lack of educational and recreational resources, high crime rates, and so on, that make temporary escape desirable. Having just spent six months in a treatment centre whose staff reminded me daily that I have a chronic, progressive disease rooted in selfishness and self-centredness, Rat Park offered an alternative paradigm through which to frame my experiences. I soon decided to become a medical sociologist, and, over the next four years, I unlearned everything treatment had taught me about eating and substance abuse disorders. I also ignored my own.

After excelling in classes, collaborating with professors on peer-reviewed publications, and working round-the-clock to make up for lost time, I completed my undergraduate degree. I lived alone, I had few friends and even fewer hobbies (beyond compulsively running and reviewing my meals, that is), but what mattered was I was smart. I planned to transition directly into a master's program, which I did, and in so doing, delay forming relationships. My impeccable grade point average more than compensated for my loneliness. Plus, after all of the damage I had done, mostly to my family, I still deserved to be punished.

However, the summer before I began my master's degree, I met Sean. I didn't mean to fall in love – I was busy and important, and love was always conditional – but every so often, one can't help these things. Our first date became a weekend, a weekend became living together, and it was so absurd and wonderful I yearned to do it forever. By the first week of my MA, I was incredibly confused: How could I want to be a professor, one whose research radically altered every societal misconception about eating and substance abuse disorders, and also want to drop out of school, move to the country, and raise foster children with Sean? Like me, Sean was ambitious. Like me, Sean was diligent. Unlike me, Sean prioritized happiness. I would watch almost anthropologically as he ate, slept, and was comfortable in his skin, but I could not participate. Ultimately, then, I sent the letter because my subconscious recognized that despite being sober, I was trapped in my own stark, windowless cage. Academic achievements were my drug of choice, and, after glimpsing Rat Park, I had to flee solitary and join in the fun.[ii]

[ii] After I sent the letter, my community psychiatrist, Phil, said that I had had a "psychotic break." He attributed my episode to biomedical aberrations induced by a combination of the antipsychotic medications I had been prescribed for my somatoform disorder and the effects of medical marijuana. As I will explain, while I don't doubt that my neurochemistry was altered, literature that frames psychosis as a response to existential distress has introduced new paradigms through which I interpret my experience.

For example, psychologist Dr. Paris Williams suggests that psychosis occurs when one's "existential dialectic" – that is, one's experience of oneself as a relatively secure, stable being – and one's "relationship dialectic" – that is, one's capacity to feel loved and accepted – are inconsistent. Falling in love (and being loved in return) after believing that I was inherently incapable of love was a profound rupture in the sense of self that I had spent years cultivating and had relied on to survive.[3]

Four

Two important things happened the night I sent the letter: First, I was put on academic leave. Second, Saphira, a spirited former coworker-cum-friend whose wildness softened me and opened my heart to magic, agreed to take me in. In many ways, it was a wonderful opportunity, one that I intentionally, albeit unconsciously, orchestrated. But I was still full of pride and fear. Rather than pause, reflect, and identify the lifestyle changes I could make, I kept running. It didn't help that for weeks afterward, I was hyperactive.

I thought and moved so rapidly that I could not vocalize my thoughts. Throughout, Saphira did everything she could to keep me safe. She made space in her bed (though it would be a while yet before I slept), she assured the cops who arrived at her door that I was not a danger to myself or others, and she promised me, even as I rambled maniacally in her bathtub and insisted that she film it, I wasn't going crazy.[iii] She rubbed my stomach, spoke to the pain, and, most importantly, did not judge my bingeing and purging. Roughly a month earlier, despite my work with Meris (or because of it) I had relapsed with bulimia. This was not my first relapse nor my last, but after five years of abstinence, it was by far the most devastating. I recognize now that my flashbacks were exacerbated by medical marijuana. I also recognize that one hour of talk therapy per week was not a sufficient way to cope with them. The unwanted memories were too vivid, too invasive, and relaying them to Meris was akin to fighting a forest fire with gasoline. I wanted to compartmentalize the hurt, force it into a tidy, coherent narrative, share that narrative between the hours of eleven and twelve

---

[iii] Since 2020, the high-profile murders of racialized and Indigenous people at the hands of police have contributed to an unusual degree of public support for defunding (or, according to more radical actors with whom I align myself, abolishing) them. Even many who still endorse policing have agreed that deploying armed officers during mental health crises is inappropriate, a position that is strengthened by the testimonies of surviving family members whose loved ones have been killed during "wellness checks." Whiteness has shielded me from the worst consequences of being Mad, formerly homeless, and a drug user, and when I reflect on my multiple police encounters over the years, I wonder if I would still be alive to write this were my skin a different colour.

on Tuesday mornings, and then strategically forget until the following week. Evidently, that's not how trauma works.

Every Tuesday, I would arrive at Meris's office and disclose one or more horrific truths but couldn't fully embrace healing. "How does the terror (or the revulsion, or the self-loathing) feel in your body?" Meris would ask, to which I always responded, sheepishly but truthfully, "There is only pain." I would leave Meris's office calm, satisfied after completing another item on that week's to-do list, but, over time, framing wellness as a task did more harm than good. The flashbacks escalated in severity, made sleep impossible, and demanded to be honoured. I now believe that had I simply allowed myself to grieve (which is easier said than done when you have spent a lifetime avoiding grief), I would not have had to start bingeing and purging or send the letter. Instead, I continued to smoke obscene amounts of pot, followed an increasingly restrictive meal plan, and when that no longer worked, fought the memories with bulimia.

Five

In addition to bingeing and purging, I spent the next days stumbling between appointments with Meris and Phil, a psychiatrist I had known while homeless who had witnessed my mania and could medicate me down. I hadn't spoken to Phil in years. I was also ambivalent about psychiatry but was spinning out of control and knew I needed to be tranquilized. I further connected with an advisor at Access and Diversity, my university's disability services department. This was a strict condition for my return, so while I felt more supra- than disabled, I attended our sessions regardless.[iv] Two years later it is difficult to describe how I felt then. My email correspondence indicates I was clearly under duress but I was also, all things considered, remarkably... sane. "Trying to be normal was killing me," I wrote to my advisor, followed by, "I'm not 'crazy,' per se, but until this point my life has been garbage. I'm pissed and I'm sad and this is what I had to do to stay alive," and, finally, "I'm so glad I figured this out a month into my master's degree so I don't have to get a PhD I don't care about." Given what has transpired since, that last sentence hurts like hell.

I wonder now how my life would have changed had I simply listened to the gentle but firm voices that have always guided me away from conventional indicators of success and toward genuine fulfillment. Writing this may help me figure that out. For now, I only know that bingeing and purging prevented me from being honest with myself. Because I was so fixated on acquiring food, consuming

---

[iv] Dorothy E. Smith's "conceptual practices of power" provides a framework through which to analyze how certain, subaltern positionings (e.g. "seriously mentally ill") are produced, transcribed, and reproduced within institutional settings. She describes how those who are given "definitional privileges" about a situation and what properly responsive conduct to it should be engage in a "cutting out" of the relevant extraneous factors that inform this situation. For example, at school, the bureaucratic requirements that my episode be documented through a structured questionnaire, condensed into a brief summary by a disability services advisor, and shared with my professors constructed a singular narrative, one that necessarily concealed motivations for my behaviour that were not easily identifiable as "mentally ill type." However, by making visible the practices that allow disparate actors to arrive at a particular meaning, some of which I try to accomplish here, one can unsettle or problematize the authority of the account.[4]

food, and expelling food, my inner wisdom was muffled by the relentless commands (*Keep going – get it out*) and vitriolic observations (*You're a sick Fuck; a pig*) of active bulimia. I now see how closely my bulimic voice resembles that of my mother, whose response to my eating disorder, particularly bulimia, has always been disgust. I've also learned that bingeing and purging doesn't appease the voices – it aggravates them. Simultaneously, the rhythmic cycle of food-in, food-out is tangible, corporeal, an anchor to reality when I'm disembodied. This in part is why it is so addictive. Bulimia may induce or exacerbate pre-existing psychotic symptoms, but it is also how I best cope with these same symptoms. Regardless, because the voices were so rapid and so multitudinous, I couldn't discern fact from fiction, love from fear. My subconscious understood that getting a master's degree would not fix me, but I remained tethered to academia because – amid the chaos – it was all that still made sense. Because of this, despite being explicitly advised not to, both by my advisor and psychiatry, I started writing my thesis.

Six

My frantic writing lasted for weeks, carrying on despite not having conducted any research. Remember, this couldn't just be any thesis – it had to be the best, most influential thesis a master's candidate had ever produced. I decided to write about how the intergenerational transmission of trauma manifests in disordered eating, substance abuse, and psychosis. These are broad, interdisciplinary topics that would need to be refined substantially to be viable for a book-length manuscript, let alone a master's paper. However, the glut of literature I had at my disposal in both the social and biomedical sciences did not deter me; it just sped me up. By then I should have known (and I would have, had circumstances been different) that being one's own research subject, particularly when one is too unstable to conduct research, is dangerous. But because my professors had been told not to respond to my emails, and because by December I was halfway across the world, I wrote (and wrote and wrote) unencumbered. I had booked a trip to Australia months earlier, after Sean had gotten hired. During the days, he worked while I wrote, and at night we delighted in the shimmering sand dunes, mountain ranges, and my lack of inhibition. I imagine Sean knew I was unwell. He had seen my chaotic affect, heard my disorganized speech, and, based on what I know of him, may have found them exciting. It's not that Sean fetishized my Madness, exactly, so much as he didn't question whether my boisterousness, hypersexuality, and disinterest in boundaries were temporary displays of something serious and sinister. I do not blame him for this – I am rocket fuel when I'm manic – but I do feel sorrow when I realize that throughout my life, men have seen me as a trope.

Something I should also mention (something I would prefer not to think about, let alone disclose) is that the insights I was having – *I'm not crazy, I'm just traumatized! My childhood* was *abusive! Mom and Dad have been gaslighting me! Fuck their privacy, I deserve to be angry!* – felt so enormous, so profound, that they spilled onto social media. I became a demented virago, once utterly obsessed with attaining my parents' approval, now determined to bring my family to its knees. By this point, I had been confused for the better part of twenty years. As a child

The Becoming

I had tip-toed around my father, the volatile son of Italian immigrants whose explosive outbursts kept me awake at night, straining to hear if he was hurting my mother. After developing bulimia and recognizing how controlling my mother was, how unrelentingly cruel she could be, I began to see myself in my father and to empathize with him. More often than not, I wished to hurt Mom, too. That said, neither of my parents has ever received a mental health diagnosis (neither of my parents has ever dared ask), and each has adeptly performed normalcy; has place-made in suburbia; has stayed there while I have binged, purged, drank, drugged, and cycled endlessly through treatment centres, homeless shelters, and mental institutions. The world should know, I told myself, what has been done to me. The world should know, I told myself, this is not my fault. Social media became my diary and the more attention I received, the more I had to say. At last, I thought, people will understand.

A funny thing happens when you air your family's dirty laundry. You quickly realize there is more of it than you thought. One load leads to two, two becomes three, three becomes four until finally your grandparents, cousins, aunts, and uncles – each has sidled up beside you at the laundromat with secrets of their own and wants to swap, borrow, lend them as if exchanging fabric softener. I do not suggest imploding on social media – I still flush with shame when I reflect on the grandiosity, verbosity, and sheer arrogance that I displayed – but after being so tightly wound for so many years I didn't see (or care) that I was causing harm. I just knew that publicly unravelling was cathartic. I was not okay, I had never been okay, and now, I thought, the world would know who was responsible.

Another funny thing about airing your family's dirty laundry: as quickly as they become engrossed in it, people forget. When I returned from Australia there were no rounds of applause at the airport. There were no angry mobs waiting, fists raised, torches lit, ready to storm my parents' mansion and exact revenge. There was only my father – depleted, weary, and willing to buy me groceries. A third funny thing about airing your family's dirty laundry, I suppose, is that once it's over – once the Facebook posts have been deleted and the sedatives have been injected and you've slept for more than an hour – your family, though disgusted, will still be your family. Dad didn't say much on the way home. Neither did I. Then, before he dropped me off at the apartment unit that he and my mother owned – the one I lived in, studied in, and destroyed myself in – my father offered to buy me binge food.

Seven

I'll clarify here that while my father knew or suspected that the hundreds of dollars' worth of groceries he bought that day would be regurgitated, we had co-signed an unspoken agreement to overlook my bulimia. This agreement had been established while I got into daily altercations with my mother as a teenager over which food belonged to whom and who had the right to do what with it. Back then, I would hide in the bushes after leaving for school and wait, nestled between moss-covered tree stumps, growing increasingly agitated as I pictured the cakes, cookies, and half-cooked slabs of meat I would soon devour. My mother always left after my father, and until she did, I would crouch, atrophied muscles aching, pulse racing, watching tiny ants swerving in zig-zag patterns on the ground. After what felt like years but was never more than minutes, I would return to the house; let myself in; disappear.

Hours later (without fail, every day I would be stunned at just how many hours had passed), I would come to, take stock of what was missing, consider replacing it, curl up in bed, instead.

Before long, my mother saw what I was doing. She worked less, changed the alarm code, and bought a combination lock. The lock lived on the refrigerator, and, at first, she covered it with a dish towel before company came over. Later, she left the lock exposed, and I watched her tell friends and relatives, between heavy sighs, forlorn glances, and crocodile tears, that her daughter was untrustworthy. Attached to the lock was a blue and green bungee cord. My mother stretched the cord from the refrigerator, upwards, across the pantry, and onto the door of the cupboard directly adjacent the pantry. Our food supply became contraband, off limits to those who could not consume appropriately. The bungee cord – its colours, its texture, the way it chafed my forearm as I wriggled my fingers through the small crack between the pantry door and the wall, searching for sustenance – is imprinted in my memory.

Bulimia radically altered our household dynamic. Whereas my mother, a registered nurse, was once a fragile victim of my father's erraticism, my eating disorder empowered her by thrusting her into the role of medical authoritarian. Her expertise in all things physical became the focal point of our interactions, and rather than approach me as a concerned mother ought to – with love and perhaps even some compassion – she tried educating me into wellness. First, I arrived home to pamphlets on my bed about tooth decay, esophageal cancer, and cardiac arrest. Then I arrived home to pocket checks, bag searches, and a room that had been turned upside down and cleared of hidden binge food. To her I was a spoiled, careless glutton. To me, she was an ignorant, insensitive dictator. Each of us had acid tongues.

Throughout this, my father, a secondary school teacher, faded into the background. During my formative years, his moods had been cyclical. He was uninhibited, convivial, giddy to the point of elation for days or weeks or months on end. Then his disposition would darken, and his good-natured jokes would become imbued with malice before stopping all together. Finally, after days or weeks of anxious anticipation, my father would morph into a monster, his impetuous rage directed first toward my mother and then me, as I tried vainly to defend her. After developing bulimia and then alcoholism, I reflected on my childhood and reconciled old beliefs about my father – that he was resentful, capricious, a villain – with new beliefs about my mother – that she was neurotic, suffocating, a tyrant. I became my father, and in so doing I replaced him in the dysfunctional dyad that was my parents' marriage. This was not a coincidence. My mother has since observed that my difficulties brought my parents together. She has noted that after years of tension, my bulimia seemed to pacify him. What I have never said to my mother – what I have never been able to articulate, at least in a way that she will hear, that is – is that bulimia pacified my father because my mother, for once, had someone else to nag.[v]

---

[v] Although there is no consensus on the role that family dynamics may play in the development of eating disorders, some research suggests that families of adolescents with anorexia nervosa tend to display high levels of interpersonal boundary problems, enmeshment, rigidity, and poor communication, whereas families of adolescents with bulimia nervosa tend to display high levels of chaos, family conflict, and distress. Although these are just a few possible correlates of eating disorder symptomology, and it would be reductive to attribute my eating disorders solely to my parents, it's worth noting that my family did regularly display patterns associated with both adolescent anorexia and bulimia.[5]

For what it's worth, my father's feigned naiveté preserved our relationship. After I became homeless, he would visit me from time to time. We wouldn't talk much, but he would buy me groceries. After I left addiction treatment in 2011 and moved into the apartment unit I picked out and my parents bought for me, he still visited. We wouldn't talk much, but he would buy me groceries. My father did not grow up in abject poverty, but I have inferred that his material and emotional needs often went unmet. And, while I can't know for sure what of his temperament is inherent versus learned, I do know that to my father, and to the majority of my family, particularly the Italian side, food is synonymous with love. When I stepped off the plane in Canada, my father's presence (and, more specifically, his suggestion to go get groceries) was his way of telling me he cared – that he was extending an olive branch. In return, I welcomed his care, snatched the branch, and like a petulant child being sent to bed before supper, lit the branch on fire and gleefully watched it burn.

EIGHT

In January of 2016, things got dark quickly. The body can only sustain extreme activation for so long until eventually and inevitably it comes down. Hard. I had been abstinent from bulimia in Australia, but while there I could feel a sense of foreboding hanging over me like a cumulonimbus cloud, one whose presence reflects atmospheric instability and suggests a storm is brewing. Even as I surfed, socialized, and wrote (and wrote and wrote), I knew my eating disorder was biding time until it could re-emerge the moment I stepped on Canadian soil, and ruthlessly at that. However, even more concerning than bulimia was that three days before I departed, for the first time in nearly five and a half years, I decided to get drunk.

The folks in Alcoholics Anonymous tell you relapsing is not a choice. Through a combination of dated biomedicine and quasi-religion, the program frames alcoholism as a hopeless condition of mind and body, one that prompts the alcoholic brain to convince the alcoholic, as if the two are distinct entities, to drink. One's only chance, according to the Big Book, is to engage in a rigorous process of repentance and sacrifice that mirrors Christian confession. And at twenty-six, I was done with this. I couldn't fully articulate why ("I don't like the god thing," I would tell AA members when I saw them in the community) but intuitively, I knew that constant reminders of my powerlessness were not the "help" I needed.[vi] I had been rendered powerless long

---

[vi] The "Big Book" of Alcoholics Anonymous (tellingly referred to as the "AA Bible") was originally published in 1939. While the text frames alcoholism as a chronic, progressive disease, it departs from today's medicalized accounts of addiction and is imbued with religious undertones. Throughout, we see the cultural categories of illness and sin converge, a trend that the current "disease model" of addiction manifestly rejects through its emphases on genetics, psychopathology, and neuroscience.

The more recent focus on the body-mind as a site of innate physiological pathology ostensibly reduces stigma by eliminating the prospect of "making bad choices" when it comes to substance use. However, not only does labelling one as "diseased" trigger social processes that lead to status loss and elicit assumptions of dangerousness and incompetence, the elimination of the perception of choice has been incomplete, at most. Specifically, neoliberalism informs the ways we individualize social problems such as poverty and addiction. For those who are visibly marginalized at the intersections of poverty and

before finding alcohol. Thus, when I drank in Melbourne, I told myself I was doing so of my own volition. I still say this, but as you will soon learn, my definition of volition has expanded to accommodate two realities – that of being an agent, and that of my agency sometimes emerging from parts of me whose motivations are obscured, at least until I have burst into flames and incinerated everything/one/where in my path.

That evening, Sean was apprehensive. "I don't think this is a good idea," he murmured as we waited for our drinks to arrive at the restaurant where it began. "Are you sure about this?" he asked as we bought bottles of wine at the liquor store afterward. But he was also intoxicated, and I sincerely promised I would not return to active addiction. Three days later, the moment my father left me in my (his) apartment, I dove into the weeks' worth of groceries he had just purchased, and between episodes of bingeing and purging, I revelled in the elation of getting to sate my thirst.

As I reflect on my rapid descent back into alcoholism, I see very distinctly that my decision to drink in Melbourne was informed by my eating habits. Just as I was incapable of abstaining from academia, the prospect of bingeing and purging once home marred my judgement to such a degree that even after three rounds of addiction treatment, half a dozen stints in detox, and countless alcohol-related psychiatric admissions, I believed I could drink normally. I still have no idea what normal drinking is, but I'm fairly certain that even the most hopeless inebriate would have deemed my alcohol intake over the next several months to be far from it.

In January, I also went back to the master's degree that I knew, deep down, wasn't a solution. I was already bingeing and purging incessantly, and within weeks I was also drinking before, during,

---

substance use status, institutionalized support revolves around compelling people to embark on self-improvement projects (what Erin Dej refers to as becoming an "entrepreneurial subject"), which requires accepting responsibility for one's social precariousness. Thus, the discourses that circulate shelters, treatment centres, and society more generally are logically inconsistent (e.g. "Addiction is a disease that no one gets on purpose or has control over, *and* the choices one makes while in addiction, including to not recover, are solely the addicted person's fault") and reframe inequalities as "consequences." We haven't moved that far from seeing people as "sinners," after all.[6]

and after classes. Sean would be in Australia until April, so I had free rein over the apartment, free rein over the food that entered and was expelled from my body, and free rein over the liquor I consumed. My life devolved into chaos, and maintaining a facade of stability grew increasingly difficult, particularly given how hard my body crashed. Weeks of euphoria had depleted me of the neurotransmitters responsible for mood regulation, such that my legs, which only days prior had frolicked through sand dunes, hiked up mountain trails, and sprinted down white sand beaches, no longer functioned. In addition to enrolling with disability services, a stipulation for my return was that I regularly reviewed my progress with the department head. I did not mind these meetings, and the professor with whom I spoke was nothing but supportive. But, given my condition, getting to them was agonizing. Each morning, I had to mentally prepare to make the three-block commute from my apartment to the bus stop. I would pause more than a few times on benches and curbsides to massage my legs, groaning and pleading with them to please, just keep going. The fact that I was consuming upwards of twenty-six ounces of hard liquor, a depressant, each day did not help. Neither, of course, did bingeing and purging.

Long before I was cognizant of it, I employed food as a mood stabilizer. As a child, I knew that restricting my intake made me feel powerful and in control of... something. I am now aware that although self-starvation serves many purposes, some of which I will return to later, I am corporeally drawn to it because it induces mania. It is a free stimulant, even stronger than cocaine, and, of equal importance, obsessing about calories, fat grams, and number of hours between each meal suppresses unpleasant memories. While ruminating on my intake, I simply lack the cognitive space for more nefarious thought. Bulimia, on the other hand, is both an upper and a downer. Fantasizing about bingeing, purchasing binge food, and setting this food *just right* in front of me is tremendously exciting, and the delight this ritual induces is more comparable to the effects of smoking crack. Tunnel vision while ingesting hit after hit of sugar is relieving and sublime. That said, as with any addiction, bulimia's return on investment is brief. The first binge of the day is always the most rapturous. Subsequent binges feel more and more like chores, until consuming becomes a task I must complete because tomorrow will be different, and I need to get all the food in, now, and then out, now, while I have the chance. After a long day of bulimia, I am depressed, exhausted, and so full of self-hatred I will do anything to alter my mood. I level myself out again by getting drunk and high.[vii]

After returning from Australia, I needed the surges of energy produced by bingeing and using substances. Other than going to campus, buying food, alcohol, and, eventually, cocaine, was the only way to get myself off the couch. At the same time, beating the shit out of myself prolonged the comedown and exacerbated the psychological and physiological implications of severe depression. As has historically been the case, then, my solutions to a major problem were major problems in and of themselves. I was in hell, and I didn't see a way out. I told myself that Sean would reinvigorate me when he got home. With his support, I would sober up, stop bingeing and purging, and be the chipper, sexy, spontaneous version of myself he had fallen in

---

[vii] The relationship between co-occurring eating and substance abuse disorders has been well-documented since the 1970s. For example, Niva Piran and Tahany Gallada analyzed a large, nationally representative sample of Canadian women using data collected by Statistics Canada in the Mental Health and Well-being cycle 1.2 of the Canadian Community Health Survey (CCHS). They concluded that alcohol dependence and interference were significantly associated with eating disorder symptoms, while there were significant associations between risk for eating disorders and life-time dependence on illicit drugs.[7]

However, while some research samples from populations that have been formally diagnosed with either anorexia, bulimia, or anorexia and bulimia, fewer studies identify correlations between specific forms of disordered eating and specific categories of substance use (e.g. whether someone with anorexia and/or bulimia is more inclined to abuse stimulants or depressants). These possible relationships are further complicated when one considers the potentially confounding influence of the presence of one or more mood disorders. In my experience, mania is a desirable (albeit frightening) state that I have historically induced, depending on contextual factors, via self-starvation, bingeing and purging, and stimulant use. When I become *too* activated, however, alcohol and opioids become mechanisms to resume equilibrium. In other words, disordered eating may replicate the neurophysiological effects of substance use. More research is needed on the embodied experiences of these phenomena, as both quantitative and qualitative work tends to emphasize prevalence rates, theoretical advances in locating disordered eating specifically as feminist empowerment or, in opposition, as a response to systemic "fatphobia." Much less work examines how these behaviours actually feel.

love with. Sean, however, was not informed of this plan, nor did he consent to it, and I soon learned that having multiple selves does not bode well for romance.

Nine

Sean arrived in Vancouver on April 1, 2016 – April Fool's Day, which fits because, in some ways, our relationship was a joke. It was sincere, yes, but it was also too rapid, too fuelled by lust, and far too optimistic. I wasn't accustomed to optimism, and I was frightened by the enormity of my need for him. He hadn't yet met my darkness. By mid-May, Sean was gone. Not out of the country or the city, mind you, but gone from the vision I had had for a future. The devastation was familiar – cathartic, even. All my life, be it with partners or family or food or flesh, I have yearned for the ache of absence.

For our reunion, I bought a costume to wear to the airport. After three months of intensive self-abuse, I knew a tight skirt and sheer blouse wouldn't conceal the bags under my eyes, my swollen lymph nodes, or my visible weight gain. Still, I tried. I tried to appear normal, whatever that means. I tried to pretend that nothing had changed, and that I was still charming, exuberant, and fun. I tried so hard, but despite a lifetime of acting, my performance was subpar. Sean saw through my props – the makeup, the clothing, the forced voice inflections that emulated mania – and knew right away he was in bed with a fraud. I was a grotesque caricature of the woman I had been the year before and was too defeated to care. It didn't help that the mask I wore was marred before I put it on.

It is not hyperbolic to say I have done exquisitely terrible things. The majority of these things – exploiting my grandmother, who had Alzheimer's disease, for tens of thousands of dollars, so relentlessly that my mother finally filed a restraining order to prohibit me from seeing her, for instance – I have not regretted. Active addiction is earth shattering. It invades you, engulfs you, and overrides any moral qualms you once had about lying, stealing, and becoming either someone else or yourself, depending on how you perceive it. This is what I have always told myself, anyway, whenever guilt has crept in, that the things I have done to secure food, booze, *reprieve*, are warranted because life has been unfair. Life *has* been unfair – it has been unfair in ways that are systematic, sustained, and have extirpated the obligation I once felt to engage in the social contract – but I am also re-evaluating this excuse, this complete unwillingness to be accountable for my actions. Again, my thoughts on volition are fluid. Part of grappling with this is admitting that I cheated.[viii]

I genuinely can't recall what I was thinking the night I slept with my ex. I wish I had a valid excuse, a compelling reason beyond, "Sean was in Australia, I was scared, and I was in an altered state," but I don't. Sean was in Australia. I was scared. I was in an altered state. My ex, Steven, and I are very much alike, and together we are destructive. Since I am more untethered, he has been able to justify our dynamic by positioning himself as my rescuer. He rescues while he berates, this seeps into our sex life, and, while there is much to unpack there, I will just say that until now, I haven't had to justify anything because feeling good is enough when one has learned to unlearn shame. That said, sleeping with Steven had consequences even I could not ignore.

I know I woke up after it happened feeling ill. I drank immediately. I also know I mentioned my betrayal to the bartender of the local pub, whom I met while purchasing and then snorting rail after rail of powder cocaine while barricaded in the pub's one decrepit bathroom

---

[viii] About my relationships, I have resonated with theories that draw broad parallels between interpersonal interactions and theatrical performances. Sociologist Erving Goffman's "dramaturgy," for instance, compares life to a play. He purports that humans consistently negotiate and re-negotiate "reality" via "impression management" (conscious or unconscious attempts to influence ways in which others see us by strategically withholding or revealing information). To do so, we employ "props," "masks," other tools, and, like Sean and I were doing by not explicitly discussing my transgression, may also engage in "teamwork" to uphold a certain, preferable version of "reality." In this way, every social interaction may be considered artificial, even when actors are not being deceptive with intent.[8]

That said, the term "masking" is also employed by the autistic community to denote the extensive output required to camouflage or hide one's neurodivergence. Masking may manifest in explicit ways such as rehearsing responses to questions, but it is often done in the moment and can require sustained, elaborate, and unconscious effort. We also know of meaningful gender differences in how people imitate neurotypical behaviour, and that these differences may explain why more young boys than girls are diagnosed with autism. For example, because girls are generally socialized into docility, we are more likely than boys to obsess over being in good standing with people and to adapt to being able to do so. Thus, because autistic girls present in more socially acceptable ways, it is more likely for this group to be misdiagnosed throughout our lives with mental health conditions such as obsessive compulsive disorder, depression, anxiety, anorexia, and psychotic disorders.[9]

stall. The bartender said that to tell Sean would be selfish, but within days I had relayed what I remembered of the truth. I did so via telephone. I said I was sorry (which I was) and I didn't expect him to forgive me (which I didn't). After hanging up and calling back, Sean agreed to give me another chance. When we met at the airport, neither of us mentioned this.

Looking back, I see Sean as also performing. Our relationship was still young enough that we wanted to present our best selves, all while assuring the other they hadn't made a mistake. I also think Sean is uncomfortable being single. He never brought up my cheating because he stays in character to a fault, so when we abruptly stopped sleeping together, I did not understand. Was our sex life not phenomenal? Had he not gone out of his way to meet my family? Most baffling, had we not discussed our long-term living arrangements? I cannot speak for Sean, but I sense that before I had my episode (that is, before I sent the letter and before both of us were forced to deal with its aftermath), Sean had seen me as stable, competent, and mature. I was "all prisms and light – fucking magic to see," is what he texted me after our first date. Unlike my parents, Saphira, or Steven, all of whom viewed me as de facto unreliable, Sean had high hopes for me – he expected more. When I let him down, I assume that it was devastating.

After Sean left – after he told me when I confronted him about his lack of affection that I was too mentally ill to be attractive – I was not surprised. Crushed, yes, but definitely not surprised. I could not verbalize it, I would not have admitted it at the time, but part of me was relieved. I could cut the act, drop the mask (which was cracked and bleeding, anyway), and binge, purge, and drink in solitude. I wanted nothing more than to extinguish the parts of me he loved. I went on a tear, sought out expressly degrading sex work, and launched an all-out assault on my body and my spirit. Somehow, though, I kept excelling academically.

Ten

I completed my master's program in April 2017 with an overall average of 90 per cent. My academic advisor (not the one who received the letter – a different professor who agreed to guide my research when I returned from medical leave) told me after I defended my thesis it was the best she had ever read. I suspect she may have said this out of pity, but then again, I've always been terrible with compliments ("You're so arrogant," says my mother whenever I try to tell her I'm smart. "You may have a few degrees under your belt, but you live like a goddamn pig.")

I don't remember writing my thesis. More often than not, I would come to after hours or days of drinking and, like magic, the introduction (and the methods section, and the discussion, and the conclusion) would be waiting on my laptop (which would invariably be covered in chocolate sauce, cookie crumbs, ketchup smears – evidence of binges I also don't remember). According to my committee, my words were novel, eloquent, and compelling. According to me, they had been conjured by a stranger. After I passed, the first and only person I texted was my mother.

The night before I defended my thesis, I white-knuckled my way through the sweats, shakes, and terror of withdrawal to arrive on time and field questions coherently. My first drink as a master's graduate was not celebratory so much as it was mandatory. By then, I was going to the emergency room on a bi-weekly basis, asking for diazepam, and, rather than detoxing, filling the scripts and continuing to drink. Mixing alcohol with benzos can be fatal, but I was not concerned. For as long as I can remember, I have felt invincible – above the trappings of human mortality. My body's capacity to tolerate abuse is matched only by my spirits. Besides, the gaping holes in my memory were a welcome break from the pain.

Looking back, I'm not surprised I did so well. Since I was imploding – that my life had become, to borrow from AA, totally unmanageable – it makes sense to have clung to routine. If nothing else, seminars and deadlines forced me to know which day it was. But being so consumed by addiction barred me from evaluating the purpose academia served. I had supressed my revelations from November 2015, and I denied that even with a perfect grade point average, peer-reviewed publications, and prestigious scholarships, I still felt deadened, numb, and hopeless. In short, I was reproducing the conditions that had caused my psychotic break in the first place. I doubled down and swore that succeeding within these same conditions would be my ticket out.

As I deteriorated, I clung to the belief that doing a doctoral degree would be my salvation. I wasn't delusional in the sense that I was happy, but I told myself I could be, eventually. I just needed a PhD. After applying to five institutions and getting accepted by all of them, I decided to go to Oxford. Oxford was impressive. Oxford was fancy. Maybe, just maybe, with Oxford on my CV I could do something to eradicate the inexhaustible, embodied screaming. This is what I told myself as I continued to wake at arbitrary times of day in arbitrary places covered in arbitrary bruises. Still, I had the insight to make a contingency plan: two books, I promised myself. I just had to write and publish two books – two *important* books – and if that didn't fix me, I could drink myself to death. Recently, I have reconsidered this plan, but I am still aware (acutely so, in darker moments) these words could be one of the books.

Eleven

The rest of April has all but vanished. It is a blur of booze, vomit, and angry correspondence sent and received. I grew increasingly incoherent and my liver started failing. I was still technically employed as the project coordinator for a research study, but though I had been physically present leading up to my thesis defence, I ceased contributing the moment it was accepted. I either arrived at meetings in a black out or I didn't arrive at all. However, I stayed alive. I promised myself that Oxford would be different, and while I didn't honestly believe this, it was easier than the truth.

I don't remember calling my cousin, but eventually, I did. I had been publicly embarrassing myself for days, but it was not shame that prompted me to ask for help. Rather, it was the certainty that death had, once again, latched onto my back and wrapped its claws around my neck. This time, it had sunk in its teeth and was sucking at the juices. My subconscious – the force that emerges when circumstances are dire, the force that is hell-bent on living, the force that wrote and sent the letter – intervenes when it has to.

I was told when I woke up in hospital the next day that my blood alcohol level had been over ninety times the legal limit. That figure still seems comical – what does ninety times the legal limit even mean? How does one live with that much ethanol in her system? – but the psychiatrist on call that morning was not amused. After he forbade me from leaving – I had screamed demonically, spoken in tongues, and had been certified under the mental health act – I was not amused, either.

That morning, as I ripped out my intravenous tubes, argued with the psychiatrist, and tried to escape, I missed my grandmother's funeral. She had spent her last years of life in a facility for people with Alzheimer's, and I rarely (never) visited. I could not contend with the flood of self-hatred spawned by memories of using her condition against her, nor could I witness my mother's tenderness as she cared for her, so disparate was this from the wrath with which my mother treated me (*What does it mean to be impaired?*). The dissonance between our three pasts and what I felt and saw in the present sucked the wind out of me – materiality melted at its seams. This is something I will live with forever, and I have strategically ignored it since. Still, I have the medical bracelet I took from my grandmother and pocketed when we last spoke. I had been drunk, and I was probably not concealing this as well as I thought I had been. I carry this bracelet with me to remind myself of the work I must do; I almost put it on the other day before hesitating and leaving it in my bag. So much cognitive, emotional, and spiritual work. For once, it will not be a letter grade that informs my progress.

PART SIX

Twelve

I spent a month in the psych ward. The fury at being held hostage was indescribable, and it compelled me to do nothing but binge, purge, and pace. Involuntarily commitment is vile. It is degrading, dehumanizing, deranged. Only bulimia created time. I would eat frantically thrice daily then circle, hawk-like, through the common area. After gorging on others' leftovers – cold, tasteless hospital food washed down with dixie cup after dixie cup of apple juice – I would purge, finish, and glare defiantly at the oblivious nursing staff. I was not once asked why I was there, nor did anyone suggest that I was suffering. The sterility was in stark contrast to my volcanism. And because institutionalization-incarceration cuts out space for softness, I acted as they saw me. I was bipolar. I was borderline. I was prone to horrific self-destruction because – as per psychiatry, my family, and AA – my brain is broken. I proved them right.

But, after exactly one week of this – after exactly one week of shouting, fainting, experiencing wildly unpredictable somatic symptoms that evaded diagnosis – I stopped.[ix] Sort of. Sobriety and abstinence from bulimia weren't so much chosen by me as they chose me, which is always how it feels when I ricochet from one end of the body-mind pendulum to the other. I began counting calories, exercising each morning on the stationary bike outside the nursing station, and eliminating condiments, liquids, anything that troubled

---

[ix] "Somatic symptom and related disorders" are a category in the DSM-5 for a cluster of distressing physical symptoms that have no organic cause that arise alongside "abnormal" thoughts, feelings, and behaviours related to these symptoms. These labels are nebulous, but a salient feature is a patient's pre-occupation with their physical symptoms and the certainty that their problems are biological. Prior to being diagnosed with a somatoform pain disorder, I underwent multiple X-rays, an MRI, a colonoscopy, an endoscopy, and hematological screening to rule out the presence of internal bleeding and cancer. Nevertheless, my symptoms persist, and are frequently accompanied by what I can only describe as an intense *pressure* inside my frontal lobe and the back of my head. I now associate this pressure with anxiety, and it has at times been sufficiently intense to facilitate fainting. Ample research has linked somatic symptom disorders to trauma, making the jurisdiction of "somatic symptom and related disorders" as "mental illnesses" suspect, given their undeniable physiological presentation.[10]

the orderly categories that food must fit into when I am not vomiting. The psychiatrists commended me.

Four months later, I flew to England. I was sober, I wasn't bingeing, I wasn't purging, my apartment was clean, my parents were pleased, and I sincerely believed that I was stable. I was not stable. After leaving the psych ward, I had immediately started to prepare my dissertation. I had compiled a reading list, refined my research questions, and devoured texts seminal and fringe on mental illness, disordered eating, and substance use. I also journaled daily, and I attended the occasional CBT-based recovery meeting, but I still didn't understand – I could not yet admit – that academia, more so than any substance, alters my mood and conceals my feelings. Had someone asked me, I would have said I felt excited. Had someone asked me, I would have said I felt content. I was neither excited nor content, but I couldn't recognize this because I hadn't ever known happiness. Had someone been around, they also would have noticed I was rapidly losing weight, was exercising compulsively, had resumed my all-day, everyday marijuana habit, was growing increasingly paranoid, and, by September, existed almost entirely in a fantasy world. What I noticed was that after the two years of hell I had just endured, to be abstinent from my most egregiously destructive addictions was enough.

Prior to leaving, the closest thing I had to a maternal figure was Meris. I still saw her each Tuesday, and I continued to be as transparent as possible, given my preoccupation with Oxford. Meris recognized before I did that something was amiss. She pointed out that while sobriety and abstinence from bulimia were enormous, running a half-marathon each morning on an hour of sleep and six hundred calories followed by continuous pot smoking was not a great alternative. I knew this too. That said, because I identified as bulimic before anorexic, I couldn't fully grasp how dangerous my actions were. Self-deprivation felt deliberate, contained, and *mature* relative to bulimia, though I now see it as the other side of the same tarnished coin. Meris has never tried to argue, but she did gift me a bracelet during our last session. "I know you don't believe in this stuff, but it's Tiger's Eye – it's protective," she said as she smiled, passing me the delicate stones. She was right – I don't believe in that stuff – but as I slipped the bracelet onto my wrist, I felt a surge of warmth. Meris would be with me. I would still feel safe. I would soon find out that safety, above all else, was what I had been seeking. And a bracelet wouldn't cut it. These realizations would nearly cost me my life.

Part Five

PART FIVE

ONE

As I hope is getting clearer, I have inhabited two selves. The first is bulimic, alcoholic Nicole. She misses deadlines, lives in filth, and hates herself. Her life is mayhem, and she is along for the ride. Addictions aside, her emotional volatility (as well as her self-soothing with food) is eerily reminiscent of behaviour she has witnessed from her father. Then something happens. She is institutionalized, she has a near-death experience, or the hustle (*Where will my next drink, my next dollar, my next hit, come from!*) gets to be too gruelling. When she reaches this tipping point, this place of total depravity, she ceases bingeing, purging, and drinking. She so dreads relapsing, however, that her behaviour becomes diametrically opposed to the chaos in its constraint. This Nicole is anorexic and a workaholic. She cannot eat anything pleasurable, lest it trigger a binge. She must read, write, and be furiously productive. She feels nothing except anxiety. She is still tormented (my god how she is tormented) but now she resembles her mother.

When I arrived in England, I was my mother. I was clinging to control as a proxy for adulthood with the vice-like grip of a toddler who clutches her caretaker's hand, dizzy in a crowd. I was terrified of strangers, the lights, the colours, the sounds, and terrified of myself. I had dreaded the flight because I was entrenched in routine, specifically as it pertained to exercise, and anticipating a time rupture immobilized me. For weeks I had planned and re-planned my first trip to a British gym, and as I staggered sleep deprived and stunned from the airport, I knew exactly where to find it. This gym – its hours of operation, the number of treadmills it had, the exact make and model of these treadmills – was more important than anything. *I was not okay*, but I didn't see this yet.

I spent three nights at an Airbnb, during which time I spoke to no one except an off-duty bus driver. Post-flight, I stowed my belongings and walked for hours through the city centre until it occurred to me that not only was I lost, I also needed to eat, quickly. Doing so in public wasn't possible, so tethered was I to the elaborate food rituals that accompany anorexia, and in an escalating panic I asked the driver for directions. When he told me that his shift had finished and offered to take me back to the Airbnb, I accepted right away. I was starving. We took a significant detour due to road construction, and after twenty minutes, it dawned on me that I hadn't slept in forty-eight hours, I wasn't carrying identification, and I was on a winding, deserted road in a foreign continent with a man whose name I did not know. The driver turned to me as if reading my mind and grinned, remarking that I might have been too trusting. My stomach dropped, and I thought about food. *Tuna and cucumber,* I promised myself; *Tonight's salad will contain tuna and cucumber, tuna and cucumber, tuna and....* I returned safely, and I spent the rest of the evening counting (and re-counting) vegetables. Before bed I texted my mother. I said I was fine and happy. Without anorexia (and without its messier, brasher sister, bulimia), solitude can be deafening.

Two

I moved into Nuffield College on day four. It is... exquisite. Stunning. Indescribable, really, though I will do my best to describe it. First, Nuffield is a relatively small, graduate-only college that was established in 1937 following a donation by motor manufacturer and philanthropist William Morris. This makes it one of Oxford's newest colleges, though as a foreigner from a young colony, it looked plenty old to me. The lawn, gardens, and courtyard at Nuffield are immaculate. The architecture is preserved, and everything is at once stoic, steeped resolutely in history, and beckoning silently but with pervasive energy for you to touch it. Touch I did, though clanging into the monolithic structures while clutching for finger-holes, my nose and knees grazing the centuries-old facades through a helter-skelter vodka haze, may have been affronting to even the most infamous of Oxford's rabble-rousing ghosts.

A few additional facts: Nuffield is composed entirely of social scientists, most completing degrees in economics, politics, international relations, or sociology. Members of my cohort were coming from positions at the British Embassy, the World Bank, and their parents' mansions. I was coming from homelessness, repressed memories, and psychiatric incarceration. Like most of the college, though, I am white.[i] I am able-bodied. I am capable of disguising my differences with elaborate language and appropriate attire, at least until I'm not (at which point the professionally staffed dining hall may as well have been the Carnegie Centre at Main and Hastings – a notorious space of

---

[i] It is no secret that institutions of higher learning perpetuate racial, ethnic, class-based, and other forms of exclusion. They do so directly and indirectly, and in the UK, Oxbridge (Oxford and Cambridge) is known for a lack of diversity. For example, after Oxford released its 2018 admissions statistics, Labour Party lawmaker David Lammy tweeted that Oxford is "still a bastion of entrenched, wealthy, upper class, white, southern privilege." Here my own position is complex. A background of homelessness, addiction, and so on doesn't often translate to high educational attainment. However, I still possess a significant degree of what French sociologist Pierre Bourdieu refers to as "cultural capital." Through careful observation, I have learned to leverage cultural resources such as the norms and values acquired through socialization to manufacture belonging in "elite" spaces, at least temporarily. My appearance also helps.[i]

abjection that I have also been escorted out of by security when at my most unwell). I performed convincingly upon arrival, but I still felt out of place. The glamour, the tradition, and the expectations, both explicit and implied, were cloying. The college also has an interesting reputation among sociologists. I was told that most Nuffield students tend to isolate. They avoid the department, speak only to peers, and think they're better than the rest, though no one said this aloud. I don't know how accurate this is – I didn't stick around long enough to find out – but I can understand why someone would arrive and never want to leave. I could barely see.

I came to Nuffield via taxi, wheeling one large and one small suitcase – my entire life reduced to essentials, packed neatly by my father. The suitcases contained clothing, running shoes, academic texts, and a postcard that read, "I am in the world to change the world," a token I had acquired at my first treatment centre over a decade prior. Otherwise, my possessions and what they symbolized were gone. I was also conflicted about which mask to wear. I wanted to be open about my past. Yet, while stating that I "had been" street-entrenched (and had, by extension, clawed my way out of street entrenchment via my own merit) was impressive, admitting that I was a few months sober (again) and had just been released from the psych ward (again) would have been too honest. Here the old adage "wherever you go, there you are" comes to mind, and while I should have recognized after twenty-eight years that I was stuck with myself, I also hoped to create an identity that wasn't rooted in pain. Complicating matters was that my research plan accepted by Oxford was about this same pain.[ii]

[ii] Some researchers incorporate lived experience into their data generation and analytic strategies, particularly during qualitative work with marginalized groups. They may do so to build rapport with participants, acknowledge their biases, or counter the hierarchical researcher-subject dynamic that emerges during data generation. Whether self-disclosure is useful or appropriate will depend on one's theoretical affiliation, among other things.[2]

PART FIVE

Three

For my master's thesis, I examined the co-occurrence of eating and substance abuse disorders among homeless youth.³ To my knowledge, mine was the first qualitative study on disordered eating to include a street-involved population. Typically, research of this nature draws from clinical samples, meaning that people have to be formally diagnosed by a provider to participate.[iii] That said, it's very difficult to access healthcare, let alone recognize, problematize, and seek treatment for self-starvation, bingeing, and/or purging, while pursuing drugs and shelter. I knew this. I had lived this. And, while my thesis topic was a departure from the ideas that had felt brilliant in Australia but were really just assemblages, the reading I did there on existentialism, deconstructionism, and the transmission of trauma through families turned out to be impactful. It came in handy when I lost it. It is coming in handy now as I slowly pick up the pieces. There are benefits and drawbacks to "me-search."

My peers at Nuffield were eager to hear about my work. I squirmed during these conversations, my cheeks flushed, because for as long as I can remember, I have been called a liar. For instance, my mother claims that being homeless was a choice. I was sent to a shelter at nineteen after going to abstinence-based addiction treatment twice. While in treatment, I was told that the solutions to my obsessions, compulsions, paralysis, memory loss, executive dysfunction, and bone-deep exhaustion were humility, prayer, and gratitude. My efforts

---

[iii] There are significant knowledge gaps about the relationships between eating disorders and social locations such as race, ethnicity, class, sex, sexuality, gender, and ability status. However, the last few decades have seen an influx of research demonstrating that disordered eating is not merely a white, wealthy women's issue. Specifically, rates of binge eating disorder and bulimia may be equivalent or higher in racialized people and people who are poor than they are in middle-upper class white people. This may partially be due to the pressure that some people feel to maintain a culturally sanctioned body weight/ shape and to still adhere to white, western beauty standards, as well as lack of access to culturally competent healthcare, lack of culturally sensitive diagnostic criteria for disordered eating, lack of economic resources to seek out healthcare, and lack of community and healthcare provider detection and recognition of eating disorder "symptoms" due to the lingering belief that racialized and/or poor people are not affected.⁴

had been Herculean. They were also futile. After another bender concluded in hospital, a psychiatrist said that to let me come home would be enabling my addictions. My mother agreed, and overnight, I went from upper-class suburbia to full street entrenchment. My parents refer to this as having "detached with love." To them, my response should have been simple. All I had to do was stop drinking, stop bingeing, stop purging, toe the line, and be normal. Throughout my life I have tried this, and each attempt has been a resounding failure. Another reason academia is so validating, then, is that it has exposed me to alternate beliefs about normalcy. *Normal is a social construct,* I can say. *Normal is produced through disciplinary power.*[iv] *Normal is neoliberal. Normal is not real.* This may be true – what is normal, anyway? – but venerating self-destruction may not be an act of resistance. Contentedness, I'm sensing, could be far more radical.

My peers were kind, but I didn't know if they would respect me. Qualitative methods are less common among Oxford sociologists than are quantitative, and in addition to eschewing statistics in favour of analyzing written and verbal data, I also have poststructuralist sensibilities. I believe that language itself is unstable, incoherent, and historically situated, and rather than convey one's "authentic" voice, it (re)produces and (re)configures dominant power relations.[6] So, while others debated the merits of certain statistical models over others, I wanted to talk about the implications of social interaction being premised on the assumption that humans are reasonable, self-knowing subjects who possess a consistent sense of self. I openly wondered whether describing oneself relays reality or creates it, and questioning the political-epistemic virtue of honesty intensified the feeling of

---

[iv] In sociological theory, normalization refers to the processes through which some mental states and modes of conduct become taken for granted as normal. Michel Foucault used the term to denote one of many tactics employed by liberal governance to construct idealized forms of citizenship. His analytics of power examined how modern punitive techniques rely less on brute force than they do subtle sanctions to wield social control. Through "disciplinary power," citizens are less inclined to resist the state than if the state were still, say, publicly torturing people, and we begin to govern ourselves on the state's behalf (e.g., by upholding rigid parameters of what constitutes normal behaviour, and ostracizing those who cannot or will not adhere to them).[5]

being an imposter.ᵛ That said, I'll never know whether my approach would have resonated or if I would have been accepted. Before I got a chance to find out (before I even attended a single seminar), the voices returned. This time, they were angry.

ᵛ Throughout the text, I adopt a Foucauldian definition of "discourse" in that I understand discourse to create systems of knowledge and meaning ("truth") that govern our social interactions and, more broadly, define and direct our collective reality.[7]

Four

In November of 2015, Phil the psychiatrist diagnosed me with bipolar disorder, type one. I contacted him while altered, and my only evidence of having done so is the email trace I left. This was some two or three days after I sent the letter, and I remember taking the bus from Saphira's house to his office as I gulped melatonin by the fistful. Phil laughed when I showed him the empty bottle, and he promptly replaced the melatonin with gluteal injections of an antipsychotic sedative. The exact diagnostic criteria for bipolar disorder (and for all mental illnesses, really) is more consensus-based than validity-based.[vi] In sum, the label implies periods of intense mood episodes ranging from immense energy and euphoria ("mania") to despair. Manic episodes are characterized by restlessness, irrationality, difficulty concentrating, reckless behaviours such as overspending and high-risk sex, and significant impairment in functioning.[vii] By then, I had known Phil for seven years. He had been one of two psychiatrists employed by Covenant House Vancouver when I arrived in 2008, and as a shell-shocked nineteen-year-old who had become homeless

---

[vi] The DSM-5 (along with all prior iterations of the DSM) has been criticized for its symptom-based classifications. Despite being understood by most as a valid diagnostic tool, it forces clinicians to rely on behavioural pattern-recognition when making diagnoses whereas other diseases are judged by biomarkers. Dr. Michael Berk uses the analogy of colour to highlight the intrinsic ambiguity of DSM classifications: "[T]he expanded DSM-5 categorisation represents a greatly expanded series of adjectives or metaphors, able to describe what we see in a manner that is defined with some reliability, even if it fails to explain why blue really is blue."[8]

[vii] Pertinent here, Dr. Stephen Strakowski, founding chair of Psychiatry at the Dell Medical School, University of Texas in Austin, uncritically explains that the symptoms of mania are diagnosed as such when they begin to cause "significant impairment in interpersonal, social, or work function; by definition, if someone requires hospitalization due to these symptoms, then mania is diagnosed."[9] By Strakowski's own admission, then, a diagnosis of mania is more closely linked to one's environment – e.g., whether they are formally employed and begin to experience difficulties generating income, or whether they are embedded in a social network that will problematize their behaviours or offer peer support instead – than measurable pathology. Had I not visited Phil, for instance, I would not have received the bipolar disorder, type one diagnosis.

overnight, I had no reason to doubt his prognosis – that I had bipolar disorder, type two. Then, in 2015, Phil skimmed the copy of the letter I had sent to my supervisor and concluded that I had been psychotic. Psychosis is considered to be a gradual or sudden break from reality, and it is what distinguishes the two bipolar disorders. Early on, it can manifest as reduced performance at work or school, unwarranted suspicion of others, less emotional expression, and anxiety. In its more severe stages, it may encompass delusions (the belief in something that isn't true or real – that one can read minds, for instance) and hallucinations (experiencing things that aren't true or real – hearing voices, for instance). Based on these criteria, I have been in varying degrees of psychosis for roughly two decades.

It is impossible to fully describe the voices. Voices may not even be the best signifier to use here, but I am stuck with language. For now, I will say this: Since childhood, I have not felt integrated. Instead, I have felt there are multiple, competing parts of me and I must mediate between each of their (our) distinct ways of being. These parts (the Nicoles, if you will) represent several age-states, and each demands love, tenderness, and validation – much of what I lacked in childhood and what my primary caregivers withhold as an adult. As of late, I have grown more adept at tending to the voices' needs, and together we live relatively harmoniously. The commands when I inhabit age-states that are distinct from my chronological age, however, are accustomed to being ignored, and they can get aggressive. When this happens, I may forget I *am* the voices, so distraught am I by their brutality. My inner world accelerates, time becomes non-linear, and stimuli are amplified. According to the psychiatric community, this is the definition of psychosis. According to people I've met who experience this, "psychosis" is a reductive version of "reality."[viii]

[viii] Although psychotic symptoms (e.g., delusions and hallucinations) are considered arbitrary products of deranged minds that have become divorced from consensus reality, research demonstrates that psychosis is strongly linked to adverse experiences in childhood.[10] Beyond this, the *content* of one's delusions and hallucinations is not usually random. A 2012 study using data generated through the 2007 Adult Psychiatric Co-Morbidity Survey (n = 7,353) determined that among those who have been diagnosed with schizophrenia, those who had been victims of rape before age sixteen were six times more likely than those who had not to report auditory hallucinations. Those who had

When the voices emerged at Nuffield, they began as they always do. They were lilting, gentle, and cautious, even. *Perhaps*, one suggested, *you can drink casually now. After all, you are thousands of miles from home, and no one here thinks you're an alcoholic.* I didn't buy it. But I was afraid by my lack of fear. A day later, this voice was joined by another, and another, all of which were confident that if I limited myself to two – three, maximum – drinks per day, and if I only drank in public, I would retain control. The voices grew louder, they became more invasive, and before long, I started to believe them. When the voices finally demanded that I incorporate alcohol into my meal plan – that I substitute, say, two ounces of vodka each day for a cup of cereal – I sensed impending doom. I was also very relieved.

---

grown up in institutionalized care (e.g., the child welfare system) were eleven times more likely than those who had not to report paranoid ideation, which makes sense when one considers the surveillance technology and the physical, sexual, emotional, and spiritual abuse that is omnipresent in these regimes of "care."[11] I will also introduce theoretical advancements from fringe and radical psychology that prioritizes the symbolic, unmeasurable meaning of psychosis.

Five

In the last few years, my relapses with alcohol and bulimia have followed a distinct trajectory. When sober, anorexic Nicole is in charge, I follow a precise meal plan, and though highly productive, I am unhappy. I have no social network; I feel no sense of community; my days are consumed by non-consumption. I restrict my food intake and, in so doing, I restrict my life in favour of calorie counting, isolation, and writing. This is not a choice the way my mother defines choice. Rigidity, routines, rituals – they are predictable and safe. Novelty, on the other hand, particularly while sober, can be an attack. I never know when I will freeze, panic, or worse. However, I am lonely. Deeply, gut-wrenchingly lonely. And, rather than acknowledge this, I toy with the idea of drinking. At first, this seems reasonable – I am, after all, tracking every calorie – and I inevitably substitute a few of my allotted food units for units of rum or vodka. *Just the caloric equivalent of my night snack*, I promise myself. *I'll barely feel a buzz.* Again, this is not a choice the way my mother defines choice. By the time the numbers take over (set always against a grey backdrop), I am somewhere else. Every time this happens, I say I will drink moderately. Never once have I.

    I followed my plan for roughly two days at Nuffield. The first time I drank, I was at a pub with college members. I was hungry but didn't feel comfortable eating in public. I planned to return to my accommodation, a stark but spacious room in a grey historic building nestled behind Nuffield's picturesque courtyard, and fix my nightly salad. I was too distracted by this salad to comprehend the questions others asked or the answers that I gave. I squirmed, my smile disingenuous, and after a few minutes of faux deliberation – during which time any lingering sense of reticence or self-preservation was replaced by a sudden, fervent, *need* to imbibe – I got myself a drink. The first sip sent a wave of ecstasy down my spine. I drank it quickly, I ordered another and, even after telling myself I would stop at two, another. Doing so woke bulimic, alcoholic Nicole who, after lying dormant for months, was famished and parched.

Six

I woke at one in the morning filled with overwhelming dread. I had unleashed something terrible and knew it. I had no friends to confide in, my parents would chastise me, so I responded how I (and my mother) always do to crises; I asked someone to fix it. I rose from my bed, head pounding, heart racing, and staggered down two flights of stairs to the cobblestone lane outside my dorm. I sent Phil a hurried email stating I was holding it together but might benefit from speaking to a doctor. I framed this message carefully, refraining from mentioning alcohol both out of embarrassment and the realization there was nothing that Phil could do. I then managed to doze restlessly before waking and heading to the gym.

After running fifteen kilometres, the events of the night before seemed more like a well-reasoned choice than a horrific mistake. *I am twenty-eight years old,* I told myself. *I have a full scholarship to Oxford. I am very smart. I can control this.* I was at once right – I was twenty-eight years old; I did have a full scholarship to Oxford; I am very smart – and (almost) dead wrong. It may seem strange to have contacted Phil given my hostility toward psychiatry. My beliefs have since evolved, but I agonized then as I do now, albeit in slightly different ways, with how to make sense of mental illness. I had developed an aversion to this identity, but I had also never lived as someone who is sane. That may sound odd, but it becomes hard to trust oneself after multiple involuntary hospitalizations. My entire existence had been pathologized, my subjectivity invaded by illness discourses that shattered my self-esteem and alienated me from myself. By the time I drank at Nuffield, I didn't know healthy from unhealthy, true from false, sane from crazy. All I knew was fear, and so I did what I have always done when frightened: I sought medical attention.

Seven

The next night, I drank again. This time, I had five ounces of alcohol after deciding to have three, and this time, after telling myself it was fine, I knew that I was screwed. I had spent the day at orientation events including a meet and greet with the sociology department, an information session with Visas and Immigration, and a seminar on what it actually means to be a doctoral candidate, all of which took place between opening a bank account, inquiring about cell phone carriers, and considering doctors. This latter task – at once a priority and easy to disregard – never came to fruition in the way I had intended.

On that second night, I attended a gathering for Clarendon scholars, an interdisciplinary, international group of graduate students who had also been deemed Oxford's most "academically able" by an admissions committee. Some people were kind, interesting, and potential friends, even. In others, their pretension and self-aggrandizement were comically overblown. I absorbed the pomp and ceremony, the lights overbearing, the sounds a swarm, and before we transitioned out of the iconic eighteenth-century building and into a nearby pub, I slammed an (expensive) glass of wine. This aroused in me the need for more, and I left the pub after two additional drinks, stopping alone before Nuffield to order another (and another) at a ramshackle tavern. I exhaled at last, which was not just due to my blood alcohol level but also to the fact that the bartender, a young Spanish man, knew nothing about academia. I told him about myself, I admitted how uncomfortable I was, and above all else, I savoured the blessed calm. That feeling would be short lived: The next morning, I woke up, skipped the gym, and considered day drinking.

Eight

Ever since Australia, I have experienced acute withdrawal symptoms immediately after drinking. In theory, I should not have woken up trembling that third morning. But I was roused by nightmares, which are a fixture of my broken sleep whether I'm drunk or sober, and I staggered to the bathroom. Shaking violently, panic clawing at my throat, and drenched head to toe in sweat, I debated buying vodka.[ix] This was bad, and I knew it.

I craved liquor for several hours and substituted wine for lunch. I was at yet another Clarendon event (my social calendar had never been so saturated or daunting), and this time, I gravitated to the bar before drinks were even poured. Three hours later the event had ended, and I was alone in a pub again. I don't remember what I was feeling – I don't remember much from this day forward – but I am certain that by the next day, I had stopped counting drinks. I didn't intentionally abandon my substitution strategy but, after ten, twelve, or fourteen vodka shots, the glee of intoxication was fast becoming more important than anything else.

[ix] As far as unusual embodiment goes, every time I have talked to a doctor about my hyper-sensitivity to alcohol, I have been assured that physiological addiction to liquor takes weeks, if not months. I hesitate to accept this. First, regarding the sensations of withdrawal, research demonstrates that prolonged exposure to alcohol prompts neurochemical changes that first manifest as autonomic hyperactivity (e.g., nausea, vomiting, agitation). This is followed by neuronal excitation (e.g., seizures and confusion) and, in severe cases, delirium tremens, too (which may also encompass auditory and visual hallucinations). This is not just uncomfortable – it is terrifying. According to the medical community, most of the symptoms I have described are linked to adaptive changes in central inhibitory and excitatory systems, meaning that one's central nervous system when detoxing becomes too activated. These changes occur over extended periods in chronic, relapsing alcoholics (which, despite intermittent periods of abstinence throughout the previous decade, I am and always will be).[12]

The kindling hypothesis also suggests that multiple episodes of alcohol withdrawal cause cumulative changes in neuronal excitability. Specifically, repeated withdrawal periods progressively worsen or sensitize ("kindle") withdrawal-induced anxiety-like behaviour. In other words, on a physiological and cognitive level, the longer you've been a drunk, the more challenging and scarier it is to stop.[13]

My memory is incomplete but I know it was this evening that I ate a slice of toast. After doing nothing but drinking all day, including bringing liquor to my room, I ate toast that caused me to exceed my daily calorie allotment. I remember telling myself I had a seminar the next morning and this one piece of toast was necessary to absorb the litre of vodka I had consumed in the hours prior. To complicate matters, I ate the toast at two in the morning, which meant that, because it was past midnight, its calories needed to be incorporated into the next day's total allotment and eliminated from breakfast. These were the rules. By this point, I was too drunk – and too hungry – to be a human calculator, and the rules, I realized with a combination of relief and foreboding, no longer mattered. This toast, then, was in every way spontaneous. It was in every way uncalculated. It was, most importantly, in every way deviant. This toast signified the death of anorexic, sober Nicole, and it became a four-week bender.

NINE

There is a Sainsbury's, the second largest of the United Kingdom's grocery store chains, very close to Nuffield. The day I moved in, I bought carrots, lettuce, and mustard. The day I began to binge and purge, I likely bought whatever was rich, sweet, and eye level. I can't actually remember this, so I assume that I was drunk. What I do remember is sneaking into my building's shared kitchen a few days later, rifling through a miniature fridge, taking what appealed to me, and running crookedly back to my room. Later, I stole a container of stir-fry, ate it with my fingers, and, after hastily regurgitating it, threw the container out the window. Stealing others' food and booze became a daily occurrence, in part because I became too sick to walk to Sainsbury's, and in part because I was drinking away remorse.

While I shook and waited for the shops to open each morning so I could get more alcohol, I was supposed to be getting a DPhil. I had gone to a few departmental events but left each of them early because they had been scheduled when I was either in mild withdrawal or already too intoxicated. That said, I had not forgotten why I was at Oxford, nor had I forgotten my desire to produce something incredible and become someone else while doing it. Falling behind instilled in me panic that I paradoxically coped with by drinking. I skipped my first cohort meeting after telling my professor that I was deeply sorry, terribly embarrassed, but I had caught the fresher's flu. I was vomiting bile, I knew I reeked of vodka, and I was far too weak to shower or brush my teeth, let alone walk to the sociology department and talk about things like research.

By this point, a week after starting to drink, I was completely addicted to alcohol. This addiction was not just psychological. I was consuming more than a litre of spirits daily, and regardless of claims that withdrawal symptoms take months to appear, my nervous system needed them. After just hours of sobriety, tremors reverberated head to toe. Each day, the woman who opened Sainsbury's asked to see my identification. I loathed this – and her – not just because she wielded such power but because I couldn't always comply. I also kept losing my bank card, and, while I waited for it to appear next to a crumpled receipt in one of my bags or drawers, I asked college members for money.

    I never got back to my room before I had to drink. I would duck into the changing room of a department store, praying I made it before seizing, or I would crouch in the most deserted alley I could find and hope that none of my colleagues saw me. I often retched between sips, chastising myself for wasting the precious liquid. Once a kindly, older gentleman witnessed me quivering outside the Nuffield gate and pushed twenty pounds into my palm. When he smiled tenderly and assured me that "all of us fall on hard times, love," I didn't admit I was a student. I pocketed the money, spent most on vodka and the rest on a McDonald's cheeseburger, and purged the cheeseburger in the McDonald's bathroom before drinking more vodka and collapsing beside the toilet, waiting.

Ten

About ten days in, I started trying to detox. However, one cannot simply enter a British emergency room and demand benzodiazepines. This didn't deter me at first. I took taxis to the A&E (the British equivalent of Canada's ER) and almost every time, I was told to go to a doctor's office or Turning Point, an outpatient treatment program.[x] I did get to Turning Point after a commute that took all morning. I kept stopping to vomit, drink, or vomit and drink, and when I finally did arrive, whimpering and sweating, an employee remarked that, given the severity of my condition, I should go to hospital.

When I was seen in the A&E, I spent fourteen hours in a cot. What the nurses didn't know, and what I could not yet say, was that something had gone very wrong in my body-mind. It was more than just withdrawal. I am used to brutally violent, racist, sexually explicit, and frankly deranged content entering my consciousness. It disturbs me, and I do not utter it aloud. However, after writhing in pain, pleading for medication, and willing away a day's worth of invasive, increasingly gruesome thoughts, the voices had taken over. I was in a psychic wrestling match, and with each passing moment, I got closer to submitting. Throughout this, whenever the words lodged in my sternum pulsated too frenetically, I lurched to the toilet and purged. They clawed; I atoned; my throat was a combat zone, ravaged and bile singed. At last, a social worker leaned over me. "You may have a problem with alcohol," she observed. Then, she reached into

---

[x] Turning Point is a social enterprise and registered charity with multiple locations throughout the UK that addresses a range of health and social issues. The location that I was directed to describes itself as "a one-stop treatment centre providing a wide range of treatment options, including harm reduction advice, structured group work programme, activities, complementary therapies, and one-to-one key work sessions to promote recovery." According to its website, it is equipped with "doctors, nurses, psychologists, recovery workers, support workers, complementary therapists, peer mentor volunteers, counsellors, and trainers." I do not know who I met with the day I arrived, nor do I know the intricacies of Turning Point's evaluation process or support trajectories. I do know that the walk back to Nuffield was very, very painful.

her pocket and handed me a brochure that read, "What to expect at Turning Point."

I left and bought vodka from an all-night gas station. Forcing it down in the parking lot, I texted Mark, who is a barometer of sorts. If he can't assuage my fear (which he definitely could not), I know my state is critical. By then, I was sufficiently desperate to do what I knew how to do – to do what always works for me. I got back. I caused a scene.

I have since deleted the text message I next sent my mother, but whatever it said prompted her to contact Nuffield. My motivation for sending it was two-fold. First, I wanted comfort. My behaviour has always been framed by my mother and psychiatry as attention seeking, and to some extent, it was.[xi] I was alone and I was spiralling. Despite my resentment and confusion about our relationship, I wanted my mother to soothe me. I was also completely – deathly – serious. Given the escalating severity of my addictions, I knew my malnourished body and unstable mind were no longer safe to inhabit. Oxford, my chance at redemption, at reinvention, was not what I hoped it would be. More specifically, *I* was not who I hoped I would be. I had left Canada filled not with optimism but with dread, and this dread, I now admitted, should have been a warning. I was broken, and I needed to be talked off the ledge. Instead, two cops showed up and nearly pushed me over.

When Nuffield's senior tutor entered my room trailed by two cops, I was startled awake. Moving to Europe had not changed my opinion about cops, and I know alcoholic Nicole, who is belligerent, may have gone on a verbal tirade. She could have ranted and raved about police brutality, state-sanctioned oppression, and race- and class-based

---

[xi] The psychiatrist I met with semi-regularly before leaving Canada informed me in no uncertain terms that I exhibit "strong 'cluster B' symptoms." In the DSM-5, "cluster B" is described as the "dramatic, emotional, and erratic" cluster, and it includes diagnoses such as borderline personality disorder (BPD), which is characterized by intense and unstable mood swings, polarized thinking, impulsivity, and ambiguous self-identity; and histrionic personality disorder, which is characterized by excessive emotionality, attention seeking, narcissism, and shallowness. Mood disorders are highly stigmatized, including by clinicians. Critics of psychiatry argue that BPD pathologizes characteristics most often associated with femininity and that BPD should be replaced in the DSM by complex post-traumatic stress disorder. It is worth noting that 75 per cent of BPD diagnosis are assigned to women.[14]

disparities in the application of deadly force. Alternately, and more realistically, given my degree of inebriation, I may have just moaned and cursed. Whatever the case, the cops did nothing but confiscate the three-month supply of lithium I had brought from Canada. I had taken the mood stabilizer each day because abruptly stopping it would have made things even worse.[xii] Another thing British emergency room doctors will not do, however, is re-prescribe medications that have been taken by police. That night, after travelling *yet again* to hospital, I waited until four in the morning. All I remember is attempting to purchase water from a vending machine, losing my debit card *yet again* and, as the sun rose, being told *yet again* by a different social worker to visit Turning Point. I laughed macabrely and returned to Nuffield, slightly more sober and in the early stages of both alcohol and lithium withdrawal. I kept drinking.

[xii] Although I had first been diagnosed with bipolar disorder nearly a decade earlier, I did not begin my first trial run of lithium, the "gold standard" medication for this diagnosis, until mid-2017. Despite reaching a therapeutic dose as determined by periodic blood testing, which people on lithium must undergo because the drug can damage one's kidneys or thyroid function over time, I hadn't noticed any effects. Everyone interacts differently with neuroleptics, but in my case, medication withdrawal (be that from anti-depressants, anti-psychotics, atypical anti-psychotics, or mood stabilizers) can manifest as mania, depression, a mixed episode (that is, being simultaneously manic and depressed), impaired cognitive functioning, and/or brain zaps (feeling as though one's brain is being electrocuted). Based on conversations I've had with others, some of whom have relayed debilitating withdrawal effects, my symptoms have usually been mild. Within the psychiatric community, medication side effects are generally viewed as nuisances that can and should be endured (often with more medication) and/or are mistaken for symptoms of additional mental illnesses.[15]

Members of the anti-psychiatry, Mad, and psychiatric survivor movements have been vocal critics of medication side effects, as well as the a priori assumption that achieving "normalcy" is worth them. Of course, there is nuance here. Some people choose to take medication because it enables them to generate income and otherwise function within the constraints of neoliberal capitalism. People in institutionalized settings may not be given a choice at all, and others still don't experience medication side effects or agree that they are a minor inconvenience. Peer-written guides for medication withdrawal are available.[16]

PART FIVE

Eleven

Phil once turned to a medical student and stated, "Nicole is the highest-functioning crazy person I know." It was insensitive, but Phil adopted a paternal role in my life while I stayed at Covenant House. We had a good rapport. At the time, I also felt a perverse sense of pride at being endorsed by Phil – at being esteemed, however patronizingly, by a medical (and, in some respects, a familial) authority. That said, Phil's statement was made about sober, anorexic Nicole. By my second week at Nuffield, he, along with my tutor, my peers, and random passersby, would have agreed I did not function at all.

In addition to taking taxis to the A&E, people at Nuffield began calling the paramedics. Once or twice, I also called them myself. Although I have thus far relayed indicators of how I drink, I have not yet explained in explicit detail why these calls were warranted. To summarize: When in active addiction, I consume alcohol like air. I need it to walk, sit upright, and breathe. At the same time, the amount I drink and the rate at which I drink makes walking, sitting, and breathing impossible. I am tethered to the stuff, always on the verge of vomiting, often unable to do anything but curl into a ball, clutch my distended abdomen, and wait until I am strong enough to do whatever I must for more. I drink straight from the bottle, I alternate vodka with vodka, I consume half a litre, a full litre, two litres, all at once. I collapse. I wake up. I do it again. Collapse. Wake up. Do it again. Collapse. Wake up. Binge and purge. Realize I am about to die. Panic. Call 9-1-1.

The day following my mother's call to Nuffield, I knocked on the door of a colleague. I had been lying in bed and struggling to breathe, listening to an indecipherable, rhythmic chant that could have emanated from the courtyard below but was likely in my mind. I screamed for help, and at some point, a porter came in. When I told him I was dying, which was not an exaggeration, he said in no uncertain terms what he thought about my conduct. This became routine – enter withdrawal, begin to hear voices, plead for someone (anyone) to fix it – but the first time that it happened, I didn't understand. I was too Mad to know I was Mad, but I was still sane enough to care.

The Becoming

I half-walked, half-crawled to my neighbour's door, where he found me hunched over and gasping for air, sweat dripping down my neck. I hadn't showered in days, but unlike the porter, the neighbour was sympathetic. He called our tutor and tucked me in his bed, rubbing my feet as we waited. He also either believed me when I said I had the flu or was polite enough to pretend. I have one clear memory from that day, which is the full bottles of hard alcohol on his shelf. *Give me one of those bottles*, I wanted to say, *and we can forget this ever happened.* I could not say this, so I closed my eyes and focused on the fact that for the first time in months, I was being touched.

PART FIVE

Twelve

These days, the phrase, "the opposite of addiction is not sobriety – it's connection" has entered mainstream culture. The saying was coined by British-based journalist Johann Hari, whose book concludes with the message that punitive drug policies (and family members) do little but alienate. They dismantle support networks, exacerbate self-loathing, and push people deeper into isolation. No kidding. Much of what Hari writes echoes the sentiments expressed in the rooms of junkie unions and drug-user networks, where members without formal education or media platforms have spent decades advocating for expanded access to harm reduction, decriminalization (and eventual legalization) of illicit drugs, and less stigmatizing approaches to heavy substance use.

The truth is, for such a contentious topic, no one really knows where addiction comes from. The term itself lacks a universally agreed upon definition, and what one may describe as drug use, others may assign the term abuse. Both the biomedical and social sciences have failed to trace loss of self-control, which is the core criterion for addiction, to a discrete set of causes, and while developments in neuroscience have nudged public perception of addiction into the realm of biomedicine, alcohol and drugs don't engender physiological or psychological dependence in most users. Even trauma exposure, a common unit of analysis when studying addiction, is inconsistently operationalized.[xiii]

[xiii] In subsequent sections, I will introduce my own (and others') theories about where (my) addictions originate. Medical sociology has informed my perspective, but it also relies too heavily on tracing stakeholder involvement in deviance designations. That is, addiction is not just or even mostly a social construction, and while our societal responses to it are, I have found medical sociology wanting when trying to understand the very real loss of self-control that I experience. The adjacent notion that "connection" prevents or encourages recovery from addiction is well-intentioned but trite. Journalist Hari, as well as Vancouver-based physician Gabor Mate, defer to trauma determinism by implying that certain adverse experiences necessarily lead to high intensity substance use.[17]

Regardless, the work done by drug user activists who care less about theory and more about practical policy change always merits recognition. This is particularly true given the staggering fatality rate of the drug poisoning crisis. In British Columbia alone, approximately five people per day have died of drug toxicity since early 2020. This is due to a combination of factors, most notably that the federal, provincial, and municipal

Trauma can be structural, systemic, and interpersonal, and what deeply affects one person may hardly faze another. I wish there was a precise, tidy etiology for my supposed pathologies, but because scientists and lay people (me included) can't even agree on what constitutes pathology, I am forced to rely on anecdotes, hunches, and ever-shifting theories about why I am the way I am. For now, I will say this: I sincerely don't know who I would be had I not felt compelled to lay awake each night as a child, pleading with god to keep my mother safe. I wonder if I would have developed the same obsessions, compulsions, and inability to connect. I don't want to suggest this is my parents' fault, in part because the laying awaking and pleading may have happened regardless, but I do wonder how else I might have passed the time, who else I could have been, had I lived in the absence of fear.

Years later, the fear I felt then is omnipresent. It creeps up on me. It makes me woozy. It has marred my ability to build friendships, go on dates, feel real. Instead, I have spent days, weeks, and months at a time alone, engaging in rampant substance use and bulimia or sequestered behind my computer screen reading, writing, and counting the minutes until I eat next. Whether alcoholic, bulimic Nicole or anorexic, workaholic Nicole is in charge, I have always been terribly – deathly – lonely. This is all to say the day my dorm mate rubbed my feet it awoke in me a primal urge for love. I was reminded of how disconnected I had been, not only in recent years but all the way back to when I still believed in god. I was reminded that I was human, that my needs, which I have never been able to think-speak-say, had always been unmet. And yet, given how unwell I was, I did not see a way out. Then, my tutor provided one for me.

---

governments continue to treat decriminalization like a political football. Five years after the province declared the "overdose" crisis an emergency, Vancouver is drafting a model of decriminalization without having consulted drug users.

PART FIVE

Thirteen

As I write this, song lyrics come to mind. I am not a singer, but when Sean still loved me, we sometimes went to choir. And, for the last day or so, all I've heard while writing is, *Be kind – everyone carries a heavy load*. Over and over. Slowly. Rhythmically. Be kind. Everyone carries a heavy load. I didn't think I had retained anything, but it's definitely from then. It's funny how memory works.

On October 18, I received an email from my mother. I didn't read it until weeks later, but its subject, "Your Current Reality," still fills me with rage. What would my mother know about my reality? The message outlines a phone conversation she had with my tutor, who explained I had three options: I could stop drinking and begin to attend classes (the ideal choice, had it been possible); voluntarily suspend my studies on medical grounds, return to Canada for hospitalization, and restart my DPhil the following year (reasonable, had it been possible); or be forcibly removed from Nuffield, expelled from Oxford, and permanently deported (bad, and still not possible – I would have died on the street). None of these things happened, but I did absorb one piece of my mother's advice: "Stop the insanity and get off the pity pot," she wrote. "Have some pride, some dignity, and do the right thing." I am not entirely sure what my mother meant by "the right thing" (I have never understood her conception of right and wrong), but I wonder if she would agree that after eliminating contact with her, I have been much saner.

Were it not for *be kind – everyone carries a heavy load*, I would also disparage myself. I would disclose that in the week before I left Nuffield, I stopped showering and brushing my teeth. I wore the same stained "Clarendon scholars" shirt and size 00 jeans. I staggered across the courtyard, unaware that others were whispering. Were it not for *be kind – everyone carries a heavy load* I would also tell you that I was, as my mother is fond of saying, a pig. I smoked indoors. I vomited in garbage cans. I willed myself to get to Sainsbury's for alcohol and stole it when too weak. I am trying to be kind. I am trying to understand how things could have gone so wrong so quickly. The only conclusion I have reached – the only conclusion that makes sense, and the one which I will spend the remainder of this book evaluating – is that I had no choice.

As I remember kindness, and that everyone carries a heavy load, I also visualize my mother. What must it have been like to receive text after text from her dying daughter? To not know whether I was serious (I was) or if I was embellishing (I never have). Only months prior, she had planned my grandmother's funeral. As I remember kindness, I remind myself I do not have a child, and I do not know maternal love – or maternal fear. I have, however, had to live with myself for decades, and I'm aware I am *exhausting*. She was also exhausted, I tell myself. The homelessness, the treatment centres, and the hospitalizations did not occur in a vacuum. She also had to cope. Be kind, I will myself. Be kind. Be kind. Be kind.

As I write this I am shaking.

Fourteen

Of my tutor's options, the third would have been simplest. She could have roused me awake, called the cops, and dropped me outside Nuffield with my luggage, passport, and a prayer. I would have stopped being her problem, and she and the college could have resumed their regularly scheduled programming. My regularly scheduled programming was about to kill me. Of that, I am almost certain. The Nicole my tutor first met – the ambitious, congenial young woman who was ready to tackle her DPhil (ready to tackle herself) – had vanished. In her place was a starved, crazed lunatic – one who screamed incoherently, lost control of her bodily functions, and had forgotten her own name. I was gone. My tutor saw this, she knew death was imminent, and she came up with option D.

The Priory Group is a network of psychiatric care facilities located throughout the United Kingdom. According to its website, it treats seventy different behavioural and mental health conditions, some addressed on an inpatient basis and some done so communally. I did not find this out until much later. I just opened my eyes one morning – October 23, though I didn't know this at the time – to see my tutor and a Nuffield porter hovering over my chest. "Try to pack your things," she said gently. "We will leave this afternoon." I had no idea what she meant. I did know, however, that rising from bed, let alone sorting through weeks of soiled clothing, would be impossible. My tutor gathered my underwear.

Minutes or hours later, the three of us were in a taxi. I was barely conscious, and I lay across the porter's lap while the taxi, which took a remarkably long time, went... somewhere. When we arrived at the Priory, I was put in a wheelchair. I was wheeled into an archaic, grumbling lift, taken to a patient room, and I watched my backpack get confiscated because it contained shards of broken glass – remnants of a stolen wine bottle I had smashed across my bathroom sink after I couldn't use a corkscrew. Then, things go dark. I would later find out I was a temporary patient and my intake had been unconventional (read: nonexistent) because I would not be part of programming. My alcoholism, eating disorder, and susceptibility to entering altered states – these were to be addressed in Canada, where I would return after completing a six- or seven-day detox. My spirit, however – the part of me that sent the letter in 2015, that has always saved my ass long after my brain has quit – made other plans.

What happened at the Priory is impossible to explain. It highlights once more the intrinsic constraints of language. And yet, to not explain it – to sit with the knowledge that I spent three weeks in hospital fighting for my life in the most intensive, excruciatingly traumatic ways imaginable – could kill me. I will endeavour, then, to make my experiences comprehensible. I will hope that someone – anyone, anywhere – is able to understand. To write about the Priory feels precarious; daunting. To not write about it would keep me there forever.

Part Four

PART FOUR

ONE

I have flashes from my first night at the Priory. I remember screaming (and screaming and screaming) as the alcohol left my system, begging for diazepam, quetiapine, *anything* that would reduce the pain and knock me out. I remember screaming (and screaming and screaming) when I was denied. I was completely bedridden, and was too weak and sick to walk, let alone communicate. Every few minutes I was breathalyzed, and I was told by a doctor that to take benzodiazepines while still so drunk would kill me. I no longer felt drunk (I was no longer obliterated, anyway), and at that point, death would have been welcome.

I didn't know it at the time, but the Priory has what is called an observation schedule. Each patient is categorized by level of perceived risk upon arrival. Those of us who are skeletal, need to be carried to the door, and reek of blood, vomit, and urine are watched twenty-four hours a day. That night, I could not process this. I was unable to understand why there was a large, Black woman seated at the foot of my bed, nor could I make sense of why she refused to leave even as I screamed (and screamed and screamed) for her to fuck off. I could have had a withdrawal "fit," as the Brits call them, and I was being watched, I eventually realized, in case I began to seize. I also learned – again, eventually – the observation schedule had many functions.

Another memory from that night is of trying to eat. I have no idea how long it had been since I had, and I see in hindsight that concerns about food had been superseded by alcoholism. Never before has substance use eliminated bulimia, but then again, never before have I drunk with such ferocity, such vigour. In the days prior my stomach had been volatile – filled with so much bile and acid and pain I must have eschewed bingeing and purging in favour of vodka and other booze. At the Priory, I was given a sandwich. I ate it in the fetal position, willing it to stay down, and I was told after being wheeled to a medical room and placed on a seated scale that at sixty-four inches tall I weighed just eighty-eight pounds. A few minutes or hours later, I asked for another sandwich. I picked at it still coiled in a ball, felt remorse, then asked the Black woman to bring me to the toilet where I purged and she watched, soundlessly, from the bathroom door.

Two

I sense it was on day three that I began to speak in sentences. My memory from this time is shattered, crudely stitched together by revisiting social media messages I don't recall sending and by reviewing my writing. There are also the people. I am still in contact with patients from the Priory. I still rely on them, in my darker moments, to remind me who I am, who I was, who I could be.

Michael arrived the same day I did, and he has told me I introduced myself by asking for a cigarette. The Priory has a gazebo-style smoking hut adjacent its side door, nestled on the lawn beside a paved area furnished with wooden tables. Along with smokes, secrets are also shared here. The same woman who watched over me wheeled me outside on one of my first nights, staring at me with disdain as I dug through an ashtray, shakily seeking hits of discarded nicotine. Michael has said I couldn't sit upright during our first encounter. I slumped sideways in my chair, the woman hovering over me in case I fell, my fingers latched onto my abdomen. According to Michael, I said I needed a cigarette and he should give me one because I was about to die. Given what happened after my first days (and what continues to happen, now), my words still frighten me. Michael obliged.

In addition to Michael, I would meet people who would unintentionally but irrevocably alter the course of my life. Before they were people, though, they were simply patients – a group of Brits to whom I was an outsider. I was a mistake, an import who had taken a wrong turn and landed in a mental hospital. This is how I saw myself, anyway. I know that after those first two days, I became semi-capable of talking. I know that whenever someone introduced themselves, I name-dropped Oxford and then stopped, pained, and began to weep instead. All I could say, over and over, was I wanted my life back.

Three

While my first week in hospital is piecemeal, I retained some information. For instance, I was told that my stay was a sort of emergency favour. I had bypassed the Priory's lengthy waitlist, and Nuffield was paying fifteen hundred Canadian dollars a day for me to be there. I also learned that no one had my medical records. I was a total stranger; an anonymous foreigner who, other than needing to be monitored while receiving pharmaceutical assistance, would be fit to pack up and ship off within the week. What no one realized, me included, was that in the coming days, weeks, and months, I would need a lot more than pharmaceuticals.

The Priory Woking, which is the nearest of the network's brick-and-mortar facilities to Oxford, has three streams. First is general psychiatry. It treats those who struggle with anxiety, depression, bereavement, and the like. Next is alcohol therapy (ATP, for short), which is twelve-step and abstinence based. Finally, there is eating disorders. This program tends to have only a few patients at a time, and its main focus is weight restoration. Members of each stream also attend individual and group-based therapies, most of which pertain to motivation for change, relapse prevention, and post-discharge aftercare. The majority of the Priory's patients are funded by England's National Health Service (NHS), which means they receive little information about when they can expect to be admitted, where they will be admitted, and, strangest of all, when they will have to leave. In the coming days, I would learn more about this infrastructure, and I would become enraged by its limitations. Initially, though, I was confused. In theory, I belonged in all of the streams. But as a patient who had been admitted only to detox, I was excluded from all of them.

The more I heard about the Priory, the more mystified I was. I had been to eating disorder treatment once, had been to addiction treatment thrice, and had been involuntarily committed (or "sectioned," as the British call it) more times than I can count. In Canada, it is rare for a facility to operate as a catch-all institution. Usually, those who have been diagnosed with eating disorders will not be admitted to treatment if they disclose concurrent addictions, while those who are admitted to addiction treatment with eating disorders are instructed to self-manage the latter or are encouraged to apply twelve-step modalities such as praying to their eating.[i] However, despite claiming to treat all conditions, the Priory still operated much like the centres I had already been to. Each stream was siloed, and patients completed a pre-intake interview so they could be divided based on their biggest concern. In practice, this meant those who had been labelled with substance abuse disorder rarely interacted with those who were general psych or eating disorder patients, general psych patients rarely interacted with those who had eating disorders or substance abuse issues, and so on. As someone who was label-less, I would float between the streams, converse with whomever I wished, and see the absurdity of reducing people to a single identity. At first, I was just distraught.

---

[i] Despite the frequency of comorbidities, most treatment centres are ill-prepared to support patients with more than one disorder. For example, the last time I attended addiction treatment, the help I got for bulimia included not being permitted in the dining room without a staff member present, signing a contract stating that I consented to being monitored (including while using the toilet) for thirty minutes after each meal, and being told that god would cure me should I want it bad enough. While I did maintain abstinence from bulimia for five years following this, I also had a list of "safe foods" I could count on one hand and none of the issues that led to my eating disorders in the first place have ever been addressed. This speaks to some assumptions made in the healthcare system about a patient's baseline cognitive abilities and neurotype.

Four

Once more, I was profoundly disoriented. Trying to reconstruct events henceforth as though they occurred sequentially feels incorrect, disingenuous, because, for most of my stay, time and space were disturbed. I am restricted by western temporal and spatial orders that conceive of both as objective, constant, and "real" – Newtonion absolutes independent of consciousness and at once fixed (space) and ceaselessly marching forward (time). But what is present? What is future? What is recurring, devastating past?[ii] My intention is not to recount a consecutive summary of what happened at the Priory. Rather, it is to *construct* a summary – all of which will be true, some of which may be only true to me – and, in so doing, demarcate boundaries, however contrived, around this opaque event. Otherwise, I may never leave.

One thing I do know is as soon as I was capable of walking, talking, and eating again, I began to binge and purge. Alcoholic, bulimic Nicole was fully in charge, which is not surprising given how I was admitted. The Priory has a gourmet food service, and for a while, bulimia kept me going. It was an emotional outlet, something pleasurable, a way to pass the time. Like previous hospitalizations, my days were structured around breakfast, lunch, dinner – tangible events with which to distract myself, soothe myself, and retain some agency over. My agency, however, while emotionally and cognitively imperative, was also killing me physically.

After reviewing my height and weight, the on-site dietician was concerned about refeeding syndrome. These are the hormonal and metabolic disturbances experienced when severely underweight people start eating again, and while they can cause cardiac arrhythmias, comas, and death, I wasn't actually digesting. Even if I had been, these

---

[ii] Western thinkers have a history of co-opting eastern and Indigenous metaphysics. For instance, representations of time as circular have influenced psychological research on the "time perspectives" of trauma survivors. Recent work on traumatic grief "re"-conceptualizes time as a cyclical process that should be measured by "meaningful" rather than chronological time, an approach that seems novel in the west but echoes cross-cultural wisdom.[1]

felt like negligible risks. Daphne, a young care aide, bore the brunt of my fury about having a reduced intake. "This is bullshit!" I shrieked when she explained why the kitchen servers had placed a half portion in front of me at lunch. "I am *not* in the eating disorders program! I am *not* here to recover! *Bulimia is all I have.*"

At the time, I was not wrong. In terms of survival, bulimia really was all I had. It was the one reprieve, the one beacon of light, amid what felt like the darkest reality imaginable. Asking someone who has no hope to suddenly abstain from a behaviour that releases endorphins is asking a lot. Too much, perhaps. I had relied on disordered eating for twenty years and could not eliminate it willingly. Having to sit with my thoughts would have been worse. After a few days of discord – one meal I had half portions, the next I was served a regular portion, following that I had a regular portion but no dessert, until finally the entire dining room was privy to an altercation between the head chef and another staff member about my meal plan – the dietician backed off. I spent my first week at the Priory losing more weight, observing the eating disorders program, and bingeing and purging just metres from where staff provided meal support.

FIVE

Around this time, my tutor came to visit. She brought toiletries, identification, and electronics. I did not care about the first two but was preoccupied with my laptop. I sensed it would be vital. My tutor sat, hands clasped, and said I had been suspended from Oxford on medical grounds. I would be allowed to restart my degree after deferring it for a year, and, while this may have been reasonable, it felt like a death sentence, existentially. I wanted to pretend the previous month simply hadn't happened. My tutor made it clear this was not an option, and then she hugged me, handed me my laptop, and left clutching a designer handbag and tear-stained paperwork.

Once she was gone, the general lounge we sat in filled with patients. It was antiquated and seemed to have been decorated a century or so before. The walls were a rich maroon, and it contained obsolescent furniture, rows of shelving units filled with peculiar sundries, and an enormous, anachronistic television. A sign on the entrance read, "Door to be left open for observation," a reminder that despite not resembling one, the Priory was still a hospital. There would be no privacy even for those grieving. As I cried, a patient named Ethan entered and asked in earnest to help. I told him that he couldn't, I very much wished to die, and, when he refused to leave, I let him embrace me, anyway.

Ethan was thirty-six and part of the general psych stream. A silver-haired bachelor who was mocked mercilessly at times for overdressing, he also struggled with substance use. We bonded one morning over our shared proclivity for chaos – our common predilection for self-destruction. This was during one of my more "stable" moments, which I soon feared I would never experience again. Under different circumstances, I might have thought Ethan was attractive. But because I was so vulnerable, was so utterly dis-interested in sex, I saw him as a brother; someone to gravitate toward when I felt unsafe. Like all patients, Ethan had his own demons – he had blown through a family fortune, was embroiled in a custody battle, his daughter had leukemia – but he concealed them under a wicked grin, ounces of hair gel, and impeccably tailored trousers. In contrast, I was destroyed. My appearance reflected this.

On the day my tutor visited, she explained that my luggage would be shipped via courier once she and a porter had packed my things. I would end up waiting over a week for clothing, but I couldn't have cared less. However, I did eventually notice my lips bleeding and my skin sloughing off. Weeks of dehydration, starvation, and neglect had aged me – had produced a garish reflection I no longer recognized when I dared peer in the mirror. Because I was still being observed (and because I was pumped too full of benzos to stand), I couldn't leave the grounds. I responded to this hostilely, swearing audaciously that I would be fine if I went to purchase moisturizer. When a doctor asked me to prove this by walking with accompaniment from one end of the Priory's lawn to the other, I begrudgingly conceded I would fall if I tried. Staff could run errands for me, and, humiliated, I did not ask so much as demand that Daphne, the care aide, borrow money from the hospital on my behalf. After she returned with lotion, I practically bathed in it. Applying and re-applying it felt sumptuous, gratifying, and indulgent, and it was here that weeks of dissociation gave way to corporeality. This was the first of many instances where I would be confronted, gently and then brutally, with the complex logistics of embodiment.

Ethan teased me often, wondering good naturedly if I planned on getting dressed. I had bigger concerns – when my next meal would be, for instance – but his ribbing did not bother me. If anything, our banter normalized things. It reminded me that others existed outside my private hell. Humour is life-affirming and mandatory when one has nothing left. I had been in similar positions before, but I was also aware that former instances of having nothing had given way to having even less: no one knew where I was, I was unemployed and suspended from school, and I was homeless in both Europe and North America. As someone who had been street-entrenched between the ages of nineteen and twenty-one, the trauma of coming full circle was calamitous. I had gone overnight from being a DPhil candidate at Oxford to being nobody – a withering drifter with no friends, family, or identity. All I had were my weighty thoughts and unbearable feelings and both of these, I would soon realize, were also not ensured.

Six

After speaking with my tutor, I thought I understood my situation. I would stay at the Priory for seven days, Nuffield would book my flight back to Canada, and, I decided, I needed a job. Where I would live wasn't yet relevant because securing employment (as a research assistant, perhaps, which would reinforce to myself and others that I was a *serious academic*) would distract me after landing. As horrific as things were, I minimized my circumstances aggressively. Rather than accurately appraise what had happened – I had torched my life to the ground and was now standing shakily among the wreckage – I started to feel unencumbered; liberated, even. I decided not to return to Vancouver. The city was too imbued with pain, and I knew I couldn't avoid reminders of my past. After having fled, the thought of explaining myself was also just... too much. I would go to Ontario or Quebec. Anywhere, really, different from where I had been. Things like formal treatment for my eating disorder, my substance abuse, or my Madness didn't even occur to me. I would pick a province, any province, and deal with housing later.

My denial expanded when my tutor said I had permission to begin the literature review for my dissertation. My advisor's offer to work remotely for the next year was a silver lining – something to cling to as a life preserver that wasn't just bulimia. I knew on some level I was in active addiction and would drink myself to death the moment I left the Priory. But I suppressed these thoughts, and whenever I felt uneasy, I told myself I would be ahead of my next cohort.

As I reflect on my journey, I remember once more to be kind – I carried a heavy load. On days four and five, I needed a reason to leave bed; a reason to keep breathing. Academia was a convenient anchor because, like bulimia, it is familiar. Unlike bulimia, it is socially acceptable. It is venerated by many, some of whom struggle with self-worth to the same extent that I do. I still believed workaholism was admirable, and its effect is ataractic. Both the voices and the disjointed, disconcerting shapes that govern my cognition dwindle when focused on a project. That said, as much as I liked the thought of producing, my impulse control was also nonexistent. I would enter the dining room, which was also jarringly formal and very British, five minutes before each meal. When my food arrived, I had already drunk a litre of juice and eaten a dozen wedges of bread, responding to others' naive inquiries ("Where do you put it all!?") with perfected performative sheepishness. This occurred alongside a reduction in my benzodiazepines, which were being tapered as I exited the most dangerous period of withdrawal. Suddenly, parts of myself with entirely different epistemologies, ontologies, and functionality collided. I was at once bulimic, chaotic Nicole, whose capacity for accomplishment is minimal, and achievement-obsessed Nicole, whose one gear is full speed ahead. I wanted to immerse myself in academia, pore over articles, and find a research position. I wanted to eat and vomit indefinitely. My somatic symptoms returned, and the overwhelming pressure in my head led to confusion and then panic. I stopped sleeping, and the voices, constant companions, also grew much louder.

Seven

Each morning at precisely seven, a chorus of, "Morning!" "Ello!" "You alright!?" echoes through the corridors. It is chipper, predictable, invasive. As it escalated in coming days, it also came from my mind. I had initially heard the chorus but hadn't consciously processed it until I stopped the benzodiazepines. Then, as the sedation wore off, I experienced hyperarousal and my amygdala, the limbic structure in charge of fear response and anxiety, triggered fight or flight. In my room, regardless of time, "Morning!" "Ello!" "You alright!?" persisted. These objectively neutral stimuli had gotten lodged in my psyche and were making me feel trapped. More strangely, each person sounded identical irrespective of age, gender, or race. "Morning!" "Ello!" "You alright!?" Over and over and over. "This is bizarre," I told Michael. "I feel like I'm on Mars." After having been dropped in the English countryside with no prior European travel experience, the Priory could have been in space.

The cognition of trauma is complex. I don't fully understand it. That said, I know traumatic memories lack spatiotemporal coherence – overwhelming emotions derived from confronting one's mortality may be purposefully forgotten, can appear without warning, and, because they are encoded in the body, may not be articulable.[iii] I also know "disorientation," though not a specific DSM diagnosis, is still seen as a bad thing. To be seriously disoriented is to experience such cognitive, emotional, physical, and affectual turmoil that persisting – simply going on – is onerous. Most view this negatively, but feminist philosophers and bioethicists have argued that disorientation also has utility. What if, while symbolizing the end of one's road, being disoriented indicates a divergence of sorts – the emergence of a new

---

[iii] There are disagreements about how memory is affected in post-traumatic stress disorder. Some argue that traumatic memory can be forgotten unintentionally or through purposeful forgetting. However, other research suggests that autobiographical memory is unintentionally enhanced by surprising, emotion-enhancing events. Generally, we know that traumatic memories tend to be less coherent than neutral memories and that writing may enable people to create more orderly narrative representations of "meaningful" time.[2]

path and with it, the ability to see the world (and oneself) through a vastly different lens?[iv]

By the last few days of my first week I was experiencing radical shifts in perception and embodiment. At times I felt elated and was phenomenally energetic, which was a stark contrast to having not been able to stand. This was followed always by despair. For example, I remember my first time walking not just the few metres to the smoking hut but continuing beyond it to the grounds. I hadn't yet taken stock of my surroundings, so overwhelmed had I been first with detoxing and then with trying to process where I was. When I did, I was in awe.

The Priory Wokingham resembles an aged, well-preserved mansion more than it does a hospital. It has a country-house exterior that is painted a tasteful off-white, and it sits atop a beautifully maintained acreage. Ethereal fog shrouds the landscape, and the atmosphere is dreamlike, especially when one already feels like they are dreaming. The hospital is also located directly beside a gun range. All day, every day, public conversations and private thoughts are peppered with what sound like cannonballs firing. I don't know whose idea this was, but a patient confirmed I wasn't imagining the baritone "pow! pow! pow!" that rumbled ceaselessly in the distance. The morning I took all this in, I was travelling alone and listening to one of my favourite songs, an uptempo anthem historically associated with fun, joy, and lust. Minutes later I had transitioned from walking to running, skipping, singing, and dancing. Life was miraculous, not because I had survived something terrible, but because I was overcome with anticipatory excitement at the prospect of eating breakfast. I liked bingeing on the talented kitchen's confectionaries, and accompanied

---

[iv] The fifth edition of the DSM states that in order to be diagnosed with PTSD, a person must experience "trauma-related arousal and reactivity" such as hypervigilance and heightened startle reaction, and it assumes that people will avoid reminders of the traumatic event. However, "trauma" may be a cumulative load derived from prolonged exposure instead of a single, discrete event. The body adapts to this over time, and the ubiquity of the diagnosis has also emerged in a socio-cultural-political context that tends to pathologize most human responses without having a shared definition of what trauma actually entails. The same can be said of disorientation.[3]

by such optimistic lyrics, I had no insight into (or interest in) what might happen after.

   When I actually started bingeing, however, I remembered it is hugely pleasurable at first and then it feels horrific. I eat (and eat, and eat) so swiftly, and until so overwhelmingly full, that I half-walk, half-run, gripping my gut in extraordinary pain and fear (*please don't rupture*), to the nearest toilet the second I snap out of it. After so many years of bulimia, all I do to purge is contract my stomach muscles and watch the contents of my digestive tract whoooosh back out of my body. I then take twenty sips and purge again. Twenty sips of water. Purge. Twenty sips of water. Purge. Again, and again, and again (*cleanse yourself*) until I am purging nothing but water, acid, and bile. After, I was gutted. Exhausted. Hopeless. The *squeezing* on my skull, rhythmic and inescapable, reduced me to a marionette, left without a puppet master and capable only of crawling back to bed while wondering deliriously when staff would finally stop saying "Ello!"

Eight

Because I couldn't see how rapidly I traversed rapture and sorrow, I focused on finding employment. Bulimia still took up most of my day, but I was determined to concoct a plan. To this end I solicited the help of Dave, a twenty-three-year-old patient who was also a tech-whiz multi-millionaire. Dave had earned his fortune buying and selling Bitcoin (alongside less savoury endeavours he did not discuss in detail), and he eagerly showed photos of his cars, summer homes, and lavish sojourns abroad. Dave was far shrewder than his bashful laugh and amiable demeanour suggested, and he was also generous. When I told him I needed a job but couldn't use my laptop, he hacked the Priory's firewall and got me access to wi-fi.

I had settled on moving out of province. I knew no one outside Vancouver, but I wanted to begin a new life. Again. On my fifth night, in the lounge with Dave, Ethan, and Michael, I tried to search for jobs. But I was too distracted. Dave always treated his friends to an after-dinner snack, and the moment I saw the Sainsbury's bag, I was overcome with an animalistic urge to consume, to shovel handfuls of crisps, boxes of cookies, mug after mug of hot chocolate mix into my mouth between ducking into the visitor's toilet to purge. I would continue this until near collapse, the squeezing in my skull intensifying with every bite, and I was not at all discreet. But no one said a thing. They politely ignored me, and, sensing their acceptance, I allowed myself to trust them.

Malnourishment is odd. I don't know to what extent my bingeing was circumstantial, habitual, and/or neurophysiological. Sustained nutrient-deprivation can have severe, deleterious consequences on cognition and behaviour, and commonly referenced is the seminal study in which Ancel Keys spent twenty-four weeks severely restricting the intake of thirty-six men.[4] Most got depressed, lost interest in sex, and relayed somatic concerns while also describing emotional distress, declines in concentration, comprehension, and judgement, and self-harming. After the experiment, they also consumed more than they had before. Sound familiar? Since then, some researchers have proposed the body has a homeostatic feedback system for regulating adiposity or fatness. This means starvation triggers the release of stress hormones linked to intense cravings – a way of demanding one return to their "set point" weight. Set-point theory is contentious, but I have no doubt that some of my bingeing at the Priory was simply due to hunger.

That said, I have explained that disordered eating serves multiple, complementary and competing functions.[v] The idea that one "listen to their body," particularly in eating disorder treatment, overlooks somatic pain, lack of interoception, and that bulimia isn't just a physical response to restriction. The adrenalin released as I'm bingeing is a natural extension of mania regardless of my weight, and, as Bruce Alexander and his Rat Park experiments have proven, deriving pleasure from self-destruction, even to the point of death, is largely environmental. I felt captive in a mental hospital; this was a hugely impactful event over which I had little – no – control, and I was employing every survival strategy I had at my disposal. Bulimia is supremely effective for avoidance, and in my first week at the Priory, I needed to avoid. Is it so surprising, then, to have relied on this behaviour to get me through?

---

[v] Body weight and shape tend to be positioned as simple, straightforward phenomena. However, not only are bodies complex machines whose weight and shape are far less predictable than most would prefer, an overemphasis on these in eating disorder treatment overlooks cognitive and somatic reasons for anorexia, bulimia, and so on. Here I am not referring to the equally reductive assumption that disordered eating is about a fear of "fatness," but rather wish to point out that disordered eating can also feel pleasurable in the body. Bingeing and purging is one of only a few activities that distracts from my somatic pain, and since I lack interoception, or the ability to feel and name my bodily processes, restriction and bulimia do elicit important senses of agency. Finally, repetitive food consumption for me is equally about textural and tactile pleasure as it is about caloric concerns.

NINE

Having binged, I was agitated, and, devoid of insight into how reckless this was, I finally called my parents. I can't remember our conversation beyond them being angry and my mother reiterating over and over how badly I'd fucked up. This triggered an extraordinary wave of grief, one that arises from unequivocal rejection, and I recall sobbing, begging, and promising to be better. I don't know what my mother's perception of this conversation would be, but through my eyes this has been our pattern: I act obscenely, I seek out comfort from my mother, and in doing so I am chastised; berated for being undisciplined; told in no uncertain terms I ought to be ashamed. Each of my accomplishments has been fuelled by this dynamic, this overidentification with how she sees me, and each of my failures has reinforced that she is right – I am a hopeless case.

After this interaction, I also sent messages to my University of British Columbia – UBC – graduate cohort. They had reached out during my time at Nuffield, but as I deteriorated, I hadn't been able to respond. I wanted them to believe I was fine; I was so busy with seminars and socializing and excelling I simply didn't have time to chat. Then, as I lost my provisional grip on "reality," I had forgotten they existed. In 2015, my cohort had watched me unravel and had supported me despite receiving days' worth of messages rife with disturbing content. I was still connected to them and knew them as safe – not able to empathize, exactly, but kind and earnest in their care for me.

The moment I greeted them from the Priory, something funny happened. I had been beside myself, but as I sat in the gazebo and composed a meandering update, I felt cheerful. Overjoyed, even. What had just been unfathomable was comical. Hilarious, really. "People, it seems that I have pulled a Nicole," I told them, giggling wildly and speaking aloud to no one in particular, "This is 2015 all over again, only this time, it's in British!" I dismissed their sympathies. I assured them I was absolutely fine, and this would be great fodder for a story. I would continue to message my cohort for the duration of my stay. The messages I sent reveal much about my splintered subjectivity. They show that part of me (the part of me that regularly joked via messenger about the surreal goings-on around me) was wickedly entertained. They also highlight how this part, though still technically Nicole, was an entirely distinct personality state from the Nicole who had arrived at the Priory, who was an entirely distinct personality state from the Nicole who would become more salient in coming days and was completely engulfed in fear.

   One of the first people I told my cohort about was Igor, the Priory's on-call physician. He was eccentric. Belgium-born, he spoke with a thick, gruff accent, he deployed unintelligible jargon, he always wore a suit, and he gesticulated erratically, his mannerisms and demeanour arbitrary, overbearing, and cartoon-esque – a parody of a cantankerous old man who happened to be a doctor. Igor had been the one breathalyzing me on my first night, and after comprehending his name and role, I saw him as an adversary. The reasons for this were multiple, but in sum, he didn't inspire confidence. My perception was influenced by his disposition and blatant disinterest as I described my mental health history. When I said I wasn't sleeping, he shrugged nonchalantly and reminded me that he wasn't a psychiatrist, I was just there to detox, and medication could be prescribed once I was back in Canada. In most contexts this approach would have been okay. I also hesitate to imply that medication would have benefited me since my journey was just beginning and could have been supressed by the introduction of foreign chemicals. But (and this is as big "but") neither Igor nor any others took seriously what I was trying to say – something (something foreign yet familiar) was happening. I was on the precipice of upheaval. Of course, I didn't have the words for this myself. When I met Igor in the wee hours, each of us pacing up and down the Priory's long, winding corridors, him trying to remain awake and me counting down the hours until breakfast, he would give me a light sedative, enough to knock me out in theory but not be drowsy afterward. The sedatives were futile, and their effect was even stimulating. Soon Igor would realize, as would I, how critical this juncture was.

PART FOUR

Ten

I couldn't work at the Priory. Being so focused on bulimia severely marred my thinking, and, while there were other, far more potent forces that blighted it, these were still hidden from consciousness. I was supposed to leave in two days but still had no place to stay, no income source, and no life acumen – no awareness of why I had done what I had done or what I should do next. I was convinced I would be more productive from town, even as I didn't really believe that my need to be alone was wholly born of pragmatism. My true motivation was wanting (needing) to buy more binge food. I couldn't accept what had happened, and the shame of returning, not with a DPhil but as a caricature of myself – cadaverous, ravaged, both mentally and physically – was intolerable. Instead, I wanted (needed) to distract.

At the Priory, each patient is assigned to a psychiatrist ("consultant") who wields a tremendous amount of power. Specifically, they dictate if patients can leave on passes, for how long these passes will be, and if they are trusted to go alone. I had heard about the consultants from disgruntled patients who had been denied pass requests, but I didn't know I had one. This was in part because my thought processes were disjointed, my memory incohesive and discordant, and also because I was neglected. Unlike other patients, I was never assessed for groups, I was omitted from individual therapy, and every time I interacted with staff (other than Daphne, who definitely remembered my rudeness), our conversations began with a puzzled prompt to remind them who I was. Rather than engage with programming, I floated. I noticed the goings-on around me, internalized very little of them, and binged to pass the time.

On my sixth day, I finally met my consultant. Dr. Herner said he knew I had come from Oxford and was supposed to soon leave for Vancouver, but, otherwise, he was uninformed of my medical or trauma history and was completely oblivious to the fact that I could barely see straight. Colours had taken on an evanescent quality, in that red became blue became purple all at once, and I could no longer discern my inner dialogue (*Morning! Ello! You alright!?*) from statements made by him, a nurse, and patient passersby. My head was in a vice (*squeeeeeze, squeeeeeze, squeeeeeze*), and because of this, even sitting was taxing.

I did not say any of this. Dr. Herner was merely an obstacle – the gatekeeper to freedom, however illusory, and I needed to convince him I was fine to leave. Fearful Nicole was supressed in favour of pompous Nicole, who assured him she (I) just wanted a quiet space to explore travel and housing. Dr. Herner agreed my timeline was urgent, he cautioned against drinking ("It would be mighty embarrassing to have to tell the folks at Oxford that we let you run off and get blottoed, Nicole," he said sternly), and after I assured him I would not, he issued me a day pass.

My pass would begin the following day, and it had the caveat that Daphne would walk me to town to show me the library. This was a wise decision on Dr. Herner's part – discombobulation aside, most people would suggest I at least be given directions – but I was so eager to binge (which I knew but would not concede) that Daphne's inclusion irked me. At the same time, I was not just annoyed. Two opposing forces clashed within me – a dialectic of intensity, indifference, desire, and disinterest. I was quasi-mindful of the fact that I was seeing and hearing things not part of consensus reality, but when I spoke with Dr. Herner I couldn't reveal my vulnerabilities even if I had wanted to.[vi] I attribute this to conditioning from both family and psychiatry. I was taught that to acknowledge weakness is to be abused or worse, ignored – dismissed outright as exaggerating and attention seeking or simply "mentally ill." Even now, the cliché "it's okay not to be okay" evokes grief and ire because in my experience, it is most certainly *not* okay not to be okay – not when one has only herself.

[vi] Here I use "consensus reality" to refer to mutually agreed upon sights, sounds, and other sensual experiences, but the idea that "reality" is generally based on appeal to consensus (versus objective fact) has been explored in philosophy, sociology, physics, literature, art, and activism. The "Hearing Voices Network," for example, hosted a public event at the Institute for the Development of Human Arts in October 2019, called "Exploring Non-Consensus Reality."

Eleven

I spent the rest of day six much as I had day five, alternating between alarm (*Morning! Ello! You alright!? Why can't I see properly — What the hell is happening!?*), apathy, and merriment. I chatted with other patients, I learned and promptly forgot details about them, and I networked with Vancouver. Sort of. That is, I received the occasional message from my graduate cohort, and while my friends interacted with me on the basis of what I had just sent them, I could never remember having been in touch. I read and re-read walls of text that were written by someone who was having one hell of a good time, and the dissonance between my social self and other selves was unnerving. I believe that each time I received one of these messages and had to re-read my own, I was influenced by the energy of my previous statements. I absorbed this energy, even digitally, and I transitioned into the personality state of someone who was indeed enjoying herself — who would then respond on this basis only to revert to fear, until a short time later, the cycle began anew.

I know as I write I am describing the characteristics of someone with a dissociative disorder. Symptoms of these at their most severe include the existence of two or more distinct identities ("personality states") accompanied by changes in behaviour and thinking, as well as ongoing gaps in memory about everyday events, personal information, and/or past traumatic events. This is widely recognized as adaptive, and those who structurally dissociate frequently report histories of overpowering, potentially life-threatening disturbances alongside severe interpersonal and environmental stressors. It is thus difficult for me to reconcile my own childhood — which was characterized by intermittent violence and definite (perceived) threats to my survival, yes, but that also included sports trips, Christmas presents, and summer vacations — with the horrific abuse associated in research and public imagination with dissociation. I don't know if I am *allowed* to claim having experienced sufficient childhood trauma to warrant this, when my trauma, compared to ritualistic torture and incest, for example, is relatively mundane.

That said, my parents' decision making later in life (and, specifically, my mother's decision to send me to a homeless shelter) is not reconcilable. I reflect now on the taxi ride to Covenant House Vancouver, and I remember feeling… nothing. Absolutely nothing. At the time, I did what I had always done (I did what was necessary to survive) in that I rapidly assessed my situation (*I am now homeless*), and I integrated this information, poorly. I could not grieve, and I realize now the "overwhelming, potentially life-threatening disturbance" I experienced that day was me. At nineteen years old, in the back of a taxi, I killed myself. I killed my naivety, my stable sense of belonging in the world, and whatever was left of childhood. I did this so my adult self could remain alive, as the pain I experienced that day and afterward would have led me to suicide had I fully acknowledged it. Instead, I hardened. I became "street-entrenched." I did "hit bottom," which, according to my mother, was supposed to motivate change, but rather than stop bingeing, purging, and drinking, I mostly bounced along bottom for another three years, smoking crack and doing street-based sex work, as I watched my friends die one by one. The person I had been pre-taxi was annihilated in an instant. "You were impossible" is always my mother's response when I challenge her decision, "You were a monster," and while she may be right – I was violent toward my mother while intoxicated as a teen – every monster needs her Frankenstein, and my violence wasn't random.

I wonder now how I may have responded or who I could have been had my mother known that anorexia and bulimia were attempts to manufacture safety in an unsafe environment. *I did this for you!* I have always wanted to say: *I dedicated my childhood to protecting you, no one asked me how I was doing – how can you be mean about this!?* Instead, there were pocket searches, refrigerator locks, and incessant reminders I was disgusting, indulgent, and spoiled. When I drank, the rage I had supressed (the rage I could not feel lest my mother need my help) erupted. It was the rage of someone whose needs have always been denied. Perhaps, I tell myself, I wouldn't have started drinking alcoholically had Mom not been so cruel. Perhaps, I tell myself, I would now be among those who are "recovered" from their eating disorders. Perhaps there would have been no taxi. Perhaps I wouldn't still crave crack cocaine because I would never have been introduced to crack cocaine, and, perhaps, I wouldn't need to write this book (perhaps, perhaps, perhaps).

Amid my confusion, I will not diagnose. In addition to uncertainty about if or when I "split," it can be difficult to distinguish the symptoms of dissociative disorders from the effects of complex trauma.[vii] Most importantly, my intention with this text is to challenge the importance of labels; what I "have" or "am" isn't up to the psy-complex. I *am* positive that my amnesia, rapid oscillation between states, and being told I have a borderline personality indicates I dissociated in 2015 on the night I sent the letter. However, whatever I have/am now was crystallized in Oxford. I reflect on the evening I spent alone in the A&E, the horror I felt at how difficult it was, both cognitively and physiologically, not to unleash a torrent of venom on the nursing staff, and I sense my inner world had changed. Dissociative identity disorder was formerly referred to as multiple personality disorder, and in my case this isn't accurate: I did/do not have multiple personalities in that I am always Nicole Luongo. What I do is regress in age (the petrified Nicole at the Priory was roughly six or seven), and before I learned to manage this, I didn't know it was happening. That said (and this is detrimental), even when I am a whimpering, snivelling, debilitated adolescent, I cannot reveal it. Since asking for help is dangerous, when I am at my most vulnerable, I am also kind of a jerk.

[vii] "Dissociation" is an encompassing term for a wide spectrum of cognition, and most people do it at least occasionally. For example, it may be as mundane as losing track of time while scrolling social media or being mildly emotionally detached. To have a clinically significant dissociative disorder, one must experience substantial distress or problems in social, occupational or other areas of functioning due to symptoms such as memory loss, immobilization, absorption in alternate realities, lack of time awareness, and/or a range of unusual body sensations. In extreme cases, sometimes referred to as "structural dissociation" or dissociative identity disorder (formerly multiple personality disorder) a person appears to become two or more people. Some argue that dissociative disorders and post-traumatic stress disorder are linked in origin and symptom presentation and should be classified within the same diagnostic category.[5]

Twelve

I was hyperactive the next morning. The prospect of leaving was all encompassing, so excited was I to finally be alone. I had an eight-hour pass and was expected at lunch to update the nurses on my progress. I didn't yet know if I would make any, but I stifled my disquiet and thought about bulimia. It was apparent by now I could not fly home (what home?) the next day, and Nuffield would fund my stay through the weekend. Rather than feel embarrassed (or anxious, or anything really beyond hunger), I interpreted this information to mean that living arrangements were only marginally important. I wanted to believe I was choosing this – that I still *could* choose – but I was no longer able to see, hear, or think audibly: Sights, sounds, and voices had hybridized into an indiscernible fusion of stimuli, and I knew there was no way I would do anything productive.

Before I left, I retrieved my backpack. This required unearthing it from a locked cupboard and watching Daphne remove shards of wine-stained glass still nestled in the bottom. After doing so, I completed a risk assessment, hurriedly hissing the answers (Would I return? "Yes." Would I drink? "No." Was I suicidal? "No.") I knew staff wanted to hear. I wasn't certain about anything, but the urge to leave was visceral. I paced, vibrating with anticipation, until Daphne was ready at last.

As we left the grounds, I began to feel uneasy. It was hard to think, walk, and breathe. I hid my escalating panic as we turned off the driveway and onto a country road, one that initially curved sharply and then straightened before becoming a four-way stop. When Daphne explained how easy getting to the shops was, I simply smiled and nodded, maintaining my composure. This was the first time I was polite, but internally I was screaming. The vice-like pain in my skull was intolerable, and by the time we reached the library some ten minutes later, I wanted to do nothing but sit, catch my breath, and curl into a tight ball on the ground. I did none of those things, and as I bid Daphne farewell, I suppressed the urge to tell her I was scared – to ask her to hold my hand and maybe give me a hug.

The library opened at eleven. I had four minutes to wait and told Daphne I would go to the café next door. The moment she left I beelined inside and ordered quiche, sandwiches, lasagna, and two large soft drinks. I was too frightened not to eat because the alternative – acknowledging my aloneness – would have been immobilizing. I proceeded to the post office and bought fistfuls of chocolate before entering the library and inhaling them, with my back to the librarian. Shoving wrapper after wrapper into my backpack, I stood to purge once the chocolate was gone. However, the faded blue door beside the librarian's desk that read "toilet" was locked. It was for disabled patrons only, but after meeting my pleading gaze and noting the stains on my week-old clothing, the librarian softened and handed me the key.

 I couldn't identify it at the time, but this was a pivotal moment. It was a turning point as I admitted subconsciously that I was not okay. I was *very* not okay. I staggered down the street, unable to remember from which direction I had come or where I should go next. I happened upon a shop and bought sandwiches, protein bars, and vegetables – foods I swore I would digest and foods I tore into the moment I left the shop. I was petrified. I referred to the number Daphne had scrawled on a business card and waited for a taxi, shaking, eyes not seeing, and eating on a bench. When I got to the hospital, I stashed my remaining purchases before greeting a group of nurses. I was expecting to be breathalyzed and to have my bag searched, but they barely noticed my presence. I then retreated to my room where I continued to eat and purge, mechanically and timorously, until I was called for lunch.

Thirteen

The plan had been to leave again after lunch, but the drawer beside my bed overflowed with food from my outing and other patients, most of whom I recognized only by face and ability to proffer snacks and cigarettes. I was carnally drawn to it, and I spent the afternoon eating, purging; eating, purging; eating, purging; crying. I admitted, finally and definitively, something was not right.

My experiences at the Priory have reinforced the absurdity of mind-body dualism. Trying to distinguish between my physical, emotional, and mental states at this time feels impossible – violent, even. Physiological processes were (are) inextricable from cognitive ones, and purging that day left me vibrating physically and racing psychically at a rate I never had before. In response to this, I kept bingeing. Doing so was rote. I wanted nothing more than to eat a real meal and sleep, and each time I purged I stared in the mirror, lifting my sweater and gaping, aghast, at what my torso had become. I could cup my ribcage, play it like a xylophone, and listen with horror as it emitted a spectral wail. I had become a ghost.

Then I was struck by a sudden, hideous thought: *Could I be dead!?* This did not feel like a question so much as I became certain in an instant that my bender had actually killed me. I had perished at Nuffield and this place, these people, my sensations of embodiment – all moribund figments of imagination, my last vestiges of quasi-coherence before the floor gave way and I landed far below. This was a sort of British purgatory – prolonged poetic justice for all the damage I had done. I probably deserved it. These thoughts arrived in rapid succession. They resonated physically, each one a conduit for the currents of shock that sped down my spine and caused my knees to buckle. I was reduced to a child, trying vainly to process a series of very adult (*abandonment-rape-alcohol-drugs-psych-wards-bulimia-homelessness-now, somehow, dead in a British hospital!?*) realities. I had been ignoring these realities for years via an endless tide of food, alcohol, drugs, men, and academia, and, now, in this bizarre, unpredictable context, they were seeping through my protective barriers, demanding that I see them. Being dead was easier.

PART FOUR

Fourteen

Though I've only introduced a few of them, the Priory had a group of patients – an ensemble cast of characters, if you will – colourful enough to rival that of any television dramedy. On my seventh day there, I needed them. Collectively, they supported me, held me up, literally and metaphorically, as my world collapsed around me. The Priory was no longer comical, I was not having fun, this was very bad. Besides Michael, Ethan, and Dave, I had met Kielan, an affable thirty-something who had been admitted for substance abuse some two weeks prior. During our first conversation, Kielan said his liver was shot and to drink again, even once, would kill him. I understood. Kielan was thoughtful but rowdy, mature but dishevelled, serious but profane. He called me "chicken" and was also, I would decide, attractive. On day seven, though, I just knew that he was soothing; that fierce and alluring as it was, I benefited from his warmth.

When the food was gone, I found Kielan in the gazebo smoking and chatting with Gretal, a vibrant Black woman who was also part of the alcohol therapy. They were waiting for visitors as I stormed toward them, gesticulating wildly. They stared wordlessly as I tried to convey the enormity of it (*I was supposed to be doing a doctorate this was supposed to be a fresh start oh my god there is so much pain how did I get here how did I get here!?*) but all I could do was quiver. My body was an assemblage of parts, rigid yet elastic, jerking and shaking with no direction or purpose. I had lost the ability to form words, and the sky disintegrated as the gunshots filled my head, louder, louder, *louder*. Kielan wrapped a protective arm around me and listened intently as I choked out I had died. He assured me, gently but assertively, I was still alive, it would not remain this activated indefinitely, and if I just *held on*, I would return to equilibrium. He was right. I clung to Kielan – the lull of his voice, the musk of his sweater – and, slowly but surely, I oriented myself.

Hyperarousal is a common symptom of post-traumatic stress. Early exposure to intimate partner violence affects child brain development by altering neural networks and modifying physiological systems. This has lifelong consequences that include exaggerated stress response.

Later, a severely traumatized person may experience involuntary muscle activity, become incapable of articulating themselves, and be incapacitated by emotion. These are natural responses, the body and brain's ways of mobilizing a person to fight, flee, or freeze, but they may not be helpful. On day seven, my physiology was in such high gear I felt I was being assaulted – the impact of what had happened, not just in England but in the years and decades prior, went beyond the range of human experience and had ended me. I wasn't entirely wrong: I had died in some ways. I was clinging to the myth of the unified, self-knowing subject – the western, rationalist assumption that people exist wholly and completely and evolve in a linear fashion – but my disparate selves had met one another and were getting acquainted.

PART FOUR

Fifteen

Kielan hugged me when his girlfriend arrived, and I was left with Gretal. She was younger than me, she joked loudly and often, and we would later recognize parallels — parallels that weren't funny — in our respective family dynamics. It was at this point, for the first time since I'd been at the Priory, I called myself psychotic. I had entered an altered state, and it was the same state I had been in almost exactly two years earlier, the night I sent the letter. Only this time, I had been psychotic for days and had been too frightened, fractured, and fragmented to notice. Then, all at once, as though struck by lightning, I couldn't *not* notice.

Gretal was aghast. She stood, said we were getting help, and led me inside and directly to a consultant. When she knocked, a slight, pale, man answered and looked me up and down quizzically. Standing beside her, I watched Gretal convey dismay as she explained I was Nicole, I was not part of her (or any) program, and I was *psychotic* (!!!) The consultant seemed… bored. Speaking to Gretal, he informed her I would have to do as every patient did, which was wait for a scheduled meeting with *my* consultant, at which point I could discuss psychosis with him. He had his own caseload, he sniffed, making it apparent as he wiped the lenses of his glasses and finally turned toward me, that he was inconvenienced. Stunned, Gretal raised her voice, insistent, and she was reprimanded for being "untoward" — too emotive and too loud, presumably, for a woman who was also labelled a drunk. I didn't know it at the time, but this benefited me greatly. Had the consultant behaved professionally — had he, for instance, inquired about my symptoms — I might have been medicated and monitored. Instead, the consultant, the care aides, and the half-dozen other staff we approached following the consultant all told me the same thing: I wasn't really a patient and could seek treatment after I'd gotten to Canada. Gretal grew more furious with each successive denial, but my temperament, though mercurial otherwise, stayed dormant through it all. The stonewalling would continue, so I thanked Gretal and retreated to my room.

The Becoming

It was here that I started writing. There was no employee to turn to. There was no one who cared to diagnose me, drug me, tell me who I was, what this meant, and what I could or should do next. There were only the Nicoles colliding. For much of my stay I would write spontaneously, only when I saw my laptop – when I entered my room in any given state, noticed it, and remembered I even had one. The moment I was finished, I would forget what I had said until I next sat down, reawakening the Nicole who relies on documentation. I had sensed this coming, and now the words arrived in a cleansing (powerful, dramatic, *painful*) flood. Looking back, the writing I did then is shocking. It is caustic, forceful, and combative. It is timid, diffident, and meek. Unlike academic prose, which is enjoyable but obligatory, writing at the Priory was cathartic – possibly divine. It was also my only anchor – tangible proof I still existed and was, despite my confusion, panic, and memory loss, Nicole(s). The first piece I wrote (all of which I still have, saved in a folder I named "Accidental Insider/ The Becoming") reads:

> I am so frightened. I have been trapped inside a carnival fun-house maze for days, with no one at the fairgrounds to hear my screams.
>
> The staff is here but they are all tending to the paying customers. Meanwhile, I have snuck in unannounced. Now that I wish to go, wish to leave this revolting nightmare, none are willing to see me out.
>
> I will find the Exit myself.

Part Three

ONE

At the Priory, it would eventually get better. First, though, as bad as it was already, it had to get much worse.

After writing, I sat back and took in my surroundings. My room consisted of a desk, a standing closet I had yet to populate, a garbage can, and a bedside table that overflowed with food wrappers. A pile of clothing given to me by another patient occupied the corner, and there was a private bathroom with a toilet, mirror, and shower. In the centre was a small, sterile cot. I knew the walls were beige, but at some point, they had stopped *looking* beige. Instead, an iridescent spectrum of colours bled into one another, their movement synergetic with my short, shallow gasps. I got scared again and went, for what felt like the millionth time, for help. The confidence and clarity I had possessed moments earlier (*I will find the exit myself*) was gone, and in its place was the conviction I was psychotic (or dead, or both) and needed medication.

These thoughts signal mental illness. Certainly, no sane person would entertain such ideas (and no sane person would see their walls melt), and according to the DSM, I am highly "mentally ill." I do not dispute this. To reduce my experience to just pathology, though, to chalk it up only to sickness, would be doing myself a disservice. My purpose with writing is to highlight that mental illness labels are not always useful, in that the more labels one accrues, the less one is trusted and the less one trusts themselves. I simply wish to offer alternate paradigms through which others may view my (and their own) experiences. These paradigms are unconventional but acknowledge that mental, emotional, physical, and spiritual distress may not be just "disease." As I see it, the DSM is one option, one version of materiality among many, and I have learned through trial and error and exquisite suffering that materiality is malleable. Of course, on my seventh day at the Priory, this hadn't fully resonated. I was drawn toward anti-psychiatry and Mad discourses, yes, but these were belief systems I had dabbled in, not ones adopted as my own. What was certain is that Phil the psychiatrist had taught me I was "psychotic" in this state, and psychosis, says common sense, is something to be corrected.

My bedroom at the Priory was at the end of the upstairs hallway, directly opposite a woman's-only lounge. I sped into the lounge with a renewed sense of urgency, pulsating with righteous anger, and yelled at staff to listen. A nurse reminded me I did not have an appointment and could not demand to see a consultant just because I felt like it. She then exclaimed, as though this required immense effort, that she would go find Igor. I did not trust Igor; I did not want to speak with him, and after the nurse fetched him anyway, he sat across from me at a table. I told him matter-of-factly I was psychotic, and he said he was not smart enough to help me. Those were his exact words: "Nicole (shrug), I am not smart enough to help you," and while I agreed, his insouciance in light of my claw-my-skin-off-pull-my-hair-out horror was maddening, independent of my symptoms. I plead to be sedated and was told by Igor, and the staff members I spoke to after him, I was overreacting. I was not, and it would be two more weeks of agony, two more weeks of shouting, kicking, begging to be heard, before I found solace within myself.

PART THREE

Two

For the rest of day seven, I was frantic. I stormed the hallways and screeched at care aides, nurses, and fellow patients, my disbelief growing with each rebuff. Staff members were apathetic, directing me to someone else or explicitly stating that they didn't know me (and implicitly, that they didn't really care). When a person believes they are psychotic – when they are hearing chanting, singing, and screaming what they know is in their mind – this is a cruel approach. I found myself in the Priory's main entrance surrounded by patients, staff, and visitors greeting their loved ones or saying goodbye. Sights, sounds, smells; the stimuli were acrid, invasive, overwhelming, and they overcame me as I sank, sank, sank, the plush carpet engulfing me and transporting me elsewhere (*I have been in this meadow before*) while I shrieked.

   I don't know how long I was on the floor, how loud I was, or if anyone noticed; I clearly remember screaming (*into the void*), but very little else. My presence went unacknowledged until I glimpsed Brent, a middle-aged care aide. His was a familiar face and seeing it reminded me I was not only frightened, I was also furious. Leaping from the carpet, I snatched a newspaper and waved it at him, barely registering the paper unravel and cascade to the floor. "What is *wrong* with you people!?" I yelled. "You British *fucks*!" and a small smile played at the corner of Brent's mouth. He thought this was funny. Unable to breathe and needing to move, I ran toward the door.

   I sped through the Priory's corridors (after seven days, I was still lost) and out the side entrance. I passed the gazebo, where a group of patients huddled, smoking to distract themselves, smoking to kill time, and I kicked a bench. Hard. "I am psychotic!" I screamed, "I have been psychotic for days, and no one here cares; this is *fucked*!" The world tilted and turned, the grass pulsating in tandem with my heartbeat and the *squeeeeezing* in my head. As though my legs belonged to someone else, I continued to the edge of the grounds where I howled inconsolably, fell to my knees, and wept. I didn't know exactly why I was weeping but doing so was vital, lustral, and good. I cried for what felt like hours, until I looked up from my crouched position to see staff walking toward me. Confused but earnest, one offered me her hand and said she would find me a cigarette. My body recoiled, but with no alternative, I rose. The grass stopped moving, I could see straight again, and for the next few moments, I felt almost "normal." These periods of calm, blessed but brief, would come and go for the duration of my stay. Appreciated as they were, pain, I would learn, is the most fertile soil for growth.

Three

Now, with the Priory behind me but still very much inside me, it is difficult to reconcile my reflections with that which seems "reasonable." If they were to be asked about this day or the ones that followed, staff would challenge my recall. Surely their version of events wouldn't (couldn't possibly) include ignoring a distraught woman, blatantly dismissing her when she clearly needed aid. But this is what I remember. Above all else, my time at the Priory is characterized by an abstruse, almost otherworldly sense of alone-ness. Without formal programming, I was physically separate from both patients and clinicians. More importantly, for the next two weeks I would inhabit a distinct *psychic* realm. I had forayed into this realm in 2015 – I had dipped my toes in, so to speak – but I had been wrenched out via tranquilizers, proximity to authority, and the logistics of addiction. This was similar: It was the first term of a graduate degree; I was driven by the need to be "exceptional" without having considered if I actually cared, and right away, I had lost it. Unlike in 2015, however, a literal and metaphorical ocean separated me from my peers, my family, and psychiatry. I had no school to return to, no medical professional was interested, and the ramifications of this breakdown were more severe than before. In other words, I had dived into unchartered waters, and now I needed to swim.

Swimming, however, would take some time. Initially, I wasn't sure that I knew how, or if I wanted to try. Instead, I looked for "logical" causes for my condition, reasoning that when I arrived in England I hadn't been drinking, I wasn't bingeing, and I ingested a mood stabilizer and anti-psychotics before bed. I had been more level, but I was still starved, smoking pot, and hypervigilant. Then, for nearly a month, I had ceased eating and consumed only alcohol. I likely experienced medication withdrawal when my neuroleptics were confiscated but didn't notice because my thirst had been insatiable. I also started hearing things, and it was difficult to keep from screaming. Then, when I arrived at the Priory, the alcohol's sedative effects wore off and my physiology would have rebounded. I became over-stimulated and over-excited because I was filled with adrenalin, cortisol, other stress hormones, which culminated in an abrupt escalation into "psychosis." I was merely hallucinating ("merely" in that I knew drugs could fix this), and I just needed the right combination of dosages.

    I found comfort in this interpretation. It was biomedical, it was rational, and parts or all of it may have been accurate. However, this was not just psychosis, and even if it had been, Igor and Dr. Herner said that beginning new prescriptions wouldn't be an option. I was thus left with... myself. With no groups to attend, no schedule to adhere to, and rather oddly – to staff, myself, and my tutor – an inability to travel, I was told Nuffield had extended my stay past the weekend but I would leave come Monday. Given where things were at, this was a lofty goal. After more yelling and more tears, none of which elicited response, my seventh day at the Priory concluded with me sitting on my bed, my thoughts churning at a rate they never had before, hearing *Morning! Ello! You alright!?* as I watched the ceiling vibrate.

Four

By now it was late October, either the day of or the day before Halloween. I wasn't conscious of this, but the season infiltrated my subconscious and impacted my impressions. Maybe. It is also possible the encounter I am about to describe would have occurred anyway because it ended up being meaningful.

After dozing briefly, I woke during my eighth night to see a witch at the foot of my bed. She was a stoic shadowy figure, her features amorphous but wicked, and though she hadn't moved, I sensed she was about to. I screamed, leapt from my bed, and fled to the upstairs lounge where I was greeted by Alice, a care aide. I had met her before and knew I admired her delicate features and amiable demeanour. However, in this moment Alice was not Alice. She was also a witch, and as she sneered, her eyes, nose, and cheeks crawled with insects. I was too frightened to speak, so I curled into the fetal position and cowered on a couch. Alice peered over me, asking what was wrong, not aware as I sobbed that her face was rotting off. My depth perception was also distorted, so while she likely maintained an appropriate distance, I felt as though she was not just adjacent me but was *entering* me from above. I couldn't watch her flesh decay and her skull emerge, her putrid breath mixing with mine, so I tried to go outside.

I made it to the downstairs corridor, but I froze once I reached the side door. The mist (the perpetual mist) enveloping the patio and gazebo repulsed me. It seemed to be a harbinger, a warning that should I penetrate it, it (the Priory) would never let me go. Utterly panicked, I kept screaming and I collapsed onto a bench. As I did so, a young woman walked toward me. She paused for a moment, averted her gaze, and retreated. Still screaming, I ran back upstairs and re-entered the lounge, where Alice the witch was waiting. Then, something remarkable happened: As I screamed, she chastised me: "Keep it down," she said snidely; "Have some self-control and think about your fellow patients! Some are in a great deal of distress, you know, and they only have sleep to look forward to!" and with this, Alice transformed again. She stopped being a witch, and as she instructed me dispassionately to take personal responsibility for my actions, she turned into the spitting image of my mother.

Five

Based on conceptions of mental illness, it would be easy to assume I fabricated this. Parts I did, but it is worth noting that Alice later apologized, that she acknowledged having been harsh, and said she regretted lecturing me when I was under duress. My recall is not solely influenced by insanity, then. I am not a crazy woman (not just a crazy woman, anyway), who was cognitively and emotionally disintegrating. I prefer to see this event, as well as those that followed, as the origins of a break-*through* of sorts; one that was astonishingly powerful, irrevocably transformative, and above and beyond all else, excruciatingly dark.

The belief that my journey at the Priory was neither arbitrary nor pathological has been theoretically explored. Thirty years ago, transpersonal psychologists Stanislov and Christina Grof introduced the idea that unusual states of consciousness accompanied by emotional, perceptive, and psychosomatic manifestations surface due to the intrinsic pursuit of wholeness.[i] They suggested these "non-ordinary states" are "spiritual emergencies," not psychosis, with the potential to catalyze healing. In their words, possible indicators of a spiritual emergency include dramatic death and (re)birth sequences, archetypical phenomena, incidence of synchronicities or extrasensory experiences, and energy. During this era, pioneering investigator on mythical states Arthur J. Deikman also coined the term "mystical psychosis" to denote accounts of psychosis aligning with reports of

---

[i] Throughout the remainder of the book, I will take liberties with how I interpret theory. Some was produced during what is considered the golden era of radical antipsychiatry that began in the 1950s (though the term itself wasn't coined until 1967). At that time, fissures between biological psychiatry and psychoanalytic psychiatry were escalating because proponents of the former viewed psychoanalysis as too time-consuming and costly. Conversely, psychoanalysts argued that scientific biomedicine was inappropriate for something as subjective as reality and that involuntary institutionalization, forced medication, and non-consensual electroconvulsive shock therapy (ECT) was unethical. This took place against a backdrop of the 1960s counterculture movement, where awareness of social inequalities on the basis of race, sex, and sexuality seeped into public consciousness. Much of the literature I cite henceforth can be broadly categorized as psychoanalytic, which is no longer the dominant mode of administering psychiatric services.[1]

mysticism. Deikman believed these experiences are prompted by "de-automatization" (undoing) of "habitual psychological structures" that "organize, limit, select, and interpret" perceptual stimuli. Much like the Grofs' indicators, the features of mystic psychosis include realness (or "stimuli of the inner world becom[ing] invested with the feeling of reality ordinarily bestowed on objects"), unusual percepts ("sensations and ideation that do not seem to be part of the continuum of everyday consciousness"), unity (experiencing one's self as one with the universe) and ineffability (the inability to express one's experiences because they are rooted in primitive memories and nonverbal sensations), all of which arise out of extreme circumstances and disrupt the subject's relationship with the world.

By now you know that I am not a strict empiricist. Mental health won't always conform to standards of systematic observation or falsifiability of hypotheses because there are things we can't and shouldn't know. However, I take scholarship seriously, appreciate rigour, and loathe new age woo. I will thus issue this caveat before proceeding: The text is about to undergo shifts in tone and form. These will include references to literature I do not use in my academic work because it requires suspending all I have been taught about deriving conclusions from the senses. It is not scientific, and more egregiously, it is individualistic. The theories I introduce situate the loci of responsibility for health and illness in the body-mind, whereas I have been trained to see these phenomena as socially and culturally constituted. The suggestion that one can "self-heal" or is "responsible for their healing" is used to sell products to people who lack the analytic tools required to know better, and in case it isn't obvious, neoliberalism is deadly. Yet in this context, none of the sociological, anthropological, feminist science, public health, epidemiological, or critical drug scholarship I studied prior to writing suffices.[ii] I have found no better way to conceive of my

---

[ii] Psychiatry's crisis of legitimacy has been partly resolved by advocacy. By monopolizing the narrative around what "mental disorders" are (e.g., the "chemical imbalance" hypothesis) and suggesting that detractors "lack insight into their conditions," it has established itself as the solution to distress. For example, Joanna Moncrieff, a senior lecturer at University College London, has reviewed the history of antipsychotic drugs and relays how they came to be regarded as "miracle cures" for a variety of human conditions despite their demonstrably negative effects among large factions of the population.[2]

Madness than through fringe psychology, even as it implicitly claims that "betterment" is a personal task or project. Please remember it is not, even as you read about how in this instance, it also kind of was.

Six

The Grofs' typology of spiritual emergencies has been evaluated, contested, and amended, but a recurrent theme in their work and that of their contemporaries is calling spiritual emergencies evolutionary crises – they are born of restricted emotional development to emancipate "vitally needed" psychic functions. Related, clinical (anti-)psychiatrist R. D. Laing proposed that psychoanalytic "defence mechanisms" (repression, denial, splitting, etc.) that unconsciously alienate one from themselves needn't stay unconscious. Rather than remain oblivious to our defence mechanisms (or become aware of them but stay powerless over them) one can "progressively realiz[e] that these are things [they] ha[ve] done to [themselves]" and, in so doing, once more become an agent.[iii]

I now interpret my encounter with Alice to have been one incident among many that occurred during a rapid, self-directed trajectory toward integration. This had started in 2015 but had been thwarted by psychiatry and my own embarrassment. Then, upon arrival at the Priory, I was met with the same admonishment when in distress characterizing my childhood, my adolescence, and my tentative (and unsuccessful) forays into adulthood. In many ways, staff at the Priory mirrored how I have been treated by my parents every time I have sought help. I have been told I am a nuisance, have been scolded for attention seeking, and have always responded with intensive self-destruction. This is why the Priory was so critical. I would soon realize, with stark, stunning clarity, for the first time in over twenty years, *this was not okay*.

According to the transpersonal psychology, spiritual emergencies necessitate therapeutic intervention distinct from that which is derived from "the pragmatically successful but simplistic worldview of

---

[iii] R. D. Laing is one of radical psychiatry's most (in)famous figureheads. His ideas were developed by working with schizophrenic patients. According to him, psychosis can be "a psychedelic voyage of discovery" that emancipates one from oppressive familial dynamics. His is a complex legacy, both because his intellectual genealogy is controversial and because he built a cult of personality that may have been saturated with nefarious elements.[3]

mechanistic science." While traditional psychiatry relies on diagnoses and medication, transpersonal psychologists claim that a "facilitator's" task is to forge nurturing, trusting relationships[iv] with one who is in an altered state. By allowing them to experience the symptoms of what appears to be "psychosis," the facilitator can support them in finding meaning in their experiences. Otherwise, should one's altered state be severe enough to interfere with daily functioning, and should they be institutionalized because of this, the result will be "sad compromises" via reductive scientism. The irony of course is that my "spiritual emergency" (or "mystic psychosis," or "spiritual awakening") may have been triggered because my history of abandonment was replicated at the Priory. While it was this that propelled me into a necessary and life-affirming state, it was also the factor that prohibited me from seeing my state as life-affirming because I had no "facilitator." All I had were Phil's words reverberating in my ears (*You are psychotic. You are psychotic*) and the sincere belief I could stay that way forever. Fortunately, though, because no one really cared, I moved toward resolution (the exit) myself.

[iv] Transpersonal psychology literally translates to "going beyond and/or through the personal boundaries of ego/identity," and it emphasizes the interconnectedness of all beings. These sensibilities echo some of today's mainstream spirituality movements, which are rightly critiqued for promoting a-historic visions of societies that have always been stratified according to race, class, sex, and so on. The belief that we are "one" or "the same" flattens the nuances of identities and their attendant differences. It is not coincidental that new-age spirituality has become associated with far-right political rhetoric. I still employ some of these theories here because they resonate with this particular experience, but I do so cautiously.[4]

Seven

I returned to bed, closed my eyes, and waited fitfully for dawn. When the sun finally shone on the dew-dropped lawn, I pounded on the upstairs office door and reiterated to the nurses and care aides inside that I was in psychosis. Helplessness consumed me. I was met with near-total disinterest, and one of the nurses assured me I seemed completely fine. Rather than keep arguing, I stomped downstairs and greeted Michael, who had woken in a jovial mood and invited me to breakfast.

  I sat with him and Ethan, and my affect mirrored theirs. They smiled; I smiled. They laughed; I laughed. I had become pliable. I absorbed my surroundings, internalized them, and radically altered my subjectivity based on context. Conflating one's inner world with that which is exterior has been described as a component of "numinous" experiences, whereby people report profound shifts in temporal or spatial boundaries. The dissolution of boundaries may also be found during "de-adaptation," when identity "becomes overwhelmed, disorganized [and] immensely confused." In other words, I no longer knew where I ended and other people began. That said, "markedly impoverished, poorly developed, or unstable sense of self-image often associated with… dissociated states under stress" is also one of the American Psychiatric Association's diagnostic criteria for borderline personality disorder – which I have been told a handful of times I have and have also been told a handful of times I definitely don't have – while psychoanalysts argue that exaggerated identification with others is due to schizophrenia.[v] For instance, the psychoanalytic concept of

---

[v] "The schizoid personality" has been a topic of great interest to psychoanalysts for roughly a hundred years. "Schizoid" is not a synonym for the clinical diagnosis of schizophrenia. Rather, it refers to "schisms," or splits, in one's personality as they pertain to longing for closeness with others. According to psychoanalysts, this is the central tension within the schizoid personality, and it looks like oscillation between states of intense emotional neediness, reactivity, intense affect and volatility, and states of blunted affect, detachment, and extreme self-sufficiency. There are parallels between this and anxious-avoidant attachment styles in attachment theory, and there are also similarities between the emotional disturbances referenced and what appears as contemporary schizophrenia.[5]

"identity diffusion" describes "disintegration of one's sense of inner continuity and sameness" and "lack of an integrated self-concept and an integrated and stable concept of total objects in relationship with the self," which, according to Melanie Klein (whose work incorporated and built upon that of Freud), is related to something called "splitting." Klein said excess splitting leads to disturbance in "the feeling of the ego" (though note that Klein and Freud's "ego" is distinct from Carl Jung's "ego") and may be a cause of schizophrenia.[vi] That said, according to Phil I have bipolar disorder, which has its own diagnostic criteria and is linked to related but distinct forms of "psychosis" than those found among people with schizophrenia (but can, like borderline personality disorder and schizophrenia, also be framed a "brain disease" derived from "chemical imbalances" in the brain). Lost yet? Yeah, me too.

I will thus continue to selectively choose information that suits my needs (my needs being the ability to feel empowered, stable, and whole), and in so doing, I will necessarily favour some truths over others. What is true regardless of which truths I employ is that during breakfast on the morning of day eight, as I giggled and grinned with Michael, the belief that I was psychotic transformed from disturbing to delightful. Between mouthfuls of pastry and cereal (I was still bingeing; everything was hyperreal), I relayed the same information to Michael and Ethan as I had to Kielan and Gretal (I was in psychosis; no one gave a damn), but now I was exhilarated. I was in psychosis! No one gave a damn! How *exciting* – how thrilling! What would my brain and I get up to? This was an *adventure*. As I excused myself and scurried upstairs to purge, writing was imperative.

[vi] Melanie Klein was born into a Jewish family. She is credited as being one of the first to use traditional psychoanalysis on young children, and her theories of childhood development both corroborated and departed significantly from those of Freud. For example, she argued that the superego is present from birth, and she insisted that aggression and violence are important motivating forces even in early childhood. Her contributions inspired much of the object-relations school of psychoanalysis, which focuses on the influence of interpersonal relations versus biologically based drives in personality development. It may also be seen as shocking. Both Klein and Freud's ideas emerged in Nazi-occupied Germany, and they reflected the political landscape of the time.[6]

Eight

Yet the brutality of purging (I am always so thorough) rendered me weak and fragile. Outside of Michael and Ethan's sphere of influence, my impetus to write was replaced by an inability to see, think, or feel beyond the need to be in bed. Psychosis was no longer exciting. Psychosis was horrifically lonely, and I wanted nothing more than for someone to assure me that I mattered. I don't know for how long I stayed there, but I remember lying on my stomach, my right arm raised and folded awkwardly under my mouth. I kissed my arm, pretending it was Sean, Steven, *anyone*, and felt an unbearable jolt through my abdomen. The somatoform pain had announced it – I – was hurting. All I wanted was human connection, but I also believed I may not even be human. No human brain could work so quickly or be so chaotic. Was I even capable of love? The more I tried to think linearly, the more circular I became. Amid the churning voices and searing pain, all I knew was I had become a monster. To describe my state as one of despair or desolation or suicidal depression does not even begin to relay how I felt. Words alone are futile, but since they are what I have, I will say that it was like my psyche had been imbued with all the suffering of humankind's past, present, and future. I was catatonic. The depth and breadth of devastation I felt in that moment and many others was unlike anything I had experienced. It (I) felt colossally, eternally *dark*, as though I had deformed spacetime and been absorbed by the blackest hole. I now floated, untethered, beneath some primordial event horizon with no reasonable hope of escape.

   I eventually latched onto the belief that I needed to eat, properly. My mind was starved, but I also hadn't digested intentionally in weeks. How would I consume a meal (I was not concerned about whether it was a small, normal, or large meal, so long as I didn't binge to the point of gastric rupture) when every time I encountered food, I attacked it – devoured it with the furor of someone who is not only ravenous but whose psyche and nervous system have ceased regulating, and who has forgotten how to respond "properly" to stimuli? I couldn't not binge, and I couldn't not purge after. Then it (re)occurred to me that the Priory treated eating disorders. The young anorexic participants I had seen slept just down the hall from me. I could ask for meal support.

I rose from bed and entered the women's lounge, invigorated by the prospect of doing something right. The nurse who ran the eating disorders program, Jen, was there, and I said I needed help. Her response – that I had not been placed on the NHS waitlist for the Priory and had by implication "skipped the line," that I had not done a formal intake for the eating disorders program, and that she neither knew nor cared who I was – still evokes rage now. It is rage that is impotent, is born of total helplessness, and arises when something (some rule, some policy, some parenting strategy) is fundamentally wrong. I argued with Jen. I pleaded with her. When she said I could sit with the eating disorder program after meals but not during, an offer that, to be of any use, would have required restraint I knew I didn't have, I returned to my room defeated. Jen had confirmed the iron cage of bureaucracy (of rationality, of efficiency, of mental health treatment) would kill me if I let it.[vii]

An excerpt from my writing that day reads:

> I am in shock. I am in a state of complete and utter disbelief at how things could have gone so wrong (am I really shocked, though)? I am questioning whether I might have permanent brain damage; whether this state of wild-eyed, frantic, need-to-run Panic could last forever. It was all I had (or so I thought).
>
> What if having nothing is better?
>
> I am frightened. I am frightened that I may no longer be human – that I may never again feel human – and, at the same time, the Pain of being human is too much to bear. The pressure.

[vii] German sociologist Max Weber used "shell as hard as steel" (translated to "iron cage") as a metaphor for the rationalization of society. According to Weber, the complex and rigid division of labour found in modern societies requires bureaucratization, whereby people are organized hierarchically and interact with each other as efficiently as possible. This is a threat to individuality and freedom, and it traps people in impersonal, rule-based systems of control.[7]

I have the option of nursing myself back to health – of becoming human. I have the option of ending it all – of having never been human to begin with.

Which do I want?

NINE

Colours, shapes, and sounds were still saturated, indistinct, fluid, and running into each other, and I knew I needed to focus. As I have always done when avoiding challenges (real challenges, that is, ones pertaining to life and death), I felt that I should work. Since I had been suspended from my DPhil (a hint that work may not have been a priority), the only outstanding task I had was editing my master's thesis. I had submitted it to an academic journal after my defence, and within a few weeks I needed to resubmit it having made revisions. It was a good distraction.

I went back to the women's lounge with my laptop. The two eating disorder patients were sprawled on the floor in baggy clothing, colouring and murmuring quietly about calories and weight gain, and I felt a surge of envy because superficially, anorexia is simple. I perched awkwardly on a couch, trembling, sweating, and sure that I was dying. The vice on my head squeezed harder than ever, and it was accompanied by persistent throbbing in my abdomen. Ignoring this, I re-read the feedback I had gotten from reviewers. One had found significant flaws throughout and had concluded that I had to completely re-structure my paper to warrant publication. At any other time, these revisions would have been tedious and may have felt insurmountable. However, I channelled my desperation into laser-like focus and edited my research as though I had never seen it before. The sentences and paragraphs became mere shapes, puzzle pieces to play with and configure into their proper arrangement. I addressed the reviewers' comments methodically, growing more jittery as my fingers clack-clack-clacked, and I drifted elsewhere, trying to stay erect. I finished just as I sensed my head might cave in, and as I did, I howled so loudly, not only did the eating disorder patients startle, one rose and called a nurse. My limbs were rigid, I vibrated, and as Jen checked my vital signs, imploring me to stop causing scenes, I looked once more at my thesis.

The original title of my manuscript was, "Disappearing in Plain Sight: An Exploratory Study of Co-Occurring Eating and Substance Abuse Dis/orders among Homeless Youth in Vancouver, Canada." I had saved my revised version as "Disappearing_Luongo." Disappearing. Luongo. I looked away and looked back again. Disappearing Luongo, Disappearing Luongo, Disappearing Luongo… Jen told me to go to my room and pull myself together, and I thought about this title. Glimpsing my emaciated frame as I collapsed onto the bed, I wondered if I would survive the night, and how long it would take staff to notice if I died there. Disappearing Luongo.

For what it's worth, my thesis was accepted for publication. I made no further revisions.

PART THREE

Ten

It was around this day that my auditory hallucinations evolved. I began to hear four syllables of the "Monster Mash," (*The moooooooonster mash*) on repeat. The morning greetings had been bad. This was somehow worse. I don't know if anyone actually played those lyrics, but at the time I didn't realize they weren't real – I just wanted them to stop.

More alarming than this was that by my eighth day at the Priory, I became aware of spending a *lot* of time in the bathroom. I wasn't urinating, defecating, or purging, but I started coming to, as one does when startled awake. I can't say for how many days this occurred, nor am I sure if it happened a few times or repeatedly. I just remember being fully clothed and squatting on the toilet, crying hysterically and emitting a disembodied whimper. I would look down and watch the veins in my arms throb (*Whose skeleton is this!?*), pulsating to the rhythm of what felt like someone else's heartbeat. As my memories from when I've been black-out drunk are disjointed, appearing as brief bursts with darkness on either side, so too is this. There is no before, there is no after, there is just residual trauma, the sensation now of my heart quickening, my chest tightening, and my lungs contracting as I relay my experiences, however inadequately, and still want to run. I have not come this far to run, so I will simply write that my moments (hours?) on the toilet, like my hours (days?) in bed, were desolate. I felt forsaken, not just left to fend for myself by staff but deserted by humanity. I found temporary solace with others, but while on the toilet and in my bed, I conceived of myself as solitary – a dissolving entity whose eventual disappearance (*Disappearing Luongo*) would culminate in... nothing.

There are many ways to interpret this. "Dissociation" is defined by "a disruption of and/or discontinuity in the normal integration of consciousness, memory, identity, emotion, perception, body representation, motor control, and behavior," with memory loss assumed to arise from "the compartmentalization of memories in separate identity states." "Dissociative amnesia" is both a symptom of "dissociative identity disorder" and an independent dissociative disorder, and I have already claimed to transition between "age-states."

The Nicole on the toilet was six or seven and was petrified without the stabilizing impact of others. Related to this, "depersonalization-derealization syndrome" also appears in the DSM as a dissociative disorder and may be characterized by difficulty recognizing one's own reflection, feeling unreal or like a spectator in one's life, feeling like general life events are unreal, and perceiving objects as changing in shape, size, or colour.

That said, I also apparently have bipolar disorder with psychotic features. Although neurocognitive deficits such as memory loss are mostly studied in schizophrenia, growing evidence indicates that dissociation is as common in those with bipolar diagnoses. Bipolar patients with histories of psychotic symptoms also perform poorly on verbal memory measures and tasks related to executive functions, which has led some to argue that bipolar and schizophrenic disorders should be classified together in the DSM due to their similar effects on cognitive impairment. In other words, whether I "am" bipolar, somewhere on the schizophrenia spectrum, or have a separate dissociative disorder doesn't really matter. What's more important is most agree that memory loss is reported by those who experienced childhood adversity, and it commonly follows traumatic life events.

It would thus be easy to attribute my dissociative experiences at the Priory to automatic adaptive coping processes of my brain, nervous system, or both, and I do to an extent. But to rely solely on biomedical explanations would insinuate challenges that are neurophysiological, permanent, and random, in which case I see no point in continuing. I will thus transition to psychiatry-adjacent explanations, and in so doing, I hope to feel less helpless.

Although much effort has been made to distinguish between psychotic breakdown and spiritual emergency, others question the use of dichotomizing them. As my own beliefs develop, I am drawn to analyses of altered states that don't deterministically define either. Need mental illness and spirituality be mutually exclusive? Frames are just schemas of interpretation. We rely on them to make sense of and respond to phenomena, and while frames have tangible consequences, they simplify reality. My realities (and there are many), are that, yes, I am Mad. And psychiatry reduces experiences and identities that are infinitely complex to little more than labels. In this vein, I find comfort in psychiatrist John Perry, who legitimates psychosis as a genuine state of being. However, he claims that it appears "[w]hen a person finds themselves in a state of acute distress, in circumstances that have assailed [their] most sensitive vulnerabilities, [and when their] psyche may be stirred into an imperative need to reorganize the self." According to Perry, what appear as symptoms of thought disorder are evidence of someone undergoing "reintegration through… disintegration." One must come undone in order to rebuild oneself, and this entails paying heed to the nonrational systems of meanings found in one's subconscious. When validated (that is, when explored and taken seriously), one's fantasies (which are not fantasies at all but are elemental expressions of one's innermost truths) elicit transformation.

    I like to think that during my seventh, eighth, and ninth days at the Priory, I was losing time on the toilet and elsewhere because the "deepest levels of [my] psych[e]" had been mobilized. I was thrust into a "mythic-world" (one in which witches became my mother) that I can't re-enter or remember clearly now because I was reconstructing my worldview. I had to break down wholly, totally, and completely so that I could rebuild – that is, become a person who didn't need a PhD to justify her existence, a person whose coping tools went beyond disordered eating, substance abuse, and workaholism. England was my opportunity. My subconscious saw this and responded without my conscious approval. It has taken time to arrive at this explanation, and it was forthcoming events that convinced me of its utility. Perry also notes that when someone is encouraged to express themselves, signs of disorder abate. Alternately, when they are pressured to be normal, one's "sense of isolation mounts, as does [their] feeling of disqualification and invalidation." "All this can only thrust [them] more into the direction of… madness and insanity," warns Perry, which "is devastating to the psyche."

Eleven

Being dismissed at the Priory was indeed devastating. It reduced me to childhood but also made me persevere. I would have my needs met, though on my eighth day I could not articulate what those needs were, nor had I deduced that staff could not meet them for me. At the same time, I began to see patients and staff less as people and more as energy, entities whose essence and intentions I could discern from far away. When I walked toward the lounge or peered at the gazebo, I would either be drawn to it or it would repel me based on who was there. It was as though I inhabited a plane of existence comparable to consensus reality but parallel. It was a world where people were sinister or benevolent, menacing or merciful, and the slightest gesture, the briefest eye contact, revealed inarticulable truths about their character. For example, Gerald was an elder who came to the Priory after attempting suicide. He shared that he had tried to end his life by train but had laid vertically on the tracks. Rather than be crushed, he had watched the train that was to kill him speed over his head. I felt secure with Gerald. He was infinitely tender, and he sat hunched in the gazebo, engulfed in fog, draped in a billowing peacoat and shrouded, somehow, in integrity that was palpable. Watching him in wordless contemplation calmed me more than sedatives ever had. He was kindness personified, and I was drawn to him as a moth is to a flame.

Perry goes on to say that people balance their conscious mind's rationality with their unconscious's nonrational systems of meaning. The two are counterparts, and each creates its own observations of realness. People tend to experience realities that are orderly, structured, and predictable because their perceptions are derived from their conscious mind. In an acute state, however, the boundaries between this and the unconscious diffuse. People may tap into symbolic landscapes in pursuit of what Jungian thinkers refer to as individuation (psychological integration).[viii] When it came to

---

[viii] Carl Jung was originally a student of Freud, but their paths diverged, as did their theories. I use him sparsely because while most of his ideas are only minimally com-

Gerald and my peers, I was aware of their singularity, but they were something more – something that transcended individuality and evoked interminable feelings of goodness. They could be framed as what Jung referred to as "archetypes" – hereditary, elemental models and forms that organize our involvement with the world and motivate our behaviour. Archetypes such as "the wise old man" appear cross-culturally in literature, art, religion, and, as for better or for worse, the delusions of psychotics.

If I subscribed to this line of thought, I would also say that people are born equipped with ancestral wisdom. Jung argued we are not tabula rasas, or blank slates upon which our identities are etched, but we possess an archive of primeval intelligence to assist us while in crisis. As a result, our mental contents in non-ordinary states reflect fundamental, archetypical information about life, death, good, and evil that can help us individuate. Of course, Jung became a sort of cult leader in part because his claims were grandiose. I am not uncritically subscribing to pseudoscience, but it is undeniable that by day eight, I had tapped into… something, and this something felt expansive. I intuited, and my mind was saturated with visions that didn't resemble anything I had seen. These visions were extraordinary yet intimate, so while the language of archetypes and individuation is not one I readily speak, I employ it here because it explains what happened at the time.

---

pelling, they do interact with some of the psychoanalytic and transpersonal canon that I cite. Perhaps more so than anyone, it is important to situate Jung within his social context. Following his split with Freud, he began to hallucinate. By the 1940s, equal parts convinced of his divine abilities and that psychoanalysis would become a redemptive worldview, he recruited a group of wealthy followers and became a cult leader of sorts. Some of his "disciples" were struggling with having to relinquish their prominent societal positions as class-based uprisings took place throughout Europe, and ultimately, many aligned with or were expressly part of the Nazi party. Jung's antisemitism escalated over time and was partly tied to career advancement. Much of his psychoanalysis, most of which was co-opted from cultures Indigenous to the Middle East, was adopted by or lent to the Nazi party and even today, pseudo-intellectuals employ him to justify reductive, biologically essentialist views on "traditional" (colonial) gender roles and more. This is all to say, take the few concepts of his within this book as tangential mentions, at most.[8]

Twelve

My eighth night ended much as the ones before it. I gathered in the lounge with a group that included Michael and Ethan, but I was so "overwhelmed with psychic events" I barely noticed who was there. This was a nightly ritual, but I never remained seated, alternating instead between the gazebo and the lounge to assess which felt safe. Afterward, a nurse entered to give us our meds. Though I asked for them, I was not prescribed a mood stabilizer or an antipsychotic, and this may be why my mind expanded.[ix] I took a moderate sedative, dozed for five or ten minutes, then woke, bewildered, and asked for medication. When I realized I had already had it, I felt a now-familiar wave of dismay roll over my shoulders and down my spine. There would be no sleep that night (nor the following, nor the following). When I was the only patient left, I went outside in search of Gerald and retired begrudgingly to my room when I saw that he was gone.

Core examples of Jungian archetypes are the persona, shadow, and self, wherein the persona is the mask we present to our peers, the shadow is the animal side of our personality (and the source of our creative and destructive energies) we repress, and the self is the unified spirit within us. Jung said the first step on the self's path to individuation was to confront and accept one's shadow because it represents all the traits one has cut-off, minimized, or disowned. It is also composed of parts of ourselves we have *learned* to reject because others rejected them first. In my case, I discerned early that fragility, verbosity, and hunger could threaten the acquisition of approval and affection. I had stifled my needs, but all at once they were impossible

---

[ix] I also include Jung because some have tried to bridge the gaps between his theories and the contemporary human sciences when theorizing serious mental illness. For example, Hallie B. Durchslag employs hermeneutics to "thematically order[] narrative material alongside quantitative data on biological and genetic underpinnings of severe mental illnesses." Drawing from their own and others' experiences of "bipolar disorder, type one," Durschlag highlights the overlap between "psychotic delusions" and Jung's archetypical clusters. They further demonstrate that psychotropic drugs modulate psychic material, and that archetypical imagery in the content of one's delusions tends to be eliminated once a person is medicated.[9]

to ignore. I *was* fragile (and verbose, and hungry), and though my behaviour was neither premeditated nor intentional, I could not make it stop. This is what distinguishes purposeful shadow work, which is a conventional practice in some psychology, from a spiritual emergency. Everything from the unconscious, including the self, may also be perceived as dangerous or demonic at first. The feeling of being attacked was compounded because I didn't have proper oversight. Not only was I not receiving trauma-informed care, no one at the Priory would even listen when I said I was psychotic.

My early relationship with Igor exemplifies this. By now, he was a match, and I was gasoline. We crossed paths during the night, and each time we interacted he refused the medication I knew would halt whatever was happening inside me. This reignited my rage, which was at once infinite, abyssal, and so close to my surface that stifling it was impossible. I would spar with Igor, watch him walk away, and, rather than run after him, shake him by the shoulders, and slap him as I envisioned doing, I would settle at my computer. Writing was all I had, especially outside of others' waking hours. My words came from part of me that didn't notice my surroundings, and trying to keep up with my thoughts demanded extraordinary control. I had the motor coordination of an infant I quivered so frenetically. It was as though an atomic bomb had been planted in my sternum.[x] This bomb

---

[x] Evoking electricity is a frequent rhetorical strategy among those discussing psychosis. For example, Morag Coate said, "My brain was like a machine which had been adapted to function normally at a lowered voltage; with the voltage suddenly raised the change in activity and intensity of experience was dramatic." While John Custance wrote: "'the lights go up,' as if a kind of switch were turned on in my psycho-physical system. Everything seems different, somehow brighter and clearer."[10]

I also wonder the extent to which these authors' prose, both of which are over half a century old, can be analyzed through dual paradigms: that of analytic psychology and that of research into trauma. We now know that overwhelming experiences live in the body and affect one's nervous system. Traumatized people may struggle to self-regulate because they contend with somatic "remembering" in the form of hyper- and hypo-arousal, even (especially) if their memories are hidden from consciousness. To put it succinctly, "the body keeps the score." As a result, we live in extremes, veering wildly between over-excitement and constriction, "mania" and shutting down. Along with physical intrusions is the constant cognitive-affective work trauma survivors must do to repress invasive flashbacks and imagery. Would it be apt to draw parallels between this tangible

was regenerative, and each conversation I had, each staff member I saw, each string of words I produced – these were nuclear reactions prompting it to detonate.

---

form of "suppression" and Jung's more esoteric subconscious "suppression?" Could it be that the "persona" one presents to the world after severe trauma (alongside the "shadow" self that grows as a result) eventually becomes so unbearable to preserve that some explode? I think this "explosion" (which appears as "psychosis") can be both spiritual and physiological. It is the refusal to maintain a facade of "normalcy" any longer, lest one die psychically, alongside a body that corroborates with volcanic testimony that *something has to change*.[11]

PART THREE

Thirteen

On my eighth night at the Priory, after seeing Igor, I wrote:

> I want my brain back. Or at least a brain – any brain – that is capable of keeping track of time and space. Every day here feels like a year (I do a year's worth of thinking every day here). At times I feel I am coming out if it ("it's almost over now"), and there will be resolution soon, but The Voices come back and my vision narrows and the soundtrack begins.
>
> For once – for perhaps the first time – I need to accept Help. And yet, when I ask for it – when I Beg for it – I am denied. The rage is reflexive – it must propel me forward (I will find the Exit myself).
>
> Is this my fault?
>
> I feel emboldened – "I will take this to the media and sue the shit out of you!" "This is Profane!" Small yet mighty, pulsating with 10,000 years' worth of pain and torment and Truth-telling Power.
>
> I feel helpless and weak. They keep telling me that I'm Safe.
>
> I am not Safe here.
>
> How could they have let this happen?
>
> Or was it me?

The words poured out of me with the fervour of a trapped animal who senses an opening in their cage and must flee before it's mended. My earliest pieces transmit enormous confusion – *Who was responsible for this? What was this? How would I get out of it? Shouldn't someone (anyone) care!?* – but before long, I would write myself into clarity. Because I was moving so quickly, conclusions about myself, the world, and my place in it, which would have under other circumstances taken decades to arrive at, were processed within hours. Everything at the Priory was condensed, and I believe this was due to my limited window of opportunity. Although my conscious mind thought I was psychotic, my subconscious – my subjugated self – saw the Priory as a time-sensitive, once-in-a-lifetime opportunity. I had to individuate now because to fly back to Vancouver still thinking Oxford had been my only chance would kill me at once.[xi]

[xi] I cannot understate the rate at which I was thinking. While the DSM defines mania as "a distinct period of abnormally and persistently elevated, expansive, or irritable mood" and "abnormally and persistently goal-directed activity or energy" that lasts at least a week, it is a cold and clinical term that is too often misinterpreted as being cognitive. The "thought intoxication" I experienced at the Priory, much like literal intoxication, circulated up, down, and through my body. An alternate explanation can be found in David Lukoff's exploration of the links between the "psychopathological category of manic psychosis" and transpersonal states of consciousness. Lukoff is cautious not to conflate manic psychosis with transpersonal states, but he suggests that the cognitive, behavioural, sensory, and energetic changes induced by mania and psychosis may overlap with the intrapsychic processes of creative, visionary, and mystical consciousness, and that the former may prompt the latter.[12]

Fourteen

When I review my writing now, the content is not what I have been taught to associate with lunacy. Although I did feel persecuted, I was not paranoid in the classic sense. I have come to see my writing as an expression of my subconscious, silent for twenty-odd years save for a few meteoric episodes, communicating with me through... myself. My arms and fingers were her (my) medium, and each time I completed a piece, I would re-read the text in a trance-like state and wonder where it came from. At the same time, I knew precisely where it came from. I had first questioned my humanity (*Am I dead!?*), and after establishing I was human, I moved onto assessing my sanity. Doing so was vital because, for decades, I had been told I was crazy and/or bad. More recently, after I met Meris and began to consider I may not have been the sole creator of my problems, my parents had doubled down. When I tried to speak with my mother about trauma, for example, either directly or by sending her article after article on how childhood adversity affects a person neurologically and physiologically, she responded in one of two ways: "Your childhood was loving, and you were a happy girl. It's not our fault you went nuts" or "Your childhood was loving, and you were a happy girl. It's not our fault you're so selfish."

If abandonment, homelessness, sexual violence, etcetera, were no one's responsibility but mine, I did not want to live. This meant my misery was not just self-induced but would continue indefinitely because mental illness is constant. On the other hand, if I was not just crazy or bad (if I had in fact been abused), I would have to unshackle myself from the chains of martyrdom. This would entail accepting I had wasted years repenting for others' sins and self-flagellation through eating disorders, substance abuse, workaholism, and loneliness was not a justified penance. These latter beliefs implied a daunting amount of work. I had no idea how to care for myself, and I wasn't sure I could learn at nearly thirty years of age. My options on the morning of day nine, then, were to either kill myself (promptly) or to begin the monumental process of healing. In some ways, I had already decided but was not cognizant of having done so. This was a "crisis of development," and this binary – live (truly live) or die – could end in one of only two ways.

My ninth day at the Priory would close with me having committed to living (truly living), but it would be several hours before I did so. Given the speed of my reality, that may as well have been months. Before breakfast, I stood at the medication counter and said again I was psychotic. The nurse passed me a handful of vitamins, poured me a small cup of water, and told me sternly to move. Immediately, I unleashed a string of expletives, and, as was consistent with this pattern, the nurse remained unmoved. Her blasé expression held steadfast, her impassivity was striking, and I shrunk, both anguished and forlorn, as I experienced déjà vu. I had never met this woman, and yet I had already known what she would say. When she shifted her attention away from me, I retreated and I screamed. "What *was* this!?" A few months earlier I had never heard of the Priory; I had never visited England; I had never even seen Europe. Yet I felt, inexorably, that I had been here all my life.

Fifteen

While I am not proud of how I acted at the Priory, I believe in the transformative potential of anger. It can serve as a pathway of influence that mobilizes adaptive behaviour, and like some feminist scholars, I compare it to a fire – destructive, yes, but also creative and illuminating. That said, I haven't always approved of anger. Before Meris, I hadn't felt it in years because I hadn't known I was allowed to. During our first session, I explained to her that while I had a history of violence while intoxicated, I had mostly resolved my ("my") issues, and other than a niggling case of anorexia, complex post-traumatic stress disorder, and a somatoform disorder that infused every moment with preternatural pain, I was mostly content. I believed anger was dysfunctional, and, because I was supremely high functioning at five years sober, it was a feeling I no longer had much use for. After all, I told Meris, I was so wanting in self-control I had drank and bulimia-d myself into homelessness. I had no right to challenge my parents' reactions to the unthinkable. This was also why twelve-step programs resonated: AA said I was diseased, I had a broken brain, and, according to treatment centres my parents paid for, I was self-obsessed, greedy, and sadistic. My first AA meeting was like coming home, the rhetoric so familiar as to be familial. After excelling in AA and making my parents proud, I had transcended anger.

In 2015, however, emotions surfaced I hadn't known I had. Unsure of what to do with them, and rife with guilt at feeling anything but gratitude toward my parents, I first tried to ignore them. I was more restrictive with my eating, I extended the length of my runs, and I sought with every tool at my disposal to stifle my growing ire. Then I fell in love, and I granted that if I was capable of something this novel – this powerful – I could be burying anger as well. This culminated in the letter, and, two years after sending it, I had left AA, had a master's degree in medical sociology, had returned to active addiction, and knew I was angry. In retrospect, though, my anger at the Priory was displaced. The wrath I directed toward staff was more symbolic than anything, and my writing – "How could they have let this happen? Or was it me?" – referred not just to events in hospital, but to my life in its entirety: How had it gone so wrong? Who was actually to blame? I will never know the true extent I was neglected while in England, but each time staff dismissed me, I was transported to speaking with my mother; to begging her to see that she had to listen. I now believe that by my ninth day at the Priory, my subconscious had decided the abuse (and it *was* abuse) from years earlier was inexcusable. When confronted with what I perceived to be parallel abuse, my various age-states – the seven-year-old who had to talk her father down in order to save her mother's life; the sixteen-year-old who was a "pig" for having bulimia; the nineteen-year-old who was sent unceremoniously via taxi to a homeless shelter; and the twenty-eight-year-old who was confused, yes, but who knew deep down that *she was not a liar* – consolidated and demanded reckoning.

PART THREE

Sixteen

This reckoning had been a long time coming, and when it arrived, it was staggering. Rather than continue turning my anger inwards, I unleashed it. I was "Mad" in the dual sense – a women/child driven to insanity through sheer, unbridled fury. That said, I could not critically reflect on the actual source of my rage. I was focused on the present, and staff's disregard *was* the withdrawal of parental love. Each care aide I saw that morning, each nurse, and each consultant was privy to a dynamic, emotive epiphany – desertion is not okay – that was really about my family.

I stood with Gerald after breakfast. As I cursed at nonexistent staff members and stomped in the gazebo, he was attentive and offered me a cigarette. Like Michael, Kielan, and Ethan, he did not say that I was fine, and he did not try to fix me. All he did was listen. Ebullient changes were simmering just below my surface but had not bubbled into awareness. Gerald watched me, unruffled, and simply said, "Oh Nicole... ," with the grave tone of someone who very clearly cares. This didn't solve my problems, but his bearing witness was important. I deserved to be heard. Now I had to decide what I was trying to say.

Looking back, I'm not surprised I was confused. Trauma is a tidal wave. It invades a person, engulfs them, overrides them, and leaves them, once it has receded, cowering amid the wreckage. One is then tasked with converting, integrating, sense making what is inherently and necessarily devoid of any sense. I excelled at self-deception, and to acknowledge that my parents had fucked up (badly) would not just undo my relationship with them but would usurp every belief I held about myself. Did I want to be exonerated from responsibility for my actions but crazy and inept? Or had I demolished my life while sane? These felt like my only choices after such conflicted communication patterns.[xii] For years, my parents had encouraged me to love myself

---

[xii] A "double-bind" is more specific than a "no-win situation," and it refers to a social versus individual phenomenon. Anthropologist Gregory Bateson introduced the term in the 1950s following research with war veterans diagnosed with schizophrenia, and he explained that double-binds involve one subject and one or more others who wield power over them. The authority figure(s) repeatedly express two orders of messaging, but their

because they had forgiven my past transgressions, which implied I had the capacity to choose transgressing in the first place. Yet every time I suggested my childhood wasn't optimal, my mental illnesses had negated my validity as a witness. "Self-love" was a command I couldn't possibly fulfill because it required admitting I had developed disordered eating and addictions on purpose, which marred any positive feelings I had about myself, *or* that I was mentally ill with no agency, which meant my addictions weren't my fault but I also had no future. Paradoxical, unwinnable circumstances never led to anything but further self-defeat.

R. D. Laing writes, "From the moment of birth… the baby is subjected to… forces of violence, called love… These forces are mainly concerned with destroying most of its potentialities, and on the whole, this enterprise is successful. By the time the new human being is fifteen or so, we are left with a being like ourselves, a half-crazed creature more or less adjusted to a mad world." This is why anger was so useful. It freed me from the constraints of perfunctory niceness, of self-annihilation in pursuit of social acceptability, and of the crazy/bad dichotomy. Either sometime before arriving at Nuffield or immediately upon arrival, my subconscious had decided to let the world (and more notably, myself) know I rejected this lack of nuance, and the result looked like insurgence.

---

first, explicit message (e.g., "you *must* do or feel X") contradicts their second, implicit message (e.g., "you *must not* do or feel X").[57] The subject, who sincerely wants to please the authority figure(s), can neither succeed nor verbalize why their task is impossible, and may be driven Mad.[13]

PART THREE

Seventeen

To see myself as both victim and agent, traumatized but not intrinsically ill, and one who has significant, unusual challenges but still has a shot at life, I needed to first get pissed. On day nine I ate breakfast hastily, smashing my cutlery on the table between each bite, talking loudly with my mouth full as I bemoaned the Priory's inadequacy. "England's pre-eminent psychiatric facility!?" I cackled, commanding the attention of the dining room. "This place is a joke!"

I sat next to the older woman I had seen every morning receiving medication in her nightgown. She was obviously a patient, but I had somehow spent over a week believing she was the Priory's director. I turned to the woman and, as fear re-emerged with a jolt, I told her I had to talk to someone. The woman, who I would later laugh with about this incident, her reassuring me that she is "just as mental as [I am]," nodded gravely and said that she would see what she could do.

I literally ran into Michael and Ethan as I finished eating, each of them inviting me to sit with them. I was too stimulated and went back outside instead, back to the gazebo, the fresh air, open sky, and resounding, apropos gunshots. The Priory suffocated me, its winding hallways, ornate decor, and perky staff, a pastiche of aberrant accessories, each contributing to my certainty this place was hazardous and things were not how they appeared. I continued my procession – *stomp, stomp, stomp* – as patients came and went, some osmosing my energy, until I had a small army of Priory detractors, each of us ranging from miffed to fuming about one or more aspects of programming. I was a whirlwind, a tornado, immune to embarrassment or any sort of social sanctions that typically interfere with "deviance." To put it bluntly, *I gave no fucks,* and this attitude compelled me to pick one last fight with staff.

This time my target was Derick, a nurse who happened to be in my way. Stomping up the stairs, I saw him in the women's lounge and grabbed him by the sleeve. "Do. Something," I hissed, and like the others, he stared at me blankly and said he did not know who I was. Rendered speechless by how ridiculous this was, I crumpled to the floor. After flailing about, my limbs wrenching and shuddering with a mind unto their own (my body knew the score), I made a crucial decision (or, rather, my subconscious did so for me); I asked to call my mother. Given what I've said about her, this likely seems quite odd. But, at the time, I didn't have the gift of hindsight. I wasn't months removed from England, wading through personal communication and reflections during ongoing sessions with Meris. I was in it, and the urge to contact family is something I now reflect on with compassion.

First, I will say this: I was not in a position to make calculated judgements. In fact, to say I "chose" anything would be an overstatement. In a rage-fuelled panic, I acted on this whim. This is the superficial assessment, anyway. A second would emphasize how complex my family is. Despite all I have said and will continue to say about them, I don't think they intentionally hurt me. This is precisely why they are so dangerous. My mother, in particular, has made caregiving the basis of her identity. She is precise, no-nonsense, and rule abiding, and while this may be useful as a nurse, thinking algorithmically is done at the expense of parenting. To her, my life has been incomprehensible – rife with chaos that she can not (will not) explain. Her response to her own anxiety has been micromanaging me, and to her the room searches, pocket checks, lock on the refrigerator, and screaming matches were born strictly out of love. As a result, I have learned to be helpless, that I lack substance, and my attempts to fully mature have been unremitting disasters. My failures validate my mother, and they reinforce that her actions (I have never left that taxi) have been appropriate and just. On my ninth day at the Priory, I was reproducing this pattern. My seven-year-old self could not see herself as a discrete, bounded object independent of her parents, and because she hadn't linked her anger to its source, she returned to the site of the wound.[xiii]

[xiii] When I was a teen, a therapist suggested that I try to reduce rather than eliminate bingeing. My mother refused to entertain this. She reviles harm reduction because it still allows for weakness, and she has imposed this worldview onto me even as I and professionals have told her over time that doing so isn't useful.

According to R. D. Laing, "ontological insecurity" is akin to having a fragile sense of self. The ontologically insecure individual lacks continuity in their boundaries between self and other and is threatened by the sense that they don't fully exist. Specifically, they are plagued by fears of "engulfment" (that exposing too much of oneself will lead to being

PART THREE

All that said, I would like to include a third dissection of my "choice." I was teetering atop a cliff, and I needed to either step off and perish below or retreat and locate shelter. My eldest age-state saw this as a test. It was one last chance to gather data, and if and when I didn't get the support I (thought I) wanted, I would have to believe my mother (that is, view myself as "bad" and/or "crazy") or shed the weight of her opinions. I was so close to integrating into conscious awareness that she was not safe, and to demystify my psyche (or, alternately, to firmly commit to dying), I needed to expose myself once more to harm.[xiv]

---

smothered or drowned); "implosion" (that others will obliterate their identity); and "petrification" (the sense of being immobilized or trapped in a world over which they have no control). According to Laing, ontological insecurity may be the product of family systems where "double-bind" patterns of communication are the norm.[14]

[xiv] Drawing from Karl Marx's concept of "mystification," which he used to describe how the bourgeoisie (ruling class) both exploited the proletariat (working class) and represented this exploitation as benevolence, Laing suggests that a similar "false consciousness" occurs within the family and affects all parties involved. Laing explained that to mystify in an active sense is to "befuddle, cloud, obscure, mask whatever is going on, whether this be experience, action, or process, or whatever is 'the issue.'" To those who are being mystified in the passive sense, this process "induces confusion in the sense that there is failure to see what is 'really' being experienced, or being done, or going on, and failure to distinguish or discriminate the actual issues." Beyond this, mystification may be compounded if, when the mystify-ed try to illuminate what is happening, the mystify-er "doubles down" and asserts that the mystify-ed's perception is "bad," "selfish," or "crazy." According to Laing, mystification often relates to who has what rights and obligations within the family, such as when a child reveals they are unhappy and is met with incredulity and accusations of being ungrateful. In Laing's words: "[m]ystification is particularly potent when it involves this rights obligations system in such a way that one person appears to have the right to determine the experience of another, or, complementarily, when one person is under an obligation to the other(s) to experience, or not to experience, [their]self, them, [their] world or any aspect of it, in a particular way."[15]

Eighteen

Derick left me in an empty room. My fear and fury formed a potent union, and I watched the walls ebb, flow, and shimmer. Before they had been vibrant, but now black swirled with greys, each tone appearing as fleeting bursts that transmuted into one another. They were ominous as I dialed my parents' number.

I had forgotten about the time-zone difference, and my mother was groggy when she answered. Her sleepy "Hello?" prompted a swell of activity, the walls throbbing faster as I howled into the phone. "I-am-psychotic-and-no-one-will-help!" to which she just sighed and said, "I know." A wave of horror washed over me – What did she know!? How did she know!? – as I tried to understand how she was privy to what was happening. As I wondered if this had been preplanned (*Had I been drugged as part of a government experiment!? Were there two-way mirrors in my room!?*), my mother said I should be grateful. Some colleges would have let me die, after all. Did I know how expensive the Priory was? At this I grew more frustrated, and she argued (why would she argue? I was so scared) that I should behave like an adult. She was tempered throughout, a stark contrast to the paroxysms I emitted as I writhed upon the couch. "Calm down," she finally interrupted with the terseness she brandishes when she feels I'm being irrational. It was this, an instruction that highlights not just my deficiencies but also her disgust with them, that seemed to break my spell. Putting down the phone I slowly stepped away and, turning, I ran back down the stairs.

I have never trusted nurses.

Nineteen

Sometime later (I now realize it was much later) I came to on the toilet. My recall of this day is jagged splinters, an incomplete mosaic of colours, numbers, words, sounds, and sensations whose edges aren't yet sanded. One image I kept returning to was of rushing toward Big Ben amid a flurry of activity, falling at its base, and blowing myself up. The explosive I would use as well as the aftermath of this action felt encoded in my body, as though I had done this already and was now a ghost reflecting on her death.

Here I will acknowledge the conceptual and practical distinctions between traumatized, crazy, and bad. I am the first, I display symptoms of the second while divesting of the premises and procedures that sustain its social meaning, and I mostly disregard the third, though I will return to this again. These labels are contested, ideological, and linked to decades (and in some cases, centuries) of interdisciplinary debate, which I was not able to sort through after speaking with my mother. I looked around, and as I tried to stand from the toilet, it was as though every negative belief about myself crystallized into a viscous substance that encased me and pushed me to the floor. I was assaulted as I sank, no more lucid than a fetus who depends entirely on its host. Everything I had avoided via substance abuse, eating disorders, and, most alluring of all, academia, loomed in concrete form. Mental illness and badness were inescapable, and in a millisecond, I embraced a lifetime of labels, deficits, and unrelenting shame.

I frame this now as my child self, the part who believed my mother, having no protection against her and inviting her in while my adult self stood guard, ready to call her bluff. I had to defy my darkness to purge it, and this first entailed letting it accost me. Across from me was the shower, and I envisioned smashing my head through it, picking up a shard of glass, and severing my jugular. My child self thought she (I) was damaged, and while she could not fix this, she could finally obliterate herself – disappear her pitiful life. Young Nicole believed she was crazy, she was evil, death was inevitable, and she should just finish it. The urge to lunge toward the shower and to have her (my) throat erupt was palpable. I just kept running.

Twenty

As I had before, I sprinted to the lounge. Brent was quietly engrossed in a book, and I likely startled him as I threw myself at his feet, begging him to handcuff me. I didn't trust child Nicole, and I cannot describe the physical effort required to stay outside my room. The mental imagery storming me felt predestined, as though I was obliged to comply with some divine plan, a sacrosanct force mandating it was time to go. Brent did not handcuff me. He did crouch beside me and listen cautiously as I sobbed, ranted, raved, and said over and over that I had to die. Given how weak I was, how depleted my frame, my energy was incredible. I *sizzled*. Not leaping upwards, propelling toward the shower, and impaling myself demanded all the fortitude I had. I likely resembled someone seizing, my movement was so spasmodic. This was combat embodied, the culmination of years of suffering clashing with my adult self's fierce guardianship, her unwillingness to relent. Brent observed my one-woman war. He assured me that he wouldn't leave me alone, but as he did so he rose from the floor, turned his back, and approached a nurse who had heard my cries and entered the room. I have memorialized this. It indicated that neither he nor anyone else had real insight into what I was experiencing – that although they were well-intentioned, staff at the Priory would not (could not) keep me safe. The choice to live (or to die) was mine and mine alone.

Brent returned after what felt like years, having recruited a nurse. Both of them stared at me as I wailed, vacillating between pleading with them to protect me by tying me to a bed and pleading with them to give me sufficient medication to fatally overdose ("a mercy killing," I called it). Brent was eerily calm. At last he asked me why I needed to die, and I heard, "It was all I had." I did not say this so much as the words were expelled from my body in a violent stream. "It was all I had it was all I had it was allIhad it wasallIhaditwasallIhaditwasallIhad." It was all I had. The chance to do a doctorate, something grand, to repent for my sins and pain had vanished. What else was there? I could not see a future. I have forgotten much of this, but I know Brent wondered if I could recall a time I had not been suicidal. To this I shrieked "Australia!" without hesitation. I had not been suicidal in Australia. I had felt tremendous joy there. Tremendous *hope*. Then, when the flood of memories was too much (the agony of bliss always trumps the agony of sorrow) and the current coursing through my body demanded that I *move*, though whether this be toward life or death I wasn't sure, I finally ran again. Brent had suggested that I rest, that I may benefit from closing my eyes, breathing deeply, and relaxing. Brent was out of his depth. I left the lounge, ran past my bedroom (and with it, the shower), ran through the corridors and back to the lawn. I screamed as I had before but louder this time, longer this time. I know my socks got wet.

    Staff members stayed behind at first. I'm not sure if this is because they sensed, as I now know, that something good was happening. Never have I cried so hard and never have I cried so honestly. Others were outside (sitting, smoking, waiting), but I only became aware of them when Kara, a twenty-eight-year-old psych patient, wrapped their arms around me. I allowed myself to feel the weight of their body on mine as they lifted me from the ground and they walked me to the gazebo, retaining a grip on my waist. Michael and Kielan were there, as were a handful of others. I continued to speak – I said over and over it was all I had – and a care aide later joined us. It was difficult not to rise, not to race back upstairs and catapult toward the shower, but the care aide began rubbing my back, and being touched felt good; being touched felt human. I smoked cigarette after cigarette, barely noticing when the filter burned my lips, and I continued to say "itwasallIhaditwasallIhad" until it was time for dinner. I couldn't not say it. Doing so was a relief valve – it diverted some of the pressure that was diffuse through my body and rattling my mind. My words, as others listened (really listened), were what kept me seated. Then the care aide asked if I was hungry – my god I was so hungry – and I made a choice: I would eat. We walked to the dining room, the care aide holding me up as I staggered forward. Ethan was there and said, "You alright?" in a way that was familiar. My food was delivered and as I ate, something occurred to me: I had not binged and purged that day. In fact, I had not binged and purged for over twenty-four hours, since Jen had barred me from joining the eating disorders program. (*I have the option of nursing myself back to health.*) If I intended to die, I told Ethan, exhausted again, I would still be bingeing. I would not be nourishing a body I was about to kill. As this dawned on me, I ate unreservedly. I did not purge. Within minutes, I felt very full and warm.

Oxford, I later wrote, was all I had:

I was homeless. I was jobless. My family was gone. I had lost my mind.

>   I.

>   Had.

>   Nothing.

>   But,

I later wrote,

>   I had a second chance.

PART THREE

Twenty-one

I would like to pause for a moment. I need to catch my breath. Unlike the first three parts, the fourth section of this book has not poured out of me. I have written and deleted, scoured theoretical work, analyzed empirical evidence, spoken with Meris, rewritten, re-deleted, disregarded it all, stepped away, returned, and, re-rewritten. I have done so in the pursuit of "truth." In order to reach pseudo-clarity (that is, the persuasion I am more than simply "crazy" and/or "bad"), I have had to negotiate and renegotiate with both social constructions of normalcy and internalized sanism.[xv] This is heavy work. My ninth day at the Priory was somehow my most memorable and is now the hardest to access. The events preceding my interaction with Brent are opaque, insulated in a remote corner of my consciousness, while the time I spent *with* Brent (and Kara, Michael, Kielan, and Ethan), will forever be defined. When I try to document it now, I instantly revolt. It is hard to sit and, restless (scared), I stand, pace, stretch, and, exasperated (scared), then I sit again. I want to drink, eat, stuff, but while those are behaviours I keep in my back pocket – assurance that should I need them, they will offer relief – the satisfaction this induces is tempered by my fear. I no longer believe I can substitute alcohol for food, nor can I use substances in a way that is contained. Should I use again there will be no moderation, and before I drink myself to death, I need to tell my story. It is my point of entry – a gateway to humanity that, more often than not, I watch from the outside looking in.

On my tenth morning at the Priory, there was a discernable shift in my affect. Dr. Herner had spoken to my tutor, who agreed to extend my stay again, and I nodded without hearing because I had seen this coming. The Priory was no longer novel, and though I still got lost, I also felt a sense of timelessness as if I had been there for many years. Something had started (*I* had started something), and I needed to stay

---

[xv] "Sanism" is a term introduced to the mainstream by the anti-psychiatry movement to denote stigma associated with mental illness labels. As with many forms of oppression (e.g., racism, classism, ableism), sanism can be both subtle and explicit, and it is often embedded into our social structures and institutions as well as the way we communicate interpersonally.

until it (I) finished. Internally I accepted this, but externally I was deranged. I roamed the corridors unshowered and unkempt, clutching the teddy bear I had brought with me to Oxford. I was hurting, and I could not (would not) hide it. The next week would be characterized by an unyielding lust for comfort and, with it, permission to be fragile. The night before had pacified me, but I desperately needed others, not just due to my emotional states; come day ten, I also required help with basic tasks.

At breakfast, I sat with Michael and Ethan. I had followed them into the dining room, unsure of their names or what they were saying, just aware they would not cause me harm. A small sandwich was placed in front of me and I stared at it, perplexed. What *was* this? Deep in my mind was the panicked realization that I had seen something like this before (many times) and should definitely know what to do with it. I began to weep as I had done on the toilet, but now, as I looked down and couldn't recognize my arms, couldn't recognize my voice, and didn't know where I was, I was not alone. Ethan ushered in staff, and Daphne walked me up the stairs. We sat together in the women's lounge, me snivelling and apologizing, trying to convey that I was not stupid but that something big was happening. Daphne asked nothing of me, but she did divide the sandwich into quarters, placing all but one piece on the counter so they were out of sight. She then produced her own food and modelled how to use utensils, apply condiments, chew, and swallow. I mirrored her, and at twenty-eight years old, I (re-)learned how to eat. The more I ate, the hungrier I became, and the hungrier I became, the more I had to say. Daphne, who days earlier had been a nuisance; an idiot; a young, dumb girl whose intellect was no match for mine, was now a sort of comrade. I described being in the taxi at nineteen, the words coming again from a place long sectioned off, and as I saw her horror – as I saw that she believed me – I felt validated, vulnerable, and seen.

PART THREE

Twenty-two

Of deep psychic exploration, Stanislov Grof writes, "biographical material is not remembered or reconstructed; it can actually be fully relived. This involves not only emotions but physical sensations, visual perceptions, as well as vivid data from all other senses. This happens typically in complete age regression." A similar premise is supported by neuroscientific inquiry into the relationship between latent infantile memory encoding and somatic dysregulation, and together these perspectives suggest that early adversities may be remembered bodily and dictate our response to crises later. Put differently, adults who lived through hard shit as kids may return to states of pre-verbal helplessness when we feel in danger. I had a difficult birth (I was technically born dead), and I believe that following the shower, I was transported back to this. I felt such despair after leaving Nuffield, such unrelenting existential hopelessness, that my spirit (my "self") discerned that survival required starting anew. The precarity with which I managed to avoid suiciding was a rebirth of sorts, and my shadow, my arrogance, the protective shields, built binge by binge, drug by drug, award by award, to mute or eliminate pain – to mute or eliminate humanness – were shattered in an instant. On a fundamental level, I was once again a suckling whose needs included only food, sleep, and love.

To claim a rebirth is dramatic, and had I not been to the Priory, I would scoff at this assertion. However, since this is my book, I will proceed as I see fit. I would soon experience radical alterations in how I viewed life, while fostering wildly different values about failure and success. It is important to note that after the shower, little had changed mentally with one critical exception: I no longer referred to myself, either silently or aloud, as being in psychosis. This is not to say I was peaceful (I wasn't) or the following days weren't awful (they were). However, by eliminating "psychosis" I was able to move beyond it – to shed its subjective limits and explore alternate ways of knowing. I was now in a position to delve into uninvestigated definitions about who and what I was.

The Becoming

On the morning of day ten, after being taught to eat, I wrote:

> I have been unhappy and unwell for a very long time. I am not crazy, nor am I psychotic. I need to return to where it all began (though in some ways, I already have). It is okay to be dis-orderly.

I was born in the city of Surrey, in the neighbourhood of Guildford. That afternoon I sat in the gazebo with a care aide and asked which part of England I was in. "Woking," was her reply. "We are in the city of Woking, which is in the county of Surrey and is close to a town called Guildford."

And for that I have no explanation.

Part Two

PART TWO

One

That near-death experiences are a catalyst for change is a common trope in literature, media, and public imagination. Reproducing it is cliché, but to use another, clichés exist for a reason. My narrative does complicate agency and causality because I (child self) facilitated this event, and the restraint I (adult self) exercised to prevent it from becoming a "full death" experience indicates I (adult self) had already changed. Almost dying then prompted me to change further, faster, and analytic psychology might say my self-image (that is, "the limited view and appraisal of [my]self that [had to] be outgrown") dissolved while doing so. Through a "mystical" (and manic) excavation process, I was now equipped to unearth (or develop, says the constructionist in me, though some may not agree) my authentic nature.[1]

Whether "authenticity" exists is debatable, but I was less performative.[i] Here I reflect on R. D. Laing's words. He writes, "If we

---

[i] The existence and definition of the "authentic self" has long been a topic of debate, and while summarizing it is well beyond the scope of this book, seminal contributors have included existential philosophers such as Jean-Paul Sartre, Soren Kierkegaard, Friedrich Nietzsche, Uriel Abulof, Erich Fromn, Simone de Beauvoir, Jean-Jacques Rousseau, and Martin Heidegger. When it comes to language use specifically, Jacques Derrida's deconstruction has been taken up by literary criticism to suggest that words cannot serve as unmediated representations of non-linguistic phenomena, and that the meaning of texts is unstable because they are founded on contradictions and internal oppositions.

A Foucauldian approach to authenticity, on the other hand, emphasizes how knowledge of self and others is always already inscribed with power relations. Foucault proposed that identities are produced through disciplinary regimes that define, constrain, and construct who we are by ascribing limits to boundaries of "normalcy" and "deviance." Externally imposed normalization classifications, or social categories, tend to be latent and are reinforced unknowingly by self and other surveillance. For instance, Foucault traced how the religious practice of confession has been appropriated by non-religious institutions such as psychotherapy and the family and become "scientized," a technique that he asserted has become "the most valuable" for producing "truth" in modern society.

Today, authenticity has become somewhat of a social imperative and a social currency. The obligation to "be oneself" is imbued with the value of contemporary individualism and, as such, it a priori excludes the external references that lead it to define it as such. Being authentic has become a commodity to buy and sell in the context of multiple, wide-scale disasters (ecological collapse, economic crises, a global pandemic, etc.) so, paradoxically, those who most wish to achieve it, for instance those who have the resourc-

can stop destroying ourselves, we may stop destroying others. We have to begin by admitting and even accepting our violence, rather than blindly destroying ourselves with it, and therefore we have to realize that we are as deeply afraid to live and to love as we are to die." Nearly killing myself illuminated the depth and breadth of my violence. It also proved that violence had been a proxy for love, and I ceded that death was alluring because life and love felt untenable. Yet I didn't want to destroy myself. I saw how my self-destruction was linked to harming others, and I transitioned away from the mutually reinforcing dynamic of self-other wreckage that had gotten me to the Priory. I started to create. In any other place I wouldn't have known how to, but outside the traditional therapeutic process, and in the span of just a few days, novel realities thrust through the barrier separating my conscious and unconscious minds. The possibilities were expansive and intense, and though I no longer called myself psychotic, I was still scared as hell.

Relationships were a source of and solution to my fear. On my tenth day in hospital, as I was consumed by vivid, archetypical imagery, and flat surfaces grew bulbous when I touched them, the impulse to seek kinship was the only thing more "authentic" than my terror. "It feels like I took truth serum," I told Michael, and in the same breath I said I didn't care about academia. "All that matters are love and connection." In the years preceding the Priory, I preferred to be alone. Others were unreliable, complicated, and messy, and since they burdened me and I them, it was best for all parties if I stayed in isolation. Then that narrative changed, and other patients became supports, whose presence unburdened me from my past, present, and obscure, indeterminate future. Not only did I need them, I couldn't not express this aloud and through my writing. This was a new type of mourning, an unpredictable, unpretentious mourning, and it was okay to be dis-orderly.

---

es to package, proffer, and acquire it via social media and elsewhere are now virtually indistinguishable. They are also imbued with Jungian or Jungian-adjacent sentiments.[2]

Two

While my group of confidantes had been small originally, come day ten I could no longer regulate with whom I communicated, how, or when. This wasn't just because I saw others as my equals figuratively; as had been the case for days, the sensation of myself as a bounded physical body with my own subjectivity was superseded by the feeling that patients were literally one entity. My genuineness thus wasn't due to being purposefully honest so much as it felt like my consciousness was extended: I was making elemental connections that echoed psychedelic states but were more extreme, occurred while sober, and may have been rooted in a pre- (or post) verbal drive to no longer be alone.[ii]

I built strange alliances, including with a woman named Gina. She arrived at the Priory after me, and she was unlike anyone I had met before or have yet to meet again. The image I have of her now is that of a box-dyed blonde in a spaghetti-strap tank-top and tattered sweatpants, a forty-something with a solid build who is perpetually dishevelled, as though having just emerged from a lengthy trek in the bush. She has a deep, protracted drawl, her hands are weathered and adorned with red acrylic nails, and she repeats the phrase "I'm feeling poorly" ad nauseam while roaming nowhere in particular. Gina had the cognitive capacity of someone younger than her age (though some may have said the same about me), and her reputation preceded her. I first heard about her from Kielan as he mocked how she asked for cigarettes. She would dig through the ashtray, as I had my first nights, collect butts in a pile on her lap, and make a show of not being able to

---

[ii] Stanislov Grof argues for the existence of a complex taxonomy of "transpersonal experiences" that may emerge during psychedelic research, "holotropic breathing," and spontaneous episodes of non-ordinary consciousness. These experiences include extension of one's consciousness either within or beyond consensus reality and space-time, while achieving one over the others depends on a variety of factors such as one's experience while in utero. Much of Grof's work demands beliefs in "god" and other obscure phenomena that have no demonstrable validity. Some of his conceptual schema has been helpful for understanding parts of my experience in broad terms, but the more intricate of his claims are dubious if not absurd.[3]

smoke them before casting her eyes around the gazebo to see if we had noticed. It was impossible not to, and someone would invariably share and be on the hook indefinitely. Gina was annoying. We were both disabled but disparately, and with differences that were so different I doubt I would have spoken to her, let alone become so invested in her, had I not been devoid of pretense. But I was and so I did.

During our first conversation, Gina said she had been admitted by her boyfriend. He was a wealthy Portuguese ("Por-tchu-geeeeze") adventurer whose class status she tried on. He was dashing, gorgeous, and young – everything she had been before she got so poorly and he committed her to hospital. The other patients debated the existence of this boyfriend, but Gina told me things about their relationship that would have proved his realness if I had been doubtful. For instance, lavish dinners and nautical escapades weren't the only ways they passed the time. He also beat the shit out of her, and when it came to sex, he got off on non-consent. She had gotten pregnant earlier that year and had complied when he scheduled her abortion. But she wanted to be a mother, and she described the abortion and her deterioration afterward with such clear-eyed regret it took my breath away. Then she misted over, and she held her hand out for a "ciggie." It wasn't just that I saw myself in Gina: When we were together, as when I was with every patient, I felt that perhaps I was Gina, that I was no longer restricted by the sensory organs of my body-ego and had subverted consensus reality to connect with organic life itself.

Lofty as this claim is, I was affected energetically by all I heard and saw, which felt like the before, during, and after of earthly sentience. About identification with others during a spiritual emergency, Grof says, "The sense of becoming another person is total and complex. It involves the body image, physical sensations, emotional reactions and attitudes, thought processes, memories, facial expression, typical gestures and mannerisms, postures, movements, and even the inflection of the voice," and though his hypotheses about the cause of this are unorthodox, neuroscience has yet to operationalize, let alone model systematically, how this happens in the brain. All I will describe, then, is a memory of listening to music as Gina approached me and screamed about wanting to leave. Instinctively, I handed her an ear bud. Within seconds, we breathed in tandem, I felt privy to her biography, and synchronized tears rolled down both our cheeks. In this moment I was not Nicole who was sitting next to Gina; we were a co-existing being, one whose fundamental yearnings (*love; connection*) were no more or less than "human."

Three

Another person who affected me greatly was Debra. We didn't formally meet until a week before I left, but our paths crossed first on three separate occasions. The most impactful was on my tenth day, when I wandered outside and gravitated toward the patio. Ethan sat with a group of outpatients, all I had seen but not spoken to, and I perched beside them because I was ruminating about the shower and this was better than my room.

In the group was a stylish blonde woman who flirted with Ethan, a brunette woman who was younger, less candid, and playing with a fidget spinner, and six or seven men. They were jovial as they gossiped and joked about their behaviours while in active addiction. I am well-versed in the language of "war stories" and the dynamics of rehab romances, and at any other time I could have introduced myself and pretended to fit in. But there were too many people, the sun was too bright, and the aggressive sexual tension felt like a violation. I smiled and laughed with them, unable to emote autonomously, until the mood turned sombre and I discerned something bad had happened.

"Is she alright?" asked Ethan, and I pieced together that Debra, who had just been admitted as part of the alcohol therapy program, was having a withdrawal-induced seizure in the lounge. Through the window I glimpsed a flurry of nurses and care aides. There was a piercing whistle, and I linked my current sense of embodiment to an experience of seizing as a teen. This had also been alcohol related, and in a second, I drew parallels between my disorientation pre-seizure years earlier and what I felt in the present. I was positive I would convulse. It also dawned on me that I had purged most of my withdrawal medication. I wrestled past the throng of people who had crowded in the entrance, a child who wished to hide from her parents' fighting but was responsible for its outcome. Debra was magnetic, and as I watched her sit up and rub the bump on her head, I couldn't tell if the fear rocketing head to toe was for her or for me.

Four

I'm not sure what Debra did after this, but I stayed focused on my body. I was filled with remorse at my carelessness, and, as constructive as it was to have disrupted the story told about psychosis, I was still tempted by the possibility of receiving a sensible, rational treatment plan that would eradicate my symptoms.

That plan never came, and to this day I don't know what if any of these symptoms were short-term sequelae of my bender. I sense they were much longer-term consequences of repeated trauma exposure, and if I were to call them signs of a trauma-related spiritual emergency, I would cite literature from transpersonal psychology on the physical properties of transformational experiences: "[T]hey are typically accompanied by dramatic physiological manifestations, such as various degrees of suffocation, accelerated pulse rate and palpitations, nausea and vomiting, changes in the color of the complexion, oscillation of body temperature, spontaneous occurrence of skin eruptions and bruises, or tremors, twitches, contortions, twisting movements and other striking motor manifestations."[4] From about day six onward, I experienced all of this and more. My mobility was impaired to the point that I fell while walking, the squeezing in my head left me perpetually dizzy, and I jittered as though I was on a turbulent aircraft (or, as I sometimes argued, like I was about to have a seizure).

However, transpersonal psychology can't explain why spiritual emergencies are physical. Attempts to do so have appeared through unlikely collaborations at the intersections of neuroimmunology, molecular biology, and the anthropology of religion. For instance, the finding that neurotransmitters linked to emotional regulation and memory are distributed throughout one's anatomy (e.g., in the nerves and plexus of the heart, the bladder, the adrenal glands, and the gastrointestinal tract) has led some to propose that scientific notions of the mind are embedded widely throughout the body. Models of decentralized or *in situ* expressions of consciousness are built on the theory that peripheral systems complement brain networks, and physical features of spirituality may be possible because the body possesses material faculties to mediate higher levels of consciousness.

The commonly assumed position of the "self" as residing in the brain is thus contraindicated by the "cross-talk" that occurs between the adrenal, nervous, immune, and limbic systems, and phenomenological epistemological approaches to embodiment suggest the intense effects of some psychosomatic practices, including spiritual emergencies, are due to this latent or "subtle" body.

Yet this analysis still may not satisfy empirically minded readers (which I am, sort of). I wish more information was available, but some physical conditions don't have known causes, and the closest we have come to legitimizing them through medicine is by creating "functional neurologic disorder." Otherwise known as conversion disorder, this captures a wide range of symptoms that are incongruent with organic disease and may be partially or wholly psychological.[iii] The term "conversion" was first used by Sigmund Freud about the substitution of somatization for a repressed idea, but long before this, Ancient Greek physicians believed that women behaved hysterically because our wombs travelled through our bodies. The DSM no longer cites "wandering womb" as the source of unexplained symptoms, but conversion is still diagnosed in women at a rate of 2:1 to 10:1 to men. And irrespective of gender, the stigmatizing premise that symptoms are "all in one's head" often translates to suboptimal or nonexistent care, which I have experienced with somatic pain.

This is all to say I can't really tell you what happened. I just know that whatever it was, physiological changes prompted intrapersonal and relational ones and vice versa, and the combination thereof ruptured the myths of Cartesian dualism and individualism.

[iii] Conversion disorder is sometimes referred to as the "modern hysteria." Until the third version of the DSM, "conversion reaction" was grouped with "hysterical neurosis" in a direct nod to its legacy as a uterine disorder (hysteria derives from "hustera," which was uterus in Ancient Greek). Not surprisingly, psychoanalytic interpretations of conversion disorder defer to unconscious drives (e.g., for sex, aggression, and so on), claiming that repressing them causes them to manifest physically. Others interpret conversion through learning models or sociocultural hypotheses.[5]

Five

Back then, witnessing the aftermath of Debra's seizure unnerved me so much that it took hours, which was the equivalent of months, for me to accept that I wouldn't have my own. I went outside after my request for medication was denied, not looking for anyone specific because when I was activated, all the patients were the same. They amalgamated into a single, life-affirming energy that mitigated the most extreme of my physical symptoms and made the cognitive-affective ones slightly more bearable until the worst had passed.

A few minutes later I processed being on a bench with Kielan. He was directing me to breathe deeply, and I heard myself call it dangerous to even think about, let alone vocalize, seizures because my mind was so powerful that doing so could trigger one. Kielan was becoming more than a friend in some abstract realm of consciousness, and this was partly because he responded neutrally to claims that I would have otherwise said were crazy. I really did believe that I would think myself into seizing. Accepting the severity of my trauma was an iterative process, and the simplest explanation for my experience was also the most difficult. I first had to cycle through periods of denial that included thinking I was dead, sub- or supra-humanness, psychotic, and feeling physically unsafe, as well as to engage in convoluted theorizing (which I have yet to conclude; it is hard to be a person) before I could admit that I just needed to *feel*.

Kielan stayed with me until my tears and gasping subsided. I reflect on these moments and interpret them as clear signs of progress. I was asking for what I needed directly, while sober, and without ulterior motives for the first time since early childhood. I also *had* to be led, and since staff were preoccupied with patient groups I was not part of, I enlisted those around me. My peers were remarkably accommodating. They stopped calling me psychotic when I did, and they took seriously the karate chop revelations tumbling from my mouth and spilling onto them. Admitting that I was unwell (to reiterate, *not* psychotic, but also not fine or bad) subverted every bit of subterfuge, every carefully coordinated deception, that had been the groundwork for decades of behaviour. It was also wholly freeing. I was now delivered from embarrassment, emancipated from posturing, able at last to kick, scream, and cry. I was also not yet at a point where doing this was a choice.

Six

I spent the rest of day ten certain I was about to have a seizure. Mid-afternoon, I also had a brief interaction with a care aide when she knocked on my door and found me crying on the bed. I had dissociated again, and when she asked if I had purged, I startled myself present by shrieking, "My body is the most precious thing in the world right now!" At the time, I wasn't exaggerating. I also had no frame of reference when the care aide brought up purging because I had forgotten what it was. Despite having been consumed for two decades with graphs, flow charts, and shapes – iron bars of a cognitive prison – dictating when I ate, how much I ate, the order in which I ate, and with whom I could (and mostly could not) eat, I could no longer define, let alone engage in, eating disorder behaviour. The conceptual schemas that had forced me to assess everything I digested through an infinite filter of checks and balances, a list of rules and regulations so complex that the only way to satisfy my impossible dietary conditions was to abstain from food entirely had been "de-automated." They were just... gone.

I wrote, "My body is not a vessel for a brain." I was becoming embodied, a term elaborated on by Laing. He describes the "embodied" and "unembodied" as existential settings and characterizes the latter as detachment from one's physical self arising from ontological insecurity. Those who are unembodied *observe* ourselves feeling instead of feeling, and we are so conscious of our responses to stimuli being correct that our sensory processes are mental. By evaluating ourselves as onlookers, we are also deprived of direct participation in activities that are mediated by sensation. This is because to be fully implicated in our body's desires, needs, and acts, and to be subject to the guilt and anxiety attendant on these, has the potential to kill us.

To elaborate, I was raised by parents who relayed the message a good child is a dead child.[iv] I was to be a straight-A student, excellent

---

[iv] On describing his interviews with the parents of psychotic adolescents and young adults, Laing explains that parents tend to frame their children's lives in three basic states or phases: The child is "good" (or even "perfect"); the child is "bad," though their

athlete, and mediator of conflicts, all of which I performed skillfully. But I was also supposed to be happy. This expectation was unspoken, and because I was so adept at fulfilling my other social roles, not being happy felt like a gruesome secret. This co-occurred with rituals; the sense that objects, not people, were my friends; and a spectrum of disordered eating that my parents only noticed when I became visibly anorexic at puberty. By then, I had played dead (happy) for so long that I was a spectator in my life, my body an "alien object" with whom my relationship was pseudo-interpersonal. Later, bulimic, alcoholic Nicole took over (and was she ever a relief), anorexic, workaholic Nicole periodically contained her, and when I reached the Priory, I had spent two decades substituting one for the other while trying to wrestle into submission my body fat and what it represented. I was done. And, away from my parents, I could discard my partially elaborated personality fragments and tend to the child beneath who needed to form relationships where she wasn't treated (and in turn, didn't treat herself) as though she were a prop.

My body is not something to adorn and present to men.

It is me; I am it. And while that may seem obvious, I had to mobilize an army of mental patients before I truly felt it.

---

behaviours are attributed to "acting out"; and the child goes "mad," so much so that their formerly intelligible actions transcend the boundaries of reason, and the child comes to be seen as irredeemable.

In *The Divided Self*, Laing explains that most parents are originally eager to "help" their child, but when asked to elaborate on the child's life trajectory and character, it is evident that the parents have grossly underestimated what their child's earliest needs would have been. "Psychotic" adolescents tend to have been praised for appearing "existentially dead" as children – devoid of biological and cognitive-affective "realness," and capable of behaving temporarily like mannequins or dolls. When the child does eventually assert their humanity, or come alive, the parents are unable to conceive of them as "real," which invariably leads to conflict and, for the child who has been trained to play dead, Madness.

About one patient Laing writes, "The common family sense accorded 'her' no existence. Her mother had to be right, totally right. When her mother said she was bad, Julie felt this as murder. It was the negation of any autonomous point of view on her part. Her mother was prepared to accept a compliant, false self, to love this shadow, and to give it anything. She even tried to order this shadow to act as though it were a person. But she had never recognized the real disturbing presence in the world of a daughter with her own possibilities."

Seven

Debra, who I later learned was a member of Britain's actual army, would be part of my imaginative one. However, on my tenth night I still knew little except she was withdrawing and she (or I?) could have another seizure. Her room was also across from mine, and, as I stared at the ceiling from bed, I was in her body (or her in mine), and I envisioned her (or me?) convulsing on the floor. I was stuck in several cognitive loops related to modifying my sensory processes, all of which revolved around the dire need to change. I also felt like I might be too late. After harming myself for decades, I wondered if the state I was in would be a sort of final form – total atavism proving in time that the shower should have been the end. The cruel irony of dying unintentionally or, worse, being stuck in a non-operating body-mind after having just decided to live, would have aligned with the impression I had of myself as cosmically unlucky, even as I knew/know that the universe is random.

After hours of this, I looked for an overnight staff member. I couldn't explain myself (or selves), but I was comforted by the idea of being observed. However, when I entered the women's lounge, Debra was already there. She lay face-down on the carpet, Derick beside her with an oxygen tank. In his hand was a vial of liquid benzodiazepine, and I watched him administer the medication intravenously as Debra shook, spat, and wheezed. It was a pained, wretched wheezing, its volume disproportionate to her petite frame, and it resembled sounds I had heard seeing a game animal get shot. I also felt like I was watching a well-worn film. I had memorized the lines many years earlier, and now I couldn't stop myself from revisiting them even though I didn't want to. *I told you!* I almost yelled, but I darted from the room before I uttered the words. I sat on the floor in the hallway, knees pulled tightly to chest, hands over ears, repeating *No, no, no, no, no,* for an untold length of time. I was once again filled with the sense that I knew more than staff, not just about my safety but about how things (big things: institutional, systemic, structural, and even celestial things) operated.

This is rather grandiose considering my state (*You have strong cluster B symptoms*), and I could tone it down (*Why are you so arrogant?*), but I am also right. I couldn't trust staff because they didn't see instances at the Priory where timing between occurrences in my inner world and externally were inexplicably harmonious, meaningfully synchronized with no obvious causal link. These "acausal connections" appeared everywhere and were more than mere delusions.[v] Yes, the universe is random, its correlations spurious, and suspending my pragmatic worldview was also necessary to adopt another. This worldview may have been achieved through psychosis, but it was infinitely gentler toward my body, psyche, and others than ones I had ever had while "sane." It enabled me to accept – no, revere – my humanity, and because I no longer had to hide myself in an environment whose creators condemned expressions of life, I could embrace the tenderness that made me who I am. By extension, I could do the same for others.

---

[v] Carl Jung echoed the "psychosomatic mysticism" model when he hypothesized that humans possess a "nervous substrate" (layer) that resides outside of our cerebrum that may also be able to "think" independent of demonstrable brain activity. He claimed that when people are emotionally or energetically heightened, our conscious minds "narrow" while our psychic instincts strengthen. This provides us with access to a priori archetypical knowledge derived from the collective unconscious. This ostensibly illuminates the relativity of time and space, and it is possible because the material world and the psyche are composed of similar energy. It goes without saying that there is no empirical evidence to support these claims, though the Grofs have made similar ones.

Of course, in biomedicine, perceiving an overabundance of meaningful coincidences is characteristic of schizophrenic psychosis. Psychotic delusions are partly defined by the extent to which these artificial connections impinge on the sufferer's world view and catalyze the emergence of new realities that engulf their daily life. Efforts have been made to identify which neurological processes are implicated in this process, but researchers have yet to reach consensus.[6]

Eight

After this, two things happened: First, I no longer thought I would have a seizure. In fact, the outcome of walking in on Debra was that after I returned to baseline (which was still akin to physical shock), I was mostly aware of being in my body and others being in theirs. Yet the residual effect of merging with them so wholly was being invested in their care. About Debra, I believed that three seizures should warrant admission to a real hospital, and, as a waiter took my breakfast order on day eleven, the matching uniforms, primness, and grating pep reaffirmed my suspicion that the Priory was staffed by actors. Frankly, I still feel like it could have been. Everything was a smoke screen. This is also true of all treatment centres; those of us whose behaviours deviate too sharply from "normality" are disappeared, forced into ritualistic mortification, and rebuilt in others' image of moral correctness.[vi] Little if any of this is actually done in service of health. The Priory was only unusual because I could detach from, critique, and reject this model of help. The second thing that happened, then, was accepting myself as an outsider. I saw that programming would have hindered my

---

[vi] In the early 1960s, sociologist Erving Goffman spent a year posing as an employee of St. Elizabeth's psychiatric hospital in Washington, D. C. His purpose was to study the subjective lives of the patients, and the ethnographic data he generated inspired his "total institution" model. According to Goffman, total institutions are places such as prisons and psychiatric hospitals where patients or inmates are physically and psychologically separated from the outside world. Their main purpose is to "resocialize" by forcefully and radically altering people's values, beliefs, behaviours, and senses of self to align with social norms.

The first stage of resocialization entails ridding people of their independence through mechanisms ("mortification rituals") such as forced psychiatric medication, referring to them by room number, solitary confinement, and strip searches. Following this, there is a systematic attempt to build new personalities or senses of self, usually through revoking and returning "privileges" (e.g., communication with outsiders, access to technology, leisure activities, being permitted to leave for brief periods, etc.). While resocialization is the goal, an unintended consequence may be the development of an "institutionalized subjectivity" – an inability to live outside of institutions because people are so unaccustomed to controlling their own lives. Goffman's text has been widely critiqued on methodological grounds, but it is still considered seminal for its theoretical insights.[7]

progress, and while I maintain that it was irresponsible to ignore me, it was also the best and only way to have benefited from being there.

With my growing confidence, I stopped seeing the value in medication. I told Dr. Herner mid-morning that I was still in and out of age-states but had never been psychotic. He stayed neutral, not affirming or rejecting my assessment, which I struggle to write about because my memories don't add up. Most would be closely supervised after begging to be handcuffed so as to not brutally maim themselves. Yet my perception is that people barely paid attention to me. I may have been on the observation schedule, but this entailed a cursory glance from a care aide once every few hours, at most. Certainly no one inquired out of concern or obligation if I still might kill myself. I question how this is possible from a liability perspective, if not a human one. I then wonder if staff saw me starting to make headway on my own. Were they aware of things I wasn't? Or was the Priory just a mismanaged institution, one whose employees were grossly underqualified and that, again from a liability perspective, are damn lucky I didn't die there?[vii] I may ask to see my patient file one day. As with every other file, though, it doesn't matter yet. And until it does, both me and you, the reader, will only have access to the reality that I am cobbling together without control groups, data triangulation, or pretending to interpret data neutrally.

[vii] A modern "total institution," the Priory Group has been found legally responsible of fatal mismanagement on different occasions. For example, fourteen-year-old Amy El-Kiera died of "the unintended consequences of a deliberate act" while receiving treatment at Ticehurst House in East Sussex. An inquest into her death concluded that despite being admitted after several suicide attempts and telling staff she was suicidal on the day she died, her "risk" rating had been downgraded to "moderate" at time of death. A jury ruled that staff did not call emergency services fast enough after she attempted suicide, they failed to call a doctor promptly, they were not trained in cardiopulmonary resuscitation (CPR), they were not adequately staffed to provide regular observation, and that they did not properly carry out risk assessments preceding El-Kiera's death. The firm was fined less than two days' worth of profit.

An investigation by the *Mirror* newspaper in 2019 also located the families of twelve young people who died while admitted to one of the Priory hospitals. Some were quoted as saying that the Priory "[puts] profits before people," and since the Priory now generates 90 per cent of its revenue from public money, including from England's National Health and Social Services, those profits are astronomical. In two deaths, falsified records were also identified as matters of concern.[8]

PART TWO

Nine

As concerned as I was about Debra, Gina, and the others, I wasn't able to think about them unless they were directly in front of me. This caused trouble in other ways, as being in the exact present meant strangers were enmeshed in my processing and I theirs, for better or for worse. After I saw Dr. Herner, I was joined in the gazebo by a recently admitted woman named Jill. She had been committed involuntarily, and her frantic energy exacerbated mine. I was overwhelmed by flashes of parallel experiences in Canada, and while I knew I was Nicole, Nicole was like Jill, and Jill was… I didn't know why Jill had been admitted, but as she spoke to a care aide, I learned that she was non-consensually enrolled in therapy, staff cited her nursing career as a reason for achieving stability, and she had internalized that she was borderline and likely never would. To me, these were policy failures. And though I usually refrain from voicing opinions about a stranger's life within seconds of having met them, then I may as well have been mainlining adrenalin because I could not shut up. Without so much as introducing myself, I interjected in Jill's conversation and told her she was being duped. She stared at me and then shut down completely. As the care aide ushered Jill inside, shooting me a backwards glare, I was overcome with shame. My heart sank, and I wondered how I was to form relationships (love, connection) when my best attempts to communicate scared people away.

Years removed from the Priory, solutions to this and other problems still do not come easily. But I am getting better at listening, and much like my abdomen, thighs, and jawline, my way of co-existing has softened over time. Paradoxically, the most effective way of getting here was to focus inward first. Perry says, "[b]ecause of the hurts and emotional injuries in early years, [one may] learn… to withhold from intimate, mutually open relationships." Those who do become more vulnerable to entering "high-arousal" states when threatened, and while medication can distract, suppress, or numb, only closeness prompts renewal. I was unmedicated, everything was a threat, and I didn't have a facilitator to interpret on my behalf what was happening. Consequently, no one had even met my adult "self." I had to retreat to find her. But because I proved that I would survive my worst moments, I was able to pursue an identity where I wasn't just seen as psychotic and/or a child.

I went to my room after this. I was guilty, but I forgot Jill, this feeling, and everything else the moment I started writing. I had been using the term "unwell" to describe myself, but it was wanting because it only allowed me to relate to others from sickness. I would expand on unwell. However, applying exact terminology to my state was more complicated than it sounds. I have been trained to think hard about frameworks, and the differences between "bad," "Mad," and their synonyms have been points of contention in considerable research for decades, if not longer.[viii] Therefore, while I am prone to overthinking during "normal" periods (e.g., now), trying to wade through discourses about the nature of mental illness while too stimulated to recognize anything around me and hijacked by everything that was and ever had been in me was like riding a derailed roller coaster.

My writing from that day is circular-but-forward-moving, extensive, and weighty. It is also rife with contradictions and redundancies, even more so than this text. It is hermeneutics clashing with structuralism interspersed with constructionism then deconstructionism meets confessional, and, while I planned to explore some of these in my dissertation, I hadn't anticipated throwing them at the proverbial wall of a mental hospital in a dissertation-length screed just to see what stuck. Sometimes these things happen. I won't describe the twists and turns my writing took because that would be another book, but I'll note the words you are reading now are an extension of that day. Put differently, my beliefs about where choice starts and ends were semi-crystallized through a written, multi-hour exorcism

---

[viii] The meanings we ascribe to deviant behaviours have changed alongside socio-political and economic transitions such as secularization, the ascendence of medical authority, and lay people's collective organizing. For example, some illicit drug users are given the option of attending court-mandated addiction treatment instead of prison. However, this fusion of carceral and benevolent sanctions denotes a new, more gentle social control that critics say still represents the punishment of difference. In the case of illicit drugs, it is telling that poor people and members of racialized groups are more likely to be incarcerated for the same actions for which white, wealthy people are sent to treatment. The distinctions between "bad" and "sick" are thus unstable, contradictory, and informed by social location.[9]

where I catalogued instances of poor behaviour that numbered in the thousands. I thematically analyzed the results just as quickly and determined that while my behavioural options had been constrained by external and internal forces, my "shadow" also acted in ways that were consistent and predictable. In short, I was unwell but capable of becoming well; I *was* becoming well. I have never achieved the same effortlessness of honesty again (*It feels like I took truth serum*), but I am now more likely to recognize when, in speaking to myself and others, I am utterly full of shit.

TEN

Two relationships I positioned beside each other that day were the one I had with my recently deceased grandmother and another with a man who began as a sex work client. Obviously, my interactions with each diverged. When the words I used to describe them were reduced from language to shapes, though, I saw the same twenty-six letters arranged in repetitive patterns and conceived of my motivations and behaviours in both as having been alike:

> I was doing what I knew how to do. I was manipulating men (one man, that is, one man who I knew was vulnerable and who I knew I could outwit, though I never had to try) to keep myself alive. I called this a fair trade because I offered something in return.

> Telling myself this, though not entirely untrue, was also too convenient. The foundation was corrupt.

> I did the same with Oma, but rather than offer her sex I offered the facade of a granddaughter (She was vulnerable, and I knew I could outwit her, though I never had to try. I called this a fair trade because I offered something in return.)

> Telling myself this, though not entirely untrue, was also too convenient. The foundation was corrupt.

> Others were collateral damage; they wouldn't have had to be if someone had just listened.

> I wanted so badly to stop manipulating, and each time the horror of what I needed to do for more became too much, I had to drink it down. That was my most accessible option because stopping wasn't possible.

> (When one is treated like an animal, one becomes an animal.)

I have been very unwell for a very long time.

I am getting well.

The foundation will be solid.

Sex work is something I have mentioned only briefly thus far because I don't want to connote it with illness. Before I continue, then, I will state that sex work is a valid form of income generation no more or less exploitative than other labour in a capitalist economy. Most sex workers are not "sick," and the criminalization of sellers and buyers, as well as the conflation of consensual sex work with trafficking, endanger people far more than the actual job requirements.[ix] With those caveats, I will also say that my economic necessity for doing sex work has only ever been due to my addictions. Bulimia and substance abuse are expensive, astonishingly so, so while many sex workers are savvy businesspeople whose work is just that – work – some of my paid relationships with men have been as chaotic and compulsive as my relationships with what I have needed their money for. *I have drunk it down.*

The man I reference here entered my life in 2016, just as Sean left it. At first, meeting him at the bar across from my parents' condo to have scripted, repetitive conversations, I enjoyed drinking double after double, like I had done with my grandmother. Drinking with my grandmother deviated in that I was still a teenager, I was the sole

---

[ix] Sex work is still considered one of society's most deviant behaviours, especially if it is full-service and street-based. In Canada, Bill C-36, the "Protection of Communities and Exploited Persons Act" (PCEPA) received Royal Assent under Stephen Harper's Conservative government in 2014. Bill C-36 draws heavily from the "Nordic Model" and treats all sex work as sexual exploitation. Because one of its stated objectives is to "denounce and prohibit the purchase of sexual services," the ramifications of Bill C-36 for sex workers have been severe. Sex work has been driven further underground, street-based sex workers must negotiate transactions in more isolated areas, sex workers are dis-incentivized to report theft and assault to police, online sex workers are less able to talk amongst themselves about safety concerns with clients or advertise their services on monitored platforms. The consequences of this are particularly pronounced in Indigenous communities and among poor, disabled, and racialized people.[10]

drinker, and my grandmother's Alzheimer's was too developed for her to remember that she had been instructed by my mother to not see me or give me money. Later, with the man, he would call his guy (whose cocaine was much purer than my guy's) sometime between our third and fourth drinks, and I would go to meet the dealer. The man would leave the bar as I left the dealer's passenger seat, a few hundred dollars lighter and equipped with enough stimulants to keep me alert and babbling through the night. We would then drink more in my parents' condo as we crushed the coke with a credit card, me snorting it through a straw from a pack of juice boxes my father once left in the cupboard. I enjoyed all of this, and even more than I enjoyed this, I enjoyed waking up after passing out to a stack of crisp bills nestled near my head. I less enjoyed the sex that occurred between the bar and waking up, and I also began to not enjoy the realization that by treating him as a friend, I had invited the man to develop feelings that compromised my access to his money. I also wanted friendship, but I needed money more, and because the conditions of our arrangement changed as regularly as my moods, things got messy, quickly.

There is nothing wrong with exchanging sex for money. However, it is best to solidify the terms of this exchange upfront so one doesn't admit too late that sex isn't really what's being sold. By the time the man started telling me he loved me and planned to leave his wife, I was doing what I had done with my grandmother – going to the bathroom when overcome with guilt, reprimanding the child voice who was aghast by my adult behaviour, and drinking from a hidden bottle until her objections dissolved into nonsense and I could float back, giggling. In both cases, I was in too deep, I needed money more than comfort, and the comfort the man's and my grandmother's money elicited when I used it for substances was also a great need. If this sounds complicated, it was. If I sound cold, I was. I also knew what withdrawal felt like. Keeping a surplus of vodka to delay it, for which money is a requirement, was more important than feelings: the man's, my grandmother's, or mine. Besides, I was offering something in return, the wait list for detox is lengthy, and, by the time I met the man, I needed alcohol to get to school – master's degrees don't earn themselves.

The lies I told to myself were not as calculated as they seem. Social and economic theories of rational choice don't fit with my experience because, as self-interested as my descriptions make me out to be, consider that in achieving the aims of one self, I have undermined those of others. I haven't wanted to do much of what I've done, and I've always known that the rewards for drinking, using, and bingeing, particularly ostracism, are identical to their punishments. So: how does one make sense of being both sadist and masochist, of pursuing goals whose outcomes keep me alive while also slowly (and quickly) killing me? My inconsistencies have inspired thousands of hours of Alcoholics Anonymous meetings, and the answers I've found there have been as lacking as ones from the rooms of academia. Being so confused, while knowing I can still acquire and integrate more hypotheses about why I am the way I am, forever, has made me not care to try. But I think, feel, act, relate, therefore I am, and because doing so is catastrophic, *I have drunk it down*.

Eleven

I will say that my theoretical ambivalence can be partially explained by family. I cite them nervously, hesitant to be seen as conniving, especially after having just described how selfish I have been. However, to not mention my parents here would also be remiss. My scheming, plotting, and self-deluding have been inextricable from theirs, and this book partly exists because I can't say this to their faces. Trust me (if possible), I have tried. I am still trying. And since communication between me and whoever reads this will be derivative, at best, I will allow you to decide for yourselves if context should be relevant. I will also understand if some readers retain little sympathy for me after all I have disclosed. These experiences are far from universal, and I have acted badly. I am trying to stop.

I can't determine what would be most relevant here, so I will simply relay this: My mother denies that I was homeless. I spent nearly three years cycling through shelters, alleyways, detoxes, psych wards, and mould-, piss- and rat-infested single room occupancy hotels on the Downtown Eastside, and when I use the word "homeless" in front of my mother, she says that I'm dramatic. I am not dramatic (though my intermittent borderline personality disorder diagnosis lends credibility to her case). I have endeavoured to speak to my mother about this, and to make her see how I have suffered, but whenever I approach her, she reminds me she has had it worse. Specifically, she has said that I embarrass her, that I compromise her reputation, and that hedonism has been a luxury not afforded to her. During these conversations I am bad and nothing more. This identity was imposed on me the moment I became bulimic, and it is one my mother returns to whenever I'm using substances. Related, substances have been the only way for me to broach this with her, even though I know by now that doing so will conclude with her assertion that compared to the deserving poor, who are deprived of housing due to circumstances they cannot control, the consequences of my actions have been natural and fair. Blaming her for them is yet another example of my badness, and it's time that I grow up.

As trenchant as this dynamic is, so too is another. Anorexia, alongside workaholism, sobriety, and the discipline people associate with them, bring out a different version of my mother. Not eating or drinking is a get-out-of-jail-free card, a white flag that diffuses the antagonism between us immediately. My containment is an upwardly mobile immigrant-settler's dream, and what gets perceived as willpower, including and especially by my mother, also permits me to embody the sick role once anorexia and workaholism go too far.[x] This Nicole is allowed to have been homeless. She obtains the right to use the word by disavowing the bulimic drunk who caused it.

The main problem with this is that since meeting Meris, the irregularities in my mother's logic have been as obvious as my own. The cracks in her foundation are clear when I reflect on her weekly visits while enrolled in addiction treatment. I was twenty-one, she woke up at dawn on Sundays to take the ferry to Nanaimo, and, during this time, I told her about my disease. I also expressed effusive gratitude that she had paid once more to save me. My mother called me sick then, and there was no doubt about my recent homelessness. This only changed when, after five years, appointments with Meris, and a sociology degree, I decided that my environment may have contributed to what I had become. Initially, telling her this looked like forwarding articles about neurodiversity, epigenetics, and the impacts of prolonged trauma exposure. Her answer was to withdraw payments for Meris ("She's turning you against us!") and to implement a vocabulary change: I had not been homeless, Covenant House had

---

[x] Sociologist Talcott Parsons' "sick role theory" posits that because health is a prerequisite of every functioning society, illness is a state of social deviance. When people become ill, the sick role is a socially prescribed mechanism that bestows upon them a series of rights and obligations with the purpose of societal reintegration. For instance, a sick person will be absolved of blame for their illness and exempt from normal role obligations (e.g., work), but they are simultaneously responsible for seeking appropriate medical care and trying to get well. However, Parsons introduced sick role theory in 1951, and its relevance has diminished significantly. Many have pointed out that Parsons overlooked chronic illness, that he undertheorized how the medical system intersects with race, gender, and social class, that he couldn't have predicted how technological advancements have reduced engagement with professionals by expanding access to self-diagnosis, and that discourses about health-promoting behaviours have become more entrenched in everyday actions.[11]

been a retreat for troubled youth, and, when I started drinking and bingeing again shortly thereafter, and was thus cavalier enough to replace the articles with screaming matches, I had been bad, not sick, after all.

Mainstream mental health discourses encourage us to share our feelings with words. Rather than express ourselves through drug-fuelled outbursts, emaciation, or by etching "help me" into our forearms, we are told all emotions are valid, and we simply need to talk. But what happens when every time we try, we elicit no response? Worse yet, what happens when talking translates to blaming, and our attempts to converse become more evidence of deviousness? I have done terrible things, and I also believe I wouldn't have had to if my parents self-reflected. I have never had the epistemic stability to pause, let alone decide who I am or could be. To underscore my point, I will provide an anecdote about my father.

He won't discuss my years at Covenant House, and I once offered him insight into the challenges of homelessness as a young, addicted woman. My attempts to have measured dialogue failed, and so, sad and frustrated, I said I don't know how many times I have been raped. To this my father recoiled and all but spat that I was already dead to him and I should be more considerate of his feelings. He then admonished me for not showing more gratitude toward him and my mother before leaving me in my/his apartment while he went to buy me groceries. After he dropped them off with a resounding, "You're welcome," I ate the groceries, regurgitated the groceries, and watched in fascination as the groceries made patterns in the toilet bowl. As I did so, I thought about my father, I thought about his feelings, and I confirmed, with relief, that now I felt nothing at all.

Is it any wonder that "reality" has been ephemeral?

This will take some time.

Twelve

If it seems like I keep circling the same issues without getting to the point, that's because I am. I have no concrete destination. Each statement that I make is accompanied by guilt. The seed of self-doubt was planted at birth and nurtured diligently for me. It became a pertinacious weed. Pruning it now as both child and old woman (one who is too aged to still be gardening) requires exceptional coordination.

No one theory will explain this.

This will take some time.

"No one can become conscious of [their] shadow without considerable moral effort," and, as I wrote, I was reminded of Alice's instruction to take personal responsibility for my actions. Her advice had been ill-timed, but after documenting what felt like every action, ever, and wanting to not repeat them, she also wasn't wrong. Accountability was important. However, after so many years of trauma and Madness, or Madness and trauma, I also couldn't parse out who I was from how others have reacted to me, and how I have reacted to those reactions.[xi] And I no longer had to try. Accountability *was* important but attempting to decouple cause from effect had been Maddening unto itself, and I saw that constant, senseless rumination about the past was more indulgent than moral. I was starting from almost the point of birth, and I could thus individuate or be more "authentic" without having to be weighed down by sickness, badness, both or neither. This wasn't the fresh start I had anticipated before Oxford, but I may have planned it all along.

My ontological security improved after such an exhaustive process, which caused me to become more embodied, which then enhanced the quality of my relationships, which then improved my ontological security even more, and so on. Perry explains that psychic integration

---

[xi] Vital to my understanding of becoming medicalized has been the idea of "secondary deviance." This is a stage in Edwin Lemert's theory of deviant identity formation, and it is deviance that has been triggered by societal reaction (e.g., stigmatization) to prior deviant behaviour. For instance, if a person commits armed robbery (primary deviance) and is caught and subsequently incarcerated, they may learn to see themselves as "criminal" and be more apt to commit further crime upon release.[12]

requires collaboration, and by my twelfth day, this cycle was fully initiated.[xii] For instance, I was able to prevent myself from speaking over Jill the next time I walked past her. This wasn't easy, and I still felt the now-familiar blurring of bodily margins when I sat too close, but now we were two people, not one. The same happened with Gina, Michael, Ethan, and Kielan. I continued to perceive movement where there was none, invert cause and effect, and be far more empathic than would be considered normal or even sane, but I recognized that I and others had cognitive-affective limits. I was thus able to warn whoever had triggered or would be triggered by traumatic flashbacks when I was about to release them. My strategy for doing so was to state, "I'm-about-to-say-some-really-fucked-up-shit-please-leave-I-don't-want-to-hurt-you," as loudly as was possible and hold my breath so those who didn't wish to hear about rape, drug use, and death had time to exit before I turned to the nearest remaining patient or staff member and unloaded. Each time this happened, I felt a surge of pride for having treated others respectfully (in my own way) and was able to do it again. People activated me past the point of being functional in daily life, but because I didn't yet have to be functional, I could practice forming relationships that were not tainted by the extractive necessity of those from before.

[xii] Perry draws from Carl Jung's archetype theory to explain that inner turmoil is resolved after being dispatched into a mutual emotional field (the "central" archetype, or the "vessel of the opus"). He claims that within this "sacred enclosed space, the individual's insights and awareness "meet and mingle" with those of the receptive listener, and this in turn promotes a deeper healing than one could accomplish independently.

PART TWO

Thirteen

That said, it still took me a few days longer than it did the others to separate from Debra. Our similarities beyond alcoholism were negligible, but even as I stayed more and more in my body-mind, I couldn't shake the sense that I was entering and exiting hers. Each time I saw her I was automatically prepared to fight, not with her but with the staff members who I believed were being dismissive at best, and more often than not unkind. I knew from Ethan that this was Debra's second time that year to have enrolled in the alcohol therapy. The first time, she had come straight from the army, completed her thirty-day stint, and gone back to drinking the moment that she left. Witnessing (reliving) her (my) shaking, sweating, and shallow breathing as she detoxed now was agonizing. So was the way the nurses patronized her, shushing her as if they knew better than she did the dysphoria induced by withdrawal. Their indifference resembled not just how they (and therefore my family) had treated me since I had been at the Priory, but also the attitudes of staff in other rehabilitation centres I had already been to.

This all came to a head on my thirteenth day, when Debra's voice and that of a nurse drew me into the hallway. After getting used to thinking, feeling, and moving at triple the rate of those around me, their animateness, which was on par with mine, almost knocked me over. I steadied myself on the wall. Sometime the day before, Debra's counsellor had given her a writing exercise from Alcoholics Anonymous. I never saw the assignment, but an educated guess is that it asked her to outline why she was powerless over alcohol and explain how this made her life "unmanageable." Debra had produced eighty-six pages amid the ongoing possibility of having another seizure. However, her counsellor had told her she had done the wrong set of questions and had barred her from sharing her responses during her group therapy session. Debra was as disoriented as she was upset, her fistful of papers waving haphazardly as she paced left, right, not going anywhere but unable to stay still. To me, this was unjust. I also recognized the nurse as the same one who had given me morning vitamins while I thought I was psychotic. To say that I disliked her doesn't begin to explain the bitterness that churned in my throat as her derisive yelling echoed down the hallway. Bright, red beams radiated from her as I heard her tell me all over again as she faced Debra that I (Debra) needed to calm down. I was fired up, alarmingly so, so I closed my eyes and forced myself to concentrate on Debra's voice before I did something irreversible.

I heard Debra say that she would leave. She would likely drink immediately, and given her medical status, I doubted she would live. This is what I believed, anyway, and the dozens of treatment centre friends I have watched do the same only to overdose or suicide within hours was the only evidence base I needed. Once more, my surroundings were no longer surroundings, and I inserted myself between Debra and the nurse while cultivating peace. That is, I made eye contact with Debra and mustered up every bodily feeling of warmth, serenity, and poise I knew resided within me, and I transmitted them to her. As our eyes locked, I mouthed "stay" and the world stood still for days, months, or years of understanding. I was a looking glass, and her affect reflected mine. For the record, I realize how this sounds. But the tenseness diffused, and Debra blinked slowly, casually remarking, "But you're not staff?" before teetering, dumbstruck, to her room. I did the same, and the day carried on, transiently calm, as though nothing had ever happened.

Fourteen

Here is a good place to reiterate that mental health, addiction, and eating disorder treatment are hierarchical by design. Staff members may have some experiential knowledge, but the transformative potential of informal peer support can't be realized when institutional mandates promise market-driven "recovery."[xiii] In other words, divisions between

---

[xiii] Peer support has an extensive history in disability rights and mental health activism. Broad in definition and practice, it denotes engaging socially, emotionally, and practically with others from a place of lived or living experience based on the principles of respect, shared responsibility, and agreement about what is helpful. Its historic purposes have been to advance the rights of mental health service users and to provide advocacy outside of biomedical or psychiatric authority.

Simon Bradstreet's typology of peer support also highlights that it emerges organically and informally wherever service users come together (i.e., inpatient wards), even if the goal of doing so is not expressly political. However, in the last two decades, services such as community mental health teams, hospital psychiatric units, and forensic units have increasingly included "people with lived experience" into their delivery models. Peer support has thus been absorbed into clinical logics that prioritize "recovery" as defined by the psy disciplines (as well as cost-effectiveness) and estranged from its radical roots.

Jijian Voronka draws from ethnographic research to point out that most paid peer support now reinforces rather than subverts pathological models of Madness. As a precarious form of affective labour, it mobilizes "experiential knowledge" to orient clients toward emotions and responses that "encourage compliance and cooperation with dominant conceptual models of mental illness." Consequently, peer inclusion reinscribes the social, legal, political, and economic regimes that organize, administer, and intervene on Madness.[13]

The meaning of "recovery" is not static or homogenous. In mainstream mental health services, it generally refers to "overcoming" or successfully "managing" the symptoms or deficits associated with serious mental illness, which we are encouraged to achieve through adherence to biomedical paradigms and complying with care plans from mental health professionals. However, anti-psychiatry and consumer/survivor/ex-patient groups have long interpreted mental illness as one aspect of an entire person, and not necessarily a negative one. Consequently, recovery may focus more on the structural and systemic "symptoms" of saneism such as poverty, institutionalization, isolation, loss of salient social roles, and all else that is linked to being seen as "crazy." Some consider that the traumatic effects of discrimination may make it impossible to return to a pre-illness state, and thus don't seek to be as we were "before." The ascendence of "market-driven" recovery is linked to mental health being increasingly commodified and defined by one's productivity within the economic system.[14]

paid, healthy employees and always-already sick patient-consumers prevent the formation of organic solidarity, as employees are more powerful than patients and discouraged from displaying a spectrum of emotions. This model is "unnatural," and while I could critique it before the Priory, it had started to feel personal. Debra was the largest canary thus far in the treatment industrial complex coal mine. She proved that the professionalization of wellness was a suppressive project, one whose outcomes led to disconnection, disenchantment, and diminution of connection.

That said, Debra was a person, not a symbol. I can write about her in the abstract or use her to signify larger issues, but I will also emphasize that I didn't just view her as a projection or a metaphor. Then and now, she was/is real. After the hallway incident, we developed camaraderie that shifted based on how charged either of us was in a given moment, which often related to our perceptions of which staff members were nearby. Some were safer than others. Both of us knew it. However, unlike Debra, staff didn't tell me to do anything, ever. Being at the Priory informally helped me see past their status as institutionally legitimized claims-makers and they became… people. This also revealed where I had been unfair. For instance, once I had confirmed that Debra wouldn't leave, I apologized to Daphne. I did so because even though she had gone out of her way to make me comfortable, I had been aggressive, patronizing, and too often, nasty. Naming matter-of-factly what I would do differently was a sort of impromptu amends. It helped me be more assured that I wouldn't repeat the patterns I had identified while writing and divest from a system that drew me in just to spit me out in a worse state than before.

Concurrently, I honed my ability to assess which staff strongly identified with their professional roles. I could see that Jen, the head of the eating disorders program, and some other nurses relished in their authority. They triggered an involuntary threat response, and I avoided them unless absolutely necessary. Given my energy, I was a live wire dipping and dodging to and fro, in and out of rooms, whenever I sensed they were on shift. Daphne, on the other hand, as well as Alice, Derick, and a few others, I registered more like equals. The voltage coursing through my body lessened in their presence, and I trusted them not to wield their titles out of spite, pettiness, or as a latent job requirement. Finally, that Igor became an unexpected source of comic relief adds to the surreal texture of my memories. I recall sitting with him in the gazebo around this time and reflecting on my admission. It was a dusty relic. "My god you screamed," he said in reference to my first night. "All you said was, 'Help Me!' [berserk pantomiming] and you went on about hearing voices." This gave me a point of comparison, and I told him that after purging for the last time, the voices had stopped as well. My thinking was alacritous and alarming, yes, but I knew that it was mine. The stories I have of Igor from myself and others are numerous and probably not that pertinent. I'll note that Michael still laughs about the time Igor berated him for smoking even as he stood beside him and lit his own cigarette, and that once I could pay attention to these things, I regularly overheard new or new-ish patients ask who Igor was because he was prone to kicking inanimate objects. He and a few other staff members defied tradition, and as I progressively saw that tradition when it came to medicine had done more harm than good, I invited those who were not married to it in.

Fifteen

On my thirteenth afternoon I wrote:

> I am no longer the person I thought I knew – the person who was determined to appear (to herself, more than anyone) competent, stable, and mature. To be an adult.
>
> I have never been an adult.
>
> A child decided to go to Oxford. A child decided that Oxford sounded important, and she thought that getting a DPhil might make her life worth something. Maybe it would impress people and maybe, with a DPhil, she wouldn't be obliged to learn to eat, or sleep, or form human connection. It was an easy out.
>
> I have decided not to take the easy out.
>
> Getting a DPhil would have been so much simpler.

At this point, I had grown slightly from helpless infancy but hadn't yet left early childhood. Onlookers may have called me eloquent in certain contexts, but this was a brief possession that ended the moment a high-intensity situation diffused. Otherwise, I was young. Tellingly, right after I wrote this, I trailed a line of patients into one of the downstairs kitchens. It was a narrow room that contained a locked fridge, sink, dishwasher, and high-end, multi-purpose espresso machine. I had watched others push buttons and press levers on the machine for almost two weeks, but it took me until then to understood what it was. I hovered, and when a new patient offered to make me coffee, I heard myself say that I wanted warm, frothed milk. I accepted it and relished in its sweetness until the words *mother's milk* resonated emphatically, stopping me in my tracks and causing me to gag. Yes, I was young. But I was chronologically almost thirty, so I also judged my

PART TWO

young-ness and the thoughts associated with it through the lens of an adult. The unfiltered discoveries ("truth serum") of my child self were unwelcome, troubling, and necessary.

Sixteen

By the end of my second week, I stopped coming to on the toilet. I was also more embodied in other ways, and congruent with being a child, I started to crave touch. Kara, the patient who had lifted me from the lawn, sensed this, and when she offered me a hug, I gratefully accepted. This became an unspoken agreement. Whenever we saw each other, a wordless nod indicated I consented to embracing, and she would envelop me so it felt like my feet were on the ground. I was unselfconscious in her arms, even as my "selves" became more unified. I can say now that before the Priory, my nervous system's ability to evaluate hazards, or "neuroception," had been warped. I rarely, if ever, felt like those in close proximity weren't about to lunge toward me and inflict physical or emotional harm. Neurobiologically, I might claim that my "mirror neurons," which are stimulated by one's first caregivers and are linked to understanding others' intent, had been undeveloped.[xiv] Alienation was inscribed into my body and

---

[xiv] "Neuroception" is a term coined by Dr. Steven W. Porges, who also introduced the "polyvagal theory." "Polyvagal" refers to the many branches of the vagus nerve, which connects the brain to multiple organs including the heart and stomach, and the polyvagal theory builds on early Darwinian insight to explain how the nuanced interplay between bodily experience and environment can trigger feelings of safety or danger. From this, Dr. Bessel A. van der Kolk has outlined the limitations of talking and talk therapy for trauma survivors, one of which is that a lack of security in one's body may manifest as feeling "chronically out of sync" with the world and its inhabitants Particularly with complex trauma, prolonged "overwhelm" destabilizes one's "neuroception" and distorts their sense of risk. The solutions that van der Kolk proposes are somatic, not verbal or cognitive.[15]

First discovered in monkey brains, mirror neurons are specialized visuospatial cells that have been found in the brain's premotor, primary somatosensory, and inferior parietal cortices and supplementary motor area. They enable us to discern other people's emotional states. They begin functioning at birth, and as infants they prompt us to imitate ("mirror") our caregivers. As we develop, mirror neurons register others' inner experiences and discharge based on what we notice (i.e., by breathing synchronously with others or by our heart rates accelerating or decelerating in tandem with another's). Mirror neurons are the source of our ability to feel empathy, and they are related to language acquisition. Related to neuroception, trauma may interfere with assessing others' intentions. We are more likely to revert to our "primitive brains" over our more rational frontal lobe regions where mirror neurons are located when confronted with even neutral stimuli.[16]

adult Nicole drank, binged, starved, ran, fucked, and achieved it away. Then, when child Nicole couldn't take this anymore, and after a period of extreme overcompensation, my different age-states converged to replicate basic attachment patterns, mediating danger. Or something.

A sign this version of events is plausible occurred on my fourteenth day in hospital. I sat with a sombre Michael and listened to him express disappointment with the general psych stream's lack of intensive care. He wanted more than what staff gave him, but he didn't know how to define what was missing, let alone acquire it. I had seen this before. I got it. It is difficult to ask for something one has been told they shouldn't need. Michael considered leaving, and had this conversation taken place a few days earlier, I likely would have reacted too intensely or not reacted at all. But I had gotten to a point where I neither overidentified with the inner worlds of others nor was I so preoccupied with my own experiencing that I forgot others had inner worlds of their own. I listened. I cared. I didn't care so deeply, however, that I confused myself with Michael, and even though I could tell he was somewhere else – somewhere dark – I also didn't say that he should stay. As we spoke, I wrestled with conflicting impulses. It was uncomfortable, but not retorting automatically, as I had done with Jill, suggests some sort of "progress." We exchanged contact information, and I knew as I watched him walk away that we would see each other soon.

Hours later, I smoked in the gazebo. This and writing were still the only ways to get through the night, and after my mass excavation, I wrote fewer words less often. I thought about Michael. I imagined him in his mother's house, drinking. I was *almost* there myself, but I stopped before being carried too far away. This worked until I got a text message I knew would be from him. Part of me had been waiting for it. And when I read that Michael had taken a near-fatal overdose of prescription medication, I exhaled deeply before skyrocketing into full-blown "mania" once more. It felt like every cell in my body was being electrocuted. I wasn't surprised to learn that Michael had done this, but slowing down temporarily had allowed me to convince myself that I didn't know as much about him as I had thought I did. This was proof that altered states were inextricably linked to honesty. And even though I didn't want to be this intuitive, I couldn't willfully turn it off.

Seventeen

Michael came back to the Priory. An ambulance dropped him off at four in the morning, and I waited in the foyer to hug him before he went to bed. This left me with a few hours to calm down. By then I had insight into how writing and talking sped me up, so I paced in circles trying to ground myself. The word "grounding" wasn't actually part of my vernacular, and at no point did I employ standard grounding techniques. But I sat firmly on my bed gripping my legs, hard and spontaneously. "I am here," I whispered; "I am here; I am real; I am Nicole." I moved upward from my ankles to my calves and then my thighs and back down again, and though it still felt like I was exploring a stranger's body ("an alien object"), one who was devastatingly thin and very, very pale, I forced myself to do this until I was less confused, electric, and wraithlike. By the time my peers woke up, I had returned to a state of what I would have called terror in the years leading up to the Priory, but compared to where I had been days before, was more like moderate discomfort.

Over the course of about four days, then, I had gone from having had my metaphysical grasp of existence annihilated to regaining (some) human finitude. The relations that structured my "self" were again more vertical than horizontal, meaning that despite being conflicting child and adult selves, I was no longer child, adult, and many other selves, rendering me self-less – usually, that is. From a transpersonal perspective, one might say I had returned from a "holotropic" state, where I had a "potentially unlimited field of consciousness," to a mostly "hylotropic" one: I saw myself as a "solid physical entity" with a more "limited sensory range" (again, usually), and, with this re-established "Newtonian [ish] image of reality," I felt more secure in my body-mind.[xv] Specifically, the walls still wavered but not as briskly.

[xv] In transpersonal psychology, "hylotropic" translates to "matter-oriented," and hylotropic mode of consciousness refers to the state of mind that we experience in everyday life. In this state, we can discern between cause and effect, we feel bounded by a physical body, we are limited by our sensory organs, and we tend to accept without question general presuppositions about the world such as "matter is solid," "two objects cannot occupy the same space," "something cannot be both true and false," and "one can only

Their colour palate had also grown subdued. Somatically, the vise grip on my head had lessened, I had regained some coordination, and I no longer felt like I was about to melt inward, float, or both. Concurrently, though, my temporal orientation was still nowhere close to "normal." I was in a time rupture, my internal rhythm near-constantly climactic, my thoughts traversing unexplored landscapes about the nature of who/what/where/why such that I aged decades every hour without moving an inch. I will discuss why this was a good thing, but it was certainly unpleasant.

I couldn't explain this to Dr. Herner when I met him after breakfast. I was taken aback when he said I had been at the Priory for two weeks because I thought I had been there about four days, if that. I also didn't remember ever not being there. About my departure, I told Dr. Herner that asking me to stay seated on a twenty-plus hour plane ride without being strapped down was laughable. His response, that I had been put on the wait list for an NHS-funded hospital bed and would be transferring to a different, public psychiatric ward when a spot became available, was staggering. I pictured myself verbally meandering in front of a faceless psychiatrist, one who knew even less about me than staff here, and weaving tangent with tangent, citing theory, my parents, and epiphanies about connection. He would think I was psychotic. He would also have the authority to put me in chemical and physical restraints, and the odds of being relegated to a padded cell, forcibly injected with antipsychotic sedatives, and wearing only paper gowns and diapers, possibly for years, were good. The gap between having self-identified as psychotic and this conversation was short in standard time, but from my vantage point it was an unbridgeable chasm; moving backward definitionally (*becoming well; unwell; psychotic; subhuman; dead...*) could be a full life sentence. Before our appointment concluded, Dr. Herner mentioned that he and my tutor hoped to move me to the hospital in Oxfordshire. This meant that I would be closer to

---

exist in one temporal framework at a time." On the other hand, "holotropic," (which translates literally to "aiming for totality" or "moving toward wholeness") consciousness refers to a state of mind in which these former assumptions about the world are inverted. It is worth noting that some of Stanislov Grof's theories are derived from having provided psychedelics such as LSD to his subjects. At one point at the Priory I wrote, "This is the longest, must excruciating acid trip of all time."

Nuffield, as well as the month I had drunk away, which was, for lack of a better term, impossible. It could not happen. I didn't say this aloud, but I left the office having promised myself I would soon be on a plane.

PART TWO

Eighteen

I don't want to imply that people can will themselves out of altered states. If we could, this book (and psychiatry) probably wouldn't exist. However, by now my adult self had just enough ascendance to take charge. Practically, this meant that as valuable as it was to "be" over "do," I had to suspend the existential and sort out more than just my mind. If I had transferred hospitals, I might still be in England. I'm not, so it goes without saying that between there and Canada I eliminated salient variables about where to go and how to get there. And, while writing will flatten the complexity of this process, I hope to convey that building a life from the confines of a mental hospital is no easy task, especially while in what could have been called psychosis.

I sat on my bed, phone in hand. Logging into my Nuffield email account, I skimmed hundreds of messages until I got to one that had been sent over a week earlier from the United Kingdom's Department of Visas and Immigration. I read that my student Visa had been cancelled, and that unless I was staying in the UK for medical reasons, I had to inform the office of my departure time. They could arrest and deport me if I didn't. I imagined asking Dr. Herner to call on my behalf and wondered what he would say about why I couldn't go. Then I cackled long, hard, and loud. Debate about the nature of psychosis, mental illness, and medicine had consequences, and as they stared back at me, inescapable, I resolved not to solicit the government's input about who I was becoming.

"Soon I will be well enough to get on a plane," I wrote. "And it is not so much the plane that I am frightened of, but that which waits for me on the other side."

There was so much maturing still to do, so many thoughts, feelings, and memories left to synthesize.

But I was out of time.

Part One

PART ONE

ONE

So far, I have alluded to the importance of time. I have explained that before I went to England, my relationship with it depended on whether I was sober and anorexic – in which case I marked its passage with meals and it crawled – or drunk, high, and bulimic, which was preferable because I lost track of it completely. I have framed the Priory as a sort of temporal paradox, my thoughts, feelings, and behaviours accelerated despite (or because of) my environment standing still. What I have described thus far is polychronism, meaning that I experienced every moment as a convergence of inner and outer events unfolding independently of the ones that came before. All of this has just been about cognition, though. What I have yet to state explicitly, but which now becomes relevant, is that time is also political. Here I am not just (re)referring to how western conceptions of it as a linear ribbon have marginalized alternative time perspectives, leading to cross-cultural conflicts at work and elsewhere, but that even where dominant paradigms are uncontested, how we view and use time is inextricable from identity, freedom, choice, and their absences.[i]

First, that people have "free time" is doubtful. Even when not engaging in formal labour, after a certain stage of development we can't forgo the social roles (e.g. mother, father, child, partner, friend, who is gendered, racialized, classed, etc.) that subtly pervade our psyche. Furthermore, contemporary capitalism has bifurcated work and leisure so stringently that indulging in the latter feels compulsory, lest we miss chances to feign reprieve from the former. Put differently, "freedom" is organized through time such that, in Theodor Adorno's words, "Neither in their work nor in their consciousness" do people

---

[i] Anthropologist Edward T. Hall described western time as "monochronic," meaning that we see it as a linear ribbon or "road" that is divided into years, months, weeks, days, hours, etc. This perception of time encourages productivity and is necessary for organizing the complex systems endemic to contemporary capitalist societies. Conversely, "polychronic" time perspectives are more common in non-western societies. Polychronic peoples are less attached to the time clock and tend to conceive of time more as "points" where multiple actions, thoughts, objectives, and people converge.[1]

genuinely dispose of it over themselves.[ii] Why do I bring this up? Because ever so briefly (and I can't even write this without citing temporality) I had no social roles, no distinction between work, play, or other, and, therefore, no time consciousness. Without this – without constantly critiquing whether I was using time "properly" or counting the minutes until I started and finished work/meals/rest – I was the "freest" I had ever been, except perhaps before learning what time was. Being only present in the truest sense of the word meant that my socially imposed selves gave way, as did the rituals I relied on to sustain the illusion of embodying them (eat, sleep, work at precise periods, or reject time and self in acutely harmful ways). I could simply "be" – in a near-total time warp.

To elaborate, in ruminating about love and connection I unearthed who I "really" was. With the time to do only this, I was no longer the high-achieving student, but I also wasn't the colossal fuck-up who regularly almost killed herself. I was just me. I was evading scientific power (my medical labels of anorexia, bulimia, alcoholism, drug addiction, and a veritable buffet of mental disorders) and governmental power (labels that were positively sanctioned but still oppressive) while being honest about what I wanted, while paying no heed to what was expected of me by virtue of what I did with time. Michel Foucault may have seen this as temporarily winning a sort of anti-authoritarian struggle. He describes these as localized interactions between people and regimes of power that materialize "in order to object to forms of subjectivization."[iii] In other words, Foucault saw

---

[ii] Adorno writes, "Free time depends on the totality of social conditions, which continues to hold people under its spell. Neither in their work nor in their consciousness do people dispose of genuine freedom over themselves. Even those conciliatory sociologies which use the term 'role' as a key recognize this fact, in so far as the term itself, borrowed from the domain of the theatre, suggests that the existence foisted upon people by society is identical neither with people as they are in themselves nor with all that they could be."[2]

[iii] Michel Foucault's "biopower" and "biopolitics" are forms of power that involve "a very profound transformation of [the] mechanisms of power of the western classic age." According to Foucault, whereas state power was once exercised repressively (e.g. through public executions), governments in the modern period take an active interest in promoting the health and stability of their subjects. The result has not been a reduction in state power, but rather the emergence of new "productive" technologies of control that join

people as being embroiled in an ever-shifting network of relations that includes rules, laws, and norms. Cumulatively, these inform the practices or technologies we employ to "produce" and "know" ourselves as "ethical," all of which are derived from the systems we're embedded in. Bluntly, no one thinks for themselves. However, the endless process of "becoming" is not just passive and predestined, and anti-authoritarian struggles arise when we refute inherited knowledge through "counter-conduct." Subversion of this nature takes many forms, but it is fundamentally immediate; it contests who and what we have been told to be, here and now, sometimes in major ways but often imperceptibly.[4] By my second week in hospital, every moment was a spontaneous de-construction of "academic" and "mentally ill Nicole(s)." Without remembering the deeds that had historically constituted her(s) (e.g. self-starvation, bingeing and purging, drinking, reading and writing for hours on end, etc.) and how people had responded to them, I *could not* see myself as anorexic, bulimic, alcoholic, a workaholic, and so on.

Yet all of this stopped when I had to leave. As the prospect of transferring hospitals loomed over me, time didn't just matter – it mattered at the expense of everything else. I knew that executing the tasks necessary to get to Canada would demand comprehension, foresight, and purposive action, and privileging these in my psyche altered my subjectivity. Gone was the space to dream, reflect, protest. The impetus to do so was strong, but it ceased being helpful the second I realized that if I went to a different hospital, I would be subsumed under its governance and made "crazier" than before. The only way to not move backward (and, I was positive, stay there) was to charge ahead, despite not being remotely prepared to re-enter a world where I behaved like an adult. This is often how subjectivization works: To

---

repressive power in enabling governments to monitor and regulate their subjects.

More broadly, Foucault championed the idea that power is everywhere. It does not just appear as discrete policies, laws, practices, or within particular systems and institutions: It is dispersed throughout the social body and pervades all of human activity, including our "personal" thoughts, feelings, and senses of embodiment. It is inescapable and invisible, and this is partially what he meant by "subjectivization" – subjects cannot be created outside of certain, dominant "truths" about what is good/bad, normal/abnormal, fair/unfair, etc., and we thus act, think, and feel to reproduce these truths even – and especially – when doing so isn't in our best interest.[3]

avoid a harsh regime of coercion, psychiatry, I had to discipline myself in less obviously restrictive ways that were repressive, nonetheless. I had to be "normal," *now*. Everything from the content of my speech to mannerisms to sense of temporality was implicated in this shift, and suddenly I wasn't just "me anymore." I was "me" who knew that every twenty-four-hour increment at the Priory cost Nuffield fifteen hundred dollars. Time was literally money, and because this anchored decisions about the length of my stay, I was once more driven by the need to be productive, though without my full consent.

Two

As much as I enjoy meandering through theory, which I admit to taking liberties with, doing so may not be effective. Grappling with "normalcy" while far from it was hard and felt and looked dis-orderly. I had no doubt I would go, soon. The question was, how? I had nowhere to live; I had no way to get there; I hadn't yet started thinking in straight lines. My ideas were lightning bolts: *Search housing ads! No, too hard! Sleep on a couch! Whose?!* interspersed with *I never wanted a PhD! Of course I ended up here! My life will not be a reactionary response to trauma!* and *Wait – where the fuck is that music coming from!?* My capacity for analytic reasoning was either over- or under-active, depending on your interpretation of being highly adept at pattern recognition for split seconds, at most, while – as every item, shape, and colour around me evoked stifled glimmers of years past – I did indeed hear music. The "Monster Mash" was now a symphony orchestra. Eight bars of a swelling chorus pulsated. An ecstatic crescendo thrummed around, in, and through me. I levitated. I felt like I had snorted one (or five) lines of cocaine too many. I was exultant, cagey, and frenetic without knowing where or how to direct my energy, but all too aware that others didn't feel what I did and held assumptions of me based on a presumed shared reality. I froze. Then, exhaling slowly, intentionally, I turned away from my laptop and started to get dressed.

Like everything, this decision was instantaneous. Much grander, more complex duties lay ahead, but how would I complete them if I couldn't change from my pyjamas? Also, like everything, what should have been simple was soon imbued with symbolism. Before I knew it, I had sorted my clothing into piles: items that encapsulated my mother, my father, others, including people from previous treatment centres and, from there, which of these had positive connotations versus ones that felt like child or sickness garments I needed to discard. I don't know how long this process took. It could have been minutes; it could have also been hours. When I finished, I was still in my pyjamas. Almost my entire wardrobe was tainted, and I stuffed it into a bulging plastic bag as though it were contaminated with biohazardous waste (which, realistically, some was). When I dragged the bag down the hallway to the women's lounge and asked a care aide if I could donate it, she looked dubious: "That's a *lot* of clothes, Nicole. Are you sure about this?" and I nodded, itchy at the prospect of ever again wearing pants made for a skeleton or tops chosen by my parents.

I did keep my Oma's jewellery. She had left me a box of gaudy costume necklaces, bracelets, and rings, and I slipped several pieces on, smiling. This was followed by jeans, a sweater, and even a touch of makeup. Peering cautiously into the mirror, I felt my sense of self bend. The fun-house distortions that produced psychotomimetic angles and chimerical deceptions ebbed and, for just a moment, I was an adult.

Alongside the orchestra, a small voice, maniacal but friendly, screeched, *She's starting to come together!*

THREE

The rest of the day unfolded similarly. One step forward, two steps back in terms of what was pragmatic versus technically superfluous but worthwhile all the same. I saw my room through older eyes, and it was a *disaster*. Besides the clothing, drool- and blood-stained bedsheets lay tousled on the floor, dirty dishes, stacked and crumb-laden, were crammed into my side table, and empty food packages were in every drawer. Cleaning was the next logical step, and I did so methodically, enamoured with the prospect of order. I was present and absent, classifying and codifying my possessions while immersed in their myriad meanings. This was about more than tidiness. By deciding what to keep, I was choosing what of my old selves I could live with – who I would retain as the dust settled, and I constructed something, *someone*, from almost (*but not quite*) nothing. I didn't do this on purpose. It had to be done. I did it. And, if pressed, I doubt I could have told anyone, least of all myself, what I was doing or why.

Looking back, I can explain my behaviour in a few ways. An optimistic interpretation is that I was more ontologically secure than I had been, especially in relation to time. I was "real, alive, and whole"[5] enough to discern which parts of my biography were desirable, and tacitly acknowledging my past, albeit outside of practical consciousness, suggests I was "in a temporal sense, a [more] continuous person"[iv] However, a more cynical, Foucauldian assessment of the same conduct would highlight that grooming, cleaning, and other hallmarks of "wellness" are examples of "technologies of the self." Again, these are the practices we employ on our bodies, minds, and souls to construct ourselves, through our own eyes, as happy,

---

[iv] British sociologist Anthony Giddens was a key figure in adapting the concept of ontological insecurity for the field of international relations. His treatment of the idea positions "practical conscious" beside "non-conscious," which he describes as "integral to the reflexive monitoring of action." One's practical conscious is "not held in mind' during the course of social activities" because actors must concentrate on tasks at hand, but unlike the "unconscious," it is also not separated by cognitive barriers from the discursive conscious. In other words, the practical conscious does not *resist* being brought into conscious awareness.[6] As a strange aside, Giddens was also Michael's uncle.

responsible citizens. They are inseparable from the obedience born of subjectivization. For Foucault, "happiness," "responsibility," and, pertinent here, "maturity," are historically and culturally located, and because subjects aren't "purely self-creating," most of what we do to evoke these feelings serves interests beside our own.[7] About health, consider that everything from clinical interventions to self-help guides to online listicles on "recovering from" or "living with" "severe mental illness" encourages showering, de-cluttering, or otherwise accomplishing as ways to manage symptoms. That we wish to function optimally at work, school, and in relationships is taken for granted, and "our" wants are shaped by neoliberal governance and the individualistic, decidedly *dis*-connected ethos it promotes. In my case, just a few weeks of abstaining from society came with an astronomical price tag. Like most people, I could never have paid for it were I not affiliated with a rich, "elite" institution, and, even then, Nuffield made clear their pockets, though deep, were hardly bottomless. This says much about our collective values, and I thus can't say for sure if "coming together" under these conditions was an "authentic" sign of progress. If economic logics hadn't dictated my trajectory, might I have benefited from more time undone, more of a chance to solidify a non-corrupt foundation before throwing together a ramshackle self atop the questionable one I had?

Both are true, I suppose. To be ontologically insecure as Laing describes it is to be a mechanical toy, one rebounding from supreme detachment to attachment that is vampire-like in its severity. One is always in motion because survival is contingent upon others' lifeblood, even as the rich inner worlds of those around us, relative to our lack of one, engulf us or cause us to petrify or implode. The days I spent merging with my peers were dire, depleting, and dread-full, and if a future event matches their intensity, I won't make it out alive. I couldn't. Yet all that happened gave me ontological autonomy, as well. After I stopped pathologizing my experience, including by substituting the term "psychosis" for "unwell" and, later, "becoming well," I was more than "a vehicle of a personality."[8] I finally felt like a person unto myself, one who didn't have to hide from others so as to not totally become them. Everything that went on was good, and, framed as a spiritual emergency, I was "rising to a new level of awareness"[9] that brought me closer to wholeness and integration. Without a deadline, I believe I would have stayed in this non-ordinary state, unbothered by social roles or time, for longer. I would have explored more about myself while under the influence of "truth serum" before re-joining consensus reality more concretely and completely – as more of a unified self. But when the deadline I did have encroached upon this process, I wasn't yet equipped to resist subjectivization. My main priority switched to not transferring hospitals, and this muddied want and need. I wanted to be(come); I had to act, and I decided who this actor was, which parts she was playing, and who the castmates were, while also writing and reciting her lines. Doing this so rapidly meant leaning on pre-existing cultural scripts, the likes of which I may not have valued had I been given room to ponder their future implications.

Four

Does any of this make sense? It does to me, but my ideas, of which there are so many, most of them half-formed, are big, abstract, and not readily wrangled through words. I am thinking in shapes again, so while the rectangle to my left aligns nicely with the triangle that hangs above it to the right, I reckon you don't see what I see.

It makes sense to me.

I'm not sure why I keep bringing in scholarship. I don't have to, and it would likely be easier for both of us if I could just tell things as they happened. But I can't extract the Foucault, Adorno, Grof *et al.* (so many *et al.*) from my psyche. They live in me as partially and with as much misinterpretation as do my parents, my experiences at school, hospitals, and homeless shelters, and everything that happened before, during, and after. It is interesting to observe this tendency within myself, this impulse to write technically(-ish), especially because, at the Priory, I was relieved to leave it all behind. Specifically, while cleaning my room, I saw the books I had brought from Canada and grimaced before hiding them from sight. I didn't like what they triggered in me, the barrage of self-analyses even the briefest glimpse of their covers evoked. I didn't want anyone else, including dead, European men, to have any say in who I was. *No more academia,* I swore, but one can't readily turn this off. And, interestingly, I see now that remembering the existence of academia actually prompted me to start thinking academically again, at exactly the same time I was glad I didn't have to. I also erred by not telling myself for how *long* I couldn't read. Thus, it was roughly six months after leaving England, while in the first of many Vancouver collective houses, which were later joined by appointments with Meris and, a year or so in, psychiatry, that I permitted myself to peek. In stops and starts I perused an essay on transpersonal psychology here, I watched a lecture on medical sociology there, and, before long, I was losing myself in full-length manuscripts but abandoning them before finishing. As a result, I (you; we) am (are) left with... this. *Does* it make sense to me? I am still trying to process what happened three (three!?) years ago, and I hope the hodgepodge of a story I have committed to telling will one day be more streamlined. Until it is, all I can do is (try to) tell you what came next.

FIVE

Believe it or not, I am significantly more coherent now than then. Then, after dressing, cleaning, and acting upon myself in other socially prescribed ways that were useful all the same, I felt ready to start looking for somewhere to stay in Vancouver. However, just as I was about to message my UBC graduate cohort to ask if I could sleep on a couch, I remembered having not paid my phone bill for months. Typically a simple procedure, I also saw that doing so from the Priory would be anything but. First, I had to send money to my cell phone carrier from a Canadian bank account. Unfortunately, I had drained this account before coming to England, and all of my money, *if there was any left,* would be in a British one. This meant I had to either add the phone company as a payee on my new account or transfer money from my new account into my old one, but because I hadn't initiated online banking with the new account, I couldn't do any of this while in hospital. How overdue was this bill? I had no idea. But as I realized that paying it wasn't feasible, I imagined what might happen if I lost access to my contacts. Particularly without consistent wi-fi, my cell phone was a lifeline. Being without it had a series of bam-bam-bam consequences that included having to transfer hospitals, getting unwell-er, being permanently detained, and being stuck in England forever. This seemed not just plausible but inevitable, and the same child who "decided to go to Oxford," took over as I lost all sense of competence and plopped on the floor, my limbs splayed and directionless, wailing.

Was I being "dramatic"? Absolutely. But alone in my room, after days that felt like years of this daunting, isolated journey, being disconnected was much too much. It was *all* too much. And between this, the email from Visas and Immigration, and the clock tick-tocking like an unhinged jack-in-the-box about to spring open and devour me, rational responses didn't come to mind. There was no more time. The walls began to liquefy. The overhead lights shimmied. My body clung to me, stuffy and uncomfortable, and I yearned to strip it off in ribbons. When I looked down, though, the extraneous flesh I usually remove when existence stifles me had already been peeled off. I had shed layers of adipose in Vancouver, the skin on top of it had shrunk and shrivelled at Nuffield, and now there was no body left to whittle; nothing to do but sit in the one I had and accept that being a body wasn't and hadn't ever been the problem. Fuck. *Nicole(s?)*, I told myself, in the same gentle but firm voice of Meris, *at eighty-something pounds, and while in a state that is definitely-maybe-not-at-all psychotic, now is not when you focus on your weight*. Now, I would take care of business as a non-psychotic person does so I wasn't shuffled to some random institution in some random town, city, county, *whatever*, where said state would possible-probably-absolutely get worse. This was the best that I could do. And, after just a few moments of my environment reanimating, the whirring and whizzing ebbed, and then it stopped completely.

Six

I decided to call the bank to bring my account online and pay my bill over my phone. This implied talking to someone, and they would have no idea why this was so huge to me. This was the first of many moments where awareness of life outside the Priory was jarring. People were going to their jobs. People were in seminars at Oxford. That others' routines had been uninterrupted – that others even had routines – made me feel like a member of another, less earthly species. (*This is all so lonely.*) I couldn't properly identify grief, but it was there, richer and more unyielding than the feelings dancing above it. The grief is still there. I am not done writing.

After searching through a stack of documents my tutor packed, I found the bank's phone number. I waited, resisting the urge to hang up. Then, after hours of elevator music, I checked out, going wholly cerebral and inviting my grown self to talk on my behalf. Trying to converse otherwise wouldn't have gotten me far. Unfortunately, neither did adult Nicole's clear explanation of the problem, which I managed to give without invoking mental hospitals or alcohol. I told the teller I couldn't remember my password and she said I could authenticate my identity by answering two security questions. I feigned confidence until she asked me to name a memorable location and, as I sputtered, "Nuffield?! Oxford?! Vancouver?! Canada?!" to no avail, I felt bashful, ashamed, and *young*. (*You don't have a home.*) I didn't hear the teller issue the next prompt, but I did cut her off and say, "The important word I gave was 'safety,'" and I was surprised to learn I was right. I am still looking for safety. I am not done writing.

Ultimately, confirming that I valued safety didn't prove that I was who I said I was, at least according to bank policy, so I hung up demoralized. I guess there's irony or a metaphor in that, which I noted then before focusing on the teller's directive – come to the bank in person. Because I had given so many wrong answers at the end of our conversation, the call had been flagged as suspicious activity. Now my account was deactivated, and I needed to bring government-issued identification to my nearest bank branch to unlock it. This added an extra, rather advanced step to paying my phone bill, and I stood, sat, and paced, my bones conduits for the intra-skeletal electric current that came, went, then came once again. I was trying so hard to be "responsible," "mature," and human, and I just felt like… crashing waves. The thoughts, feelings, responses to instructions – all of it was just… waves, and they galvanized into tsunamis with every adverse stimulus. I am still water. I may never finish writing.

Seven

After the call ended, I navigated the corridors in search of Dr. Herner. I needed permission to leave the grounds again, though my desire to do so now was different than it had been earlier in my stay. I was no longer detached from my motivations, which had been to binge and purge the week before, and I was also aware that environmental factors triggered the onset of psychotic-like symptoms. Because of this, being in public could have serious, adverse outcomes. I didn't want to conceal this risk, nor would I have been able to even if I'd tried. My movement was whip-like and repetitive, and I emulated an animal stalking its prey as I treaded up, down, and around the stairs. The orchestra climaxed again and again, and the halls narrowed as my eyes darted back and forth, flickering past everyone and everything that wasn't Dr. Herner.

A nurse intervened during my dozenth or so lap of the interior perimeter. My speech was staccato, and it was a few minutes before she grasped the relationship between going to the bank, paying a phone bill, and being permanently institutionalized as I understood it. She didn't agree with my assessment or share my sense of urgency, but even if she had, Dr. Herner had gone home. Ahead of me was another long night, and I felt like a deranged chef had shoved me into a pressure cooker. "Why do you people only treat me like a patient when you're covering your asses?" I snapped, and while I may have had a point, my reaction wasn't fair, and I knew it. Mumbling an apology, I had rounded the corner by the time the words fully left my mouth.

Overall, I was redirecting my frustration from individual staff members to the policies they enforced. This started once I had cleaned my room. And, as strange as this sounds, I think that seeing my academic books incited a paradigm shift. I became more attuned to meso- and macro-levels of critique, and instead of raging indiscriminately, I saw how my interpersonal interactions were shaped by institutional rules, practices, and values, as well as the extent to which enduring patterns of societal relations, or social structures, had organized these rules, etcetera, from the top down.ᵛ In short, I was adding the political to the personal. I got less belligerent, less reckless with my emotions, and as my energetic peaks and valleys became less pronounced, so too did the sense of bleeding into the body-minds of others. The only problem was that observing the Priory through eyes that had also been exposed to anti-psychiatry and Mad studies movements made me want to start organizing the other patients. This was antithetical to getting out.

ᵛ Micro, meso, and macro are scales used in social analyses. Macro-level research focuses on widespread social processes that most or all of society are implicated in (e.g. the economic and political systems), whereas micro-level analyses explore how macro-structures are reified, reproduced, and contested during interpersonal or small-scale interactions. Meso is intermediary, and research at this level of analysis may explore how groups and social organizations constitute and are constituted by macro-level social order, as well as how they impact and are impacted by micro-level processes.

Related, that the personal, or private, is also political was a rallying call of second wave feminist movements throughout the 1960s and 70s. The slogan speaks to the fact that people's lives are always shaped by politics, and that experiences we often consider private tend to be shared across social groups. It was originally used in the context of "women's troubles," but its meaning has shifted based on context. No one claims authorship of the phrase, but it was popularized in a 1970 edited collection that included an essay with that title by Carol Hanish. It has also featured prominently in work by Black feminists.[10]

Eight

A concrete example of what I mean by making the personal political, and why this was both valuable and an inconvenience, took place when my pacing brought me into the women's lounge. It was sometimes used for meal support, and there were two eating disorder patients huddled together, whispering. Their brows furrowed, and I didn't have to hear them to know they were talking either about food or some aspect of their Priory-mandated behavioural modifications as they pertained to food. After all, this is what it is always and never about. The pursuit of edification through eating, not eating, and/or eating in highly specific ways obscures, exacerbates, and reflects the turbulence beneath. *It is always and never about the food.* This is why it was so miraculous that my once-strained relationship with it was still in remission. I hadn't cared about what I'd eaten for days, nor had I felt tempted to engage in idiosyncratic practices of any kind during meals, *nor* would I have remembered to even if I'd tried. The inpatients' body language invoked the food-related harms I had deployed on myself that, because time was so stretched, I felt I hadn't used in decades. My memories of starving, bingeing, and purging were as confronting as the self-inflicted slaps I had resorted to when they started not to work.

In front of the patients was a meal plan form. They spotted me before I could look too closely at it, but I had seen enough to feel disdain for the glaring indicators of eating-disorder-specific treatment that were everywhere all of a sudden. How had I not noticed the lists of food groups stuck to a bulletin board, the rules about eating etiquette beside it, or the gendered words of encouragement taped to every extant surface? Their hollowness was vulgar. And, as I took in what it would have meant to be a proper patient, power that had been rationally invisible because it was embedded into each locked cupboard, motivational quote, and measuring cup, was blinding. What had been a kitchen was now a panopticonic arena of discursive struggle.[vi] In it, young women were stripped of their self-definitional

---

[vi] The word "panopticon" is derived from the Greek word for "all seeing" (panoptes). In the 1800s, British social reformer and founder of utilitarianism Jeremy Bentham designed

privileges, taught to read themselves through the historically arbitrary lens of anorexia, and implanted with strict, neoliberal ideologies about "proper wellness" while acting as unwitting accomplices in self-subjectivization.[vii] Put differently, while some have used "technologies of the self" as an analytic tool for describing eating disorders, treatment for them, at least here, wasn't any better. In fact, "recovery" appeared as coercive, unattainably perfectionistic, and crazy making as sickness did, and while I had been "nursing myself back to health" unconventionally and incidentally, a war was raging right under my nose over who was even authorized to define and enact this term. Under the garish light of "truth serum," I promised that when it came to disordered eating, especially getting "treated" for it, I wouldn't ever do this shit again.

This moment helped me greatly. Its clarity was undeniable. However, its emancipatory potential was also at odds with looking for a couch to sleep on. I yearned to pull up a chair, gossip about Jen, the nurse, and prove I could relate. We had so many things in common; they could

---

an institution that was originally intended to house prison inmates. It was circular with a centralized guard tower and enabled a single guard to monitor inmates through the walls of this tower without being seen themself. Prisoners couldn't know whether the guard was present or not, and so they were trained into regulating themselves in accordance with institutional norms. Bentham described his plans for a panopticon prison as a "new mode of obtaining power of mind over mind, in a quantity hitherto without example."

Thinkers since have credited Bentham's design – a tool of such "monstrous efficiency" that it left no room for humanity – with paving the way for totalitarian states. In the 1970s, Foucault adopted the metaphor of the panopticon to build upon how modern societies similarly discipline their subjects through "rationally invisible" power. This refers to what I have discussed about modern states "conducting our conduct" by convincing us that we have the "democratic freedom" (and obligation) to rule ourselves on its behalf.[11]

[vii] Feminist sociologist Dorothy Smith's seminal article "K is mentally ill" analyzes a written account by Angela, one of her students, about an acquaintance, K's, development of mental illness. Throughout, Smith elucidates how shared assumptions about "mental illness" are taken for granted by the author and the reader. Because of how the text is organized, including by stating at the outset that K is mentally ill, it guides the reader to this conclusion while "cutting out" possible alternative explanations of the same events, including by K. In terms of how this relates to mental health treatment, patients are always already perceived of as "ill," while resistance to the label of "illness" is seen as yet another symptom of it. This automatically eliminates the opportunity to self-define except by way of the pre-ordained "sick role" scripts that one is given.[12]

have been my friends. Yet I was also the conductor of a raving orchestra, and my position at the helm kept its musicians, who were also me, from rescinding their instruments, ambling into the audience, and forgetting how to play. I needed to prioritize. This tension epitomized how bodies are "political fields" whose presence at the intersections of (post)modernity, capitalism's concomitant time pressures, and the "qualified liberty," or illusion of freedom, this affords us, subordinates our interests.[viii] I was palpably drawn to the young women, my legs aching to follow the promise of love, connection, and community, and I was technically "free" to do this. But the mantra *time is money* also flowed through me, and I knew what would happen if I didn't labour diligently in the next minutes, hours, and days. Thus, while no one physically forced my limbs to backpedal, the unspoken threat of what

---

[viii] Foucault's work, and his later work especially, is mostly concerned with power that is enacted on subjects who retain some agency. He emphasizes that for power relations to exist, the subject on whom the governance or conduct is exercised must have a range of possible reactions to choose from. Unlike physical violence or the total restriction of movement and behaviour that is found in extreme authoritarian situations, Foucault's subject possesses the "qualified liberty" to choose from a field of possibilities that are nevertheless constrained by invisible power.[13]

A feminist, Foucauldian perspective on eating disorder treatment would point out that its disciplinary tactics rely on encouraging patients to "see" how and why their thoughts, feelings, and practices are disordered, but rarely or never are we permitted to interrogate who has been given the authority to decide this for us. Requirements such as eating in very specific ways at very specific times in very specific amounts are ostensibly put in place to "liberate" patients, but because psychiatry itself derives its power from patriarchal whiteness, these spaces can be rigid and proscriptive. Many patients do resist through bodily practices such as secretly exercising, purging, hiding food, etc., but a "successful" treatment trajectory tends to reduce or eliminate these expressions of resistance over time. Thus, the recovery narratives that receive the most praise are ones that begin with having resisted before subscribing fully to one's treatment plan with all the attendant markers of (female) docility and obedience it entails.

Of course, more so than any "mental disorder," our understanding of anorexia is "historically arbitrary." Before it was included in the DSM as a symptom of a "feeding and eating disorder," and even long before the DSM existed, reports of extreme self-starvation were relatively prevalent among religious women during the Middle Ages. Between the 13th and 16th centuries in particular, widespread Christianity and Gnostic philosophy encouraged a cultural ethos that dichotomized "evil" bodily pleasures from the holiness of souls. Fasting was viewed as a marker of spirituality, and "anorexia mirabilis," or "Holy anorexia," was described as a way for women to imitate the suffering of Jesus Christ.[14]

might happen if I "chose" not to guided me into my room, alone. I stood in front of my desk, my left hand clutching a pen so tightly it nearly snapped in half, and I redirected my vision to a still-blank to-do list.

(In case I haven't explained these concepts clearly, including how they are relevant to daily life, I will describe the present moment: This book is all over the damn map. I know it, you know it, but every time I tell myself to revise it further, my stomach revolts and acidic echoes of what I last ate tinge the back of my throat. My body-mind is saying, *No – I don't care to be perfect, and my work need not define me*. I am certain this response is "organic," it comes from my rejection of ideological authoritarianism in both my environment and my psyche, and after months of editing, I am entitled to being fine with what I have. However, the inevitability of imperfection – the inevitability of being and producing what capitalism has told me I must not be or produce, lest I waste the one chance I have to be bright, worthy, and salvageable – is keeping me awake. As tired and nauseous as I am, then, I still cannot sit, let alone lay, down. *Drink coffee*, is where my mental processes lead me, *Purposefully induce more anxiety, sublimate these feelings into a greater volume of better work, and then*, then *you'll have earned the right to rest*. To whom do we belong?)

NINE

Tearing myself from the eating disorder patients' energetic field produced sharp, physical pain around my abdomen. I suppressed it by doodling. Drawing might have been good were it not for time consciousness, but since abstract sketches of plump, feminine figures weren't about to leap from the page and look for housing, I shifted gears, groaning. Whose couch would I land on? I almost sent a group text to members of my UBC graduate cohort. But I was impressionable, and I determined that being so close to research-related activities could get in the way of deciding who I was without them. I didn't have a plan, let alone a back-up plan, and as the orchestra played on, I wanted to get it right.

   I messaged Mo, a friend who had also left a graduate program before getting a PhD. He was the only person in my network to have shown me that life – nice life – was possible after the ivory tower, and as a trumpet soloed near the back of my head, reminiscing about him felt warm. Mo rented a one-bedroom apartment a few blocks from where I lived before I left for England. I now viewed this condo as belonging to my parents only, and I figured that going back to the neighbourhood, the same but different, would emblematize having grown. Time was a flat circle but closing this particular loop didn't feel absurd at all. In fact, I quite liked its prospective symmetry. And, when Mo welcomed me with almost no questions asked, I also felt… proud. I had done something that I hadn't dreamed of doing until I did it, and this showed me that while the exit wasn't yet in sight, I was getting closer.

   After confirming that I had a place to go, my bodily sensations changed. I felt embodied again, so much so that I had the urge to rest. I closed my eyes still upright at the desk and my spine curved forward, my fists unclenched, and my cell phone clanged onto the floor. The sound it made on impact startled me as though I had been deeply asleep for hours. Then, my "vision narrowed" and the orchestra played once more. In this moment I made the express connection between completing a task, the confidence this elicited, and momentarily realigning with consensus reality, so, as the noise took over, I fought off despair by wondering what else I could get done.

Ten

My response in this scenario didn't truly belong to "me." I doubt my exchange with Mo would have been as impactful if I hadn't been so rushed, and I'm almost positive I would have found a couch, and perhaps his exact couch, even if the *pressure* hadn't seeped into every thought and feeling. If so, I wouldn't have had to get so charged so frequently, and the tell-tale signs of coming down from mania might not have gotten as severe later on. Had this been the case, I might have gotten away with only a few months of totalizing depression after I got to Canada, instead of being immobilized for almost an entire year. Of course, this is just one of many things I cannot know for sure.

As the evening progressed, there wasn't much to do except hope I got to the bank soon. I didn't want to be by myself but "usual input from the mundane [wa]s positively painful," and "discrepanc[ies] between the ordinary and the non-ordinary worlds" were more obvious while with company.[15] Specifically, as my encounter with the eating disorder inpatients had illuminated, "the systematic ordering, controlling, recording, differentiating, and comparing" of patients enacted through the Priory's policies and procedures set me off, fast.[16] Watching others be subjectivized, which was now my interpretation of goings-on, made me so angry, so readily that I lost track of getting on a plane. Virtually every detail of formal programming seemed rooted in "paternalistic professional dominance" and I wasn't able to control my aversion to this.[17] I also couldn't deal with more psychosomatic whiplash. I was thus caught in a tug-of-war between my head, which said to hide from the painful "abyss of separation" between me and everyone else, and my heart, which screamed that I was capable of bridging it.[18] I was already bridging it, after all.

To recap, then, which I am doing as much for my benefit as I am yours: After detoxing I thought I died. This was followed by a period of calling myself alive but psychotic. After nearly killing myself, which was a kind of condensed near-death rebirth, I moved away from medical labels and referred to myself as "unwell." However, I outgrew this terminology because illness was accompanied by disembodiment, lack of personal continuity, and nonexistent emotional or behavioural regulation. Throughout, I recognized that, in Grof's words, "the inauthenticity of [my] life [wa]s not limited to certain partial segments that [we]re contaminated by specific childhood traumas, but that [my] entire... life strategy ha[d] been... misdirected in a very basic way."[19] My physical symptoms were also so odd I expected to have a seizure, but when this failed to materialize, I came to see my phenomenological experiencing as being linked to spirituality. Simultaneously, I accepted that I would need to change how I related to my parents, myself, and everyone/thing/where else, and though still erratic and afraid, I felt not just prepared but eager to formulate love, connection, and peace. As I grew more ontologically secure (or, alternatively, as I was more embodied, or as my differently aged selves merged) I achieved some "inner consistency, substantiality, genuineness, and worth,"[20] which freed up mental space to take note of my environment. And as I concluded that programming would have disempowered me, I began to see the promise of inter-patient solidarities; programming didn't seem to be very useful for anyone else, either. But then I had to go. Still in a non-ordinary state, but less so than before, I scrambled to steady my body-mind at the expense of self-discovery, alliance building, or rest. I felt proud of myself as I did so, but I may have over-corrected while "choosing" not to be "sick." I also lacked the time to establish my behavioural and other improvements as permanent ways of being.

(Here, I want to apologize. What have I gotten us into!? This is like being asked to braid my own hair. Except each tendril is alive, sentient, and roaming from one section of scalp to another, and missing just one could cause the whole thing to unravel. *[I need to describe it as it is happening because so much is happening – so much is happening, all at once – that I often forget to relay important things [[things that would otherwise seem major, but, because there are so many things to keep track of, I cannot possibly remember each of them.]] I am only human, after all.]* Interior and exterior; individual and interpersonal; cognitive, affective, and corporeal – they aren't really at variance, but words pigeon-hole me into implying heterogeneity where there is none. If "the medium is the message," which it is in this case, my digressions, repetition, and propensity for "bump[ing]...[you] around, chiropractically" are a window into the game of whack-a-mole that was/is psyche.[21] I so wish I could express myself through drawing, painting, or, even better, had given up on being seen, but my thirst for validation still has not been quenched. *I am only human.*)

PART ONE

Eleven

I spent the rest of that evening in my room to avoid stimulation. Again, this was bad and good. It was "bad" because I couldn't be with others, and if I see this as having succumbed to normalizing power, doing so was equally a failure to be more "authentic." It was "good" because my knee-jerk aversion to sitting with myself, which had taken root as a young, young person, was gone. The orchestra took an intermission, and as I turned in slow, methodical circles, the walls and floor stayed put. I was... okay. I was okay... while... alone. I wasn't sure what to make of this. Aloneness usually made me feel like a caged animal who would claw her way out or die. However, the brassy, sometimes glittering, always lurid stimuli that converted the Priory into a pinball machine had been replaced by stillness – profound, numinous stillness. And I was overcome. I also decided that despite planning to "work," there wasn't anything to do. Seamlessly, I expanded and altered my definition of "work" to include anything that would help me be *more* okay in my body-mind, not just in hospital but once I got to Canada. What did prolonged, enduring okay-ness look like? What did it mean to be safe? I had never seriously thought about this, nor had I ever cared to, but in my room, which was motionless and magical, I started to find out.

I stretched my hands in front of me, palms resting on my knees. The crash-boom-bang synesthetic tendencies linking colours to numbers to sounds in wavy patterns dwindled, and then they went away. Every line in my bedroom now seemed perfectly parallel or perpendicular to the others, and the surrealist symmetry of it all was visually and viscerally pleasing. Was this... calm? In hindsight, I was much more than "calm;" the ambience was borderline hypnotic. But I didn't question it, this feeling, because I had no reason to. This stage of "becoming well" was better, so when I instinctively started doodling again, I didn't stop myself. Doodling became colouring, and then I did end up writing a list. Its title, "Things I like," is self-explanatory, but the thrill of first figuring out it was the only one that mattered, followed by the rush of adding what at any other time would have been trite (e.g., the list began with pears) is not. I still see this as radical. This was my only time contemplating, let alone documenting, how I might be happy. Furthermore, while "self-discovery" in previous treatment centres entailed filling out forms, ticking boxes on spreadsheets, and submitting assignments I completed with all the diligence of a straight-A student and none of the will to succeed, this was entirely new: I had grasped that "recovery" wasn't something to typify, quantify, or plan. It was an existential setting, one I couldn't pass or fail.

For me to do myself (and you, the reader) justice, I need to make space for the inherent contradictions and complexities that underscore(d) this sequence. Making the familiar strange is maybe my biggest goal with this text, aside from my substantially more egoistic mission of *having you fucking hear me*. So, rather than skim over what seems like a mere plot point, I will, as the academics say, unpack the last two paragraphs.

First, qualifiers like "before," "after," and "what I had been like" versus "what I hoped it would be" imply a linear grasp of time. But everything until this, including donating my clothes earlier in the day, had been done without one. I hadn't known what I was doing except while doing it, and I use "know" only in the most dissociated, depersonalized sense of the word. This includes the writing I had done, the conversations I had had, as well as the mental operations that had powered them which, while "me," were a "me" that had "partially abandoned my body and its acts" at some point along the way.[22] I had been an infinitesimal seed of a self, one whose soil was so nutrient depleted I couldn't ponder who I was, engage with others, find a place to go, stop having an eating disorder, etcetera, and remember any of this while doing it.

Here, though, I clearly anticipated a not-so-distant future. I was comfortable, content, and aware of who I was, who I had been, and who I had the potential to be if, to quote Alcoholics Anonymous, "I did the next right thing." This was progress because I was embodied, secure, and agentic, all traits that served me well then and have also done so since. But nothing is that simple. Karl Marx is often quoted as saying, "Beyond the realm of necessity begins the true realm of freedom," and my conduct here wasn't that of a free person. I was role-conscious enough to know I was Nicole, who would soon be in Canada, who psychiatry would say had been psychotic, who also needed to not drink, binge, or do anything irreparable once I got there, and so embodiment, security, and agency had become necessities. Each activity was oriented, even if not on purpose, around not being hospitalized again or dying. In Adorno's words: "Even where... people are at least subjectively convinced that they are acting of their own free will, this will itself is shaped by the very same forces which they are seeking to escape."[23]

In sum, then, I was improving because I was closer to being who and what we are told we should aspire to be. But I also long for a world where one can be bat-shit, stark-raving, can't-even-begin-to-talk-let-alone-function Mad and still be held tenderly, without recourse. If we were to blow social conventions and the structures that underpin them wide open, not just on a personal level but collectively, if we burned those fuckers to the ground – what could freedom (and goodness, health, self-love, and so on) start to look like then?

(It makes sense to me.)

Twelve

The standards of freedom laid out thus far are unattainable to anyone who is sentient, let alone self-aware. I know that. So, working within the confines of what we must want and need, I was doing fine, at least until the morning. This was my sixteenth day at the Priory, and the tranquility I felt overnight vanished once the others had woken up. The bustle in the corridors was an engine revving, gingerly at first and then faster, faster, while I made my way to breakfast. When I got there, I saw food in a way I hadn't since before I had been admitted. The cereal, toast, and fruit on a table in the corner were carbohydrates, the steaming plates of sausage, egg, and baked beans that passed from hands of kitchen staff to patients were proteins and fats, and the ketchup, marmalades, and assortment of other condiments lined neatly into serving tins were messy, *scary*, additives that didn't fit easily into boxes. I shuddered, greeting Michael and half-embracing, half-deriding the troubling reassurance of my eating disorder.

    This didn't last for long. When a staff member intercepted my toast making to tell me about an appointment with Dr. Herner, I remembered my phone bill and having to go to the bank. To my surprise and delight, Dr. Herner said I could take a taxi there. Daphne would come with me. Unlike our earlier trip, during which I had all but flown away, I was relieved to have support. "Do you think you'll be able to manage?" Dr. Herner asked, and I laugh-yelped a very honest, "I don't really know, but I sure as shit hope so!" I didn't really know. I sure as shit hoped so. And when I filled out the nurse's risk assessment form afterward, I was equally transparent: Was I suicidal? No, but who knew if I would stay that way; Did I want to drink? No, but I still could. Overall, I still don't believe that Dr. Herner and the other staff comprehended the extent to which my experience of reality was unlike theirs, especially when I look back on this time now. If they had truly realized what was happening, if they had had full insight into how extreme all of this was, would they have still let me go? Would they have even left me alone? Or would they have unilaterally determined that I was to be admitted indefinitely, not at the Priory but wherever a psychiatrist was willing and able to administer huge quantities of drugs? (Or, alternately, was none of this even worth examining to them – did anyone care at all?)

One person who did care was Gerald. We had a cigarette together before the taxi arrived. When I admitted how scared I was, he beckoned me close with a crooked index finger and pressed a crumpled bill into my palm. I stared until he stated that after buying me cigarettes for over a week, it was my turn to shop for him. He said this frankly, and when I did a quick tally of having given him my debit card, never doubting he would use it as expected, I agreed. This was a gesture of respect. It signified that my position in the hospital's patient hierarchy had moved up a few notches and, at least in Gerald's eyes, I was dependable in ways I hadn't been before. "You'll remember that I want a pack of Marlboro Gold," he said, and this was not a question.

Thirteen

When Daphne and I got into the taxi, I took stock of the pangs rippling through my chest, the undulating near my abdomen, and the squeezing in my head. I almost changed my mind – I almost yelled I had changed my mind – and then I told myself as frankly as Gerald had that I could not. *Is this* really *panic?* I asked myself, *Or is this just apprehension?* Today, I would interpret what I felt then as much more than panic, but my window of tolerance had expanded into what wasn't a window but more of an open gateway.

Bob Marley's "Everything's Gonna Be Alright" blared from the radio. Daphne smiled and sang along, and as we made eye contact, I could almost believe the lyrics. Since going out the last time, I hadn't dared venture down the long, winding driveway that led toward the road. Now the taxi's right-turn signal clicked in tandem with my heartbeat, and when the song ended, "apprehension" became "panic" which gave way to cymbals clanging, drums beating, and a silent voice screaming to turn around. I put my head between my knees, gasping.

When we got to the bank, it took several minutes of sitting on the curb outside before I could go in. Sweat beaded down my temples and onto my neck, and my legs couldn't bear the crushing weight of what I wanted them to do. Daphne was sweet, patient, and a bit confused, as she had been all along, and when she wondered aloud why this was so hard, I couldn't get across that *I was no longer the person I thought I knew.* The gravity of having to align with the "Nicole(s)" of months' past made the parade of people walking by seem like extras on a movie set. I didn't know that I would have the restraint or linearity of thought to speak clearly. What if the bank confiscated my passport? I lifted myself up, accepting Daphne's outstretched hand as my head throbbed and the passersby faded into confetti specks of colour, noise, and sound.

When it was my turn in line, I approached the young man behind the counter. First, he was nonchalant, but he soon became more formal. My hands shook. I asked him to repeat himself, and I wrote his instructions in my notebook with a child's printing. After a few minutes he directed his gaze to Daphne, and I saw myself through his eyes – the confusion and pity there induced a cascade of gut-punch shame. Slowly, the three of us got what I had come for – four digits that would allow me to activate an online banking account. I clutched my notebook as though it were a prized possession, and we walked back outside to people going about their business, none of whom noticed me or saw that I felt egregiously out of place.

Next, I asked to go to a nearby Sainsbury's. The refrigerated food jostled me into having an eating disorder again, but this didn't elicit strong emotion. It was a simple, neutral fact. And, as I reached for a chicken sandwich, my impulse to read the label was not as strong as the desire to no longer care about labels, here or anywhere. I told Daphne that I would buy a snack for later. Soon I would be choosing, purchasing, and preparing my own food again, and I said more to myself than her that I should start trying this now. Gerald's cigarettes were on a shelf behind the cashier next to a selection of hard liquor. This was my first time in days considering alcohol, but even as the bottles stirred something, somewhere, in me that was deep, dark, and malignant, I was not afraid. As with my eating disorder, alcoholism existed. It lived in me; it always would; I was becoming well. These were simple, neutral facts.

Fourteen

This sequence of events proved that institutionalization would be finite. After, I chatted easily with Daphne. She told me about herself, and I felt a funny twinge as I realized I was older than her by at least a few years. I *felt* much older as she described her undergraduate degree and career goals, but as soon as we got back to the Priory, straight lines tilted, sounds echoed where they shouldn't have, and the aromas emanating from the kitchen bounced from one side of the room to the other, all of it stop-drop-and-gasp-for-air too much. I was young again. Why was everything worse here? I could answer this in several ways, but theory matters a lot less than having recognized the "I-see-you-seeing-me and we are sick!" dynamic I had fostered with the patients permeated everything.[ix] This was important and it was also sad. I had grown to love my peers and even some of the staff members, but I knew this love would morph, dissipate, and be unfairly filtered through the distorting lens of memory as soon as I was discharged.

It is fair to say I felt love when I saw Gerald huddled in his gazebo. It was almost mid-November, and the chill made it so that only the serious smokers, of whom Gerald was perhaps most serious of all, stayed outside for more than a few minutes. Right away, "the subtle interplay between the visceral experiences of [my] own bod[y] and [his...] face... " caused a sort of dual unity between us, and I knew he was upset.[x] I had taken his emotional consistency for granted,

---

[ix] American sociologist Charles Horton Cooley introduced the concept of the "looking glass self" in 1902 to explain how people's sense of self evolves out of micro-level, or interpersonal, interactions. The idea consists of three components: a) people imagine how they appear to others in social situation; b) they react to what they believe others' judgement of their appearances to be; and c) their sense of self changes as they respond to others on the bases of their perception of others' perceptions. In other words, social interaction is like a "looking glass" (mirror), and while we can't know what others are thinking, our beliefs about what others are thinking and our responses to these beliefs are sufficiently powerful to fundamentally alter how we view ourselves and how we engage in the world.[24]

[x] Cooley's looking glass self doesn't try to explain the physiological mechanisms associated with self- and other-identity development. There are many ways to do so. A very different take on similar ideas is the existence of "dual unity," which is characterized by

so to sense his alarm as I walked toward him imbued me with the same. Gingerly, I asked what was wrong. He replied that the National Health Services (NHS), which funded his admission, had found a cheaper hospital for him, and he would be leaving that same day. He didn't know where he would go, but both of us had heard the almost unbelievable stories of patients being roused awake in the middle of the night and taken by ambulance to wherever a bed was open. Gerald was apprehensive. He said as much. In fact, this was his only word, and he used it echolalically. By dinner, he was gone. I have not heard from him since, but I think about him often. I hope he is well and never learned what it feels like to lay horizontally instead of vertically on a set of tracks as a speeding train approaches.

I also felt deep affection when I stepped inside to get Gerald a lighter and Ethan emerged from the lounge. His face was beet-red, his usually perfect hair was tousled, and he had changed into a t-shirt, shorts, and sandals, which was more casual than I had seen him. He beamed. "Have you been for a swim?" he shouted, and when I asked what he was talking about, he pointed toward the hospital wing that was for men only. "The pool! It's refreshing!" It didn't occur to me that he might be joking. And, as I barged into a room and was met with stares from two men, one a counsellor and the other on the verge of tears, Ethan giggled hysterically, as did Kielan who had joined him. I had been pranked. I was delighted. I distinctly remember thinking, *This is what friendship is*, as the two beamed at me. That they cared enough about me to do this was somehow more significant than even their support in the worst moments. It filled me with such elation that it almost – almost – made everything else feel worth it.

Stanislov Grof as "the loosening and melting of the body-ego" (p. 45). However, unlike the total and complete identification that occurs with other people in similar but distinct transpersonal states, people who experience dual unity retain awareness of their own, distinct identities. Grof documented a prevalence of this state during LSD trials, though he also claimed that psychoactive substances were not the only way to achieve it, and acute, traumatic, or blissful experiences could lead to similar results.[25] More scientific explanations of how subjectivities are co-constituted is found in the language of polyvagal theory and mirror neurons (see Part Two).

That night, after Gerald was gone and I had eaten the sandwich from Sainsbury's, I wrote:

I came in as a drunk, and I have now gone from believing that I died, to wondering if I count as human, to thinking that I'm in a schizophrenia- or bipolar-induced state of psychosis, to seeing that I'm unwell and could use some help, to understanding that I'm Mad and am having a spiritual experience.

All of these may be true; all of them may be false.

No human should be categorized.

PART ONE

Fifteen

On my seventeenth morning, I reviewed the previous day with Dr. Herner. I told him I was almost ready to go to Vancouver but had to practice being alone, away from the hospital, first. As I decelerated internally, external events would not. And once my flight was booked, there could be no more dissociation, no more regression in age, and certainly no more feeling or saying anything about psychosis. Between the Priory and Canada were hurdles that wouldn't usually have been hurdles. However, mired in intrusive, all-encompassing visions of leaping from my seat on the plane, overpowering the pilot, and crashing everyone on board into the Atlantic Ocean, preserving myself would require strategic planning.

Of course, one's choices are limited when they have no time. I still think that to truly resist all that made me unwell, I needed a longer admission. This is because the sentiment that I was more than "a collection of chemical imbalances… to be corrected" which I injected into most interactions, had diffused through my peer network.[xi] For example, my conversations with Debra shifted to the cyclical nature of for-profit addiction treatment. Jill also inquired about links between personality disorders and trauma, and then she passed this information on to someone who arrived after she did. With so many diagnoses, I fit into each of the Priory's three patient streams and could delineate the threads that bound us together. We were engaged in rudimentary, informal consciousness raising, and our convergences formed a visuospatial topography that informed my movement, generated power from the bottom up, and affirmed the self I was creating. Yet with this kind of intimacy still came enantiodromia – the tendency to pursue a psychic and spiritual state that is diametrically opposed to

---

[xi] One of the first things that introductory sociology students are taught is that the discipline is useful for connecting personal troubles (biography) to public issues (history). This awareness of how individual or micro-level experiences are shaped by meso-level systems and institutions and macro-level structures is referred to as using one's "sociological imagination," and it is applicable to everything, everywhere. Fundamentally, this text has been an attempt to encourage sociological thinking about "mental health."[26]

the one that hasn't worked.[xii] I over-compensated for my loneliness by identifying too strongly with others' emotions and probable outcomes, and doing this, while uniquely therapeutic, retraumatized me, as well. Here, "authenticity" was not conducive to safety.

I told Dr. Herner that I would use my last few days to eat, walk, talk, and think without supervision. He endorsed this, which, again, could have been lazy, irresponsible, or insightful, and then he leaned back in his chair and eyed me up and down. "So?" he said, in a way that felt as though this was being asked outside the usual psychiatrist-patient relationship dynamic, "How do you feel about everything?" I couldn't respond to this. I wanted to, but I also knew that if I started, I might never stop. I paused and, disarmed, I wondered instead what he had observed from me. This was not a relinquishment of agency so much as it came from a place of certainty that his opinion wasn't relevant. And when Dr. Herner held my gaze and responded with, "Nicole… perhaps what has gone on here is not exactly… psychiatric," he validated what I already knew.

[xii] Jung adopted the term "enantiodromia" from the pre-Socratic Greek philosopher Heraclitus to reference a so-called psychological law that describes "running toward the opposite." He claimed that after developing extreme, binary tendencies that devalue important parts of one's psyche, equally strong "counter-tendencies" will germinate unconsciously. In other words, repression begets resistance, and the more rigid one's position, the more likely they are to be "attack[ed]… from the rear" by its antipole.[27]

Foucault believed that anti-authoritarian resistance to be sustained, it must not be subsumed under external power. While he mostly analyzed large-scale revolutions, he also spoke to the impact of resistance that appears as "a swarm of points" – irregular, transitory reactions to power that "furrow… across individuals themselves, cutting them up and remoulding them, marking off irreducible regions in them in their bodies and minds." This web or network of micro-resistances may spread across body-minds, generating something bigger, but for them to become meaningful collective struggle, single expressions of resistance need to be codified and repeated (which requires time…).[28]

PART ONE

Sixteen

Dr. Herner said a medical attendant could accompany me on the plane. It was a reasonable suggestion, one I mulled over briefly before declining. Sick people needed medical attendants. I was not sick. And over the next seventy-two hours, I proved this. First, I went to town again, now without an aide. I listened to music as I walked, and when the disarranged onset of light bursts pushed me over the narrow threshold of just okay enough to not, the melody washed over me; I let it restore my sight (*My vision narrowed* – I expanded it – *The soundtrack began* – I replaced it with another). I was fully embodied, so much so that the songs seeped into my nerve endings, capillaries, and bloodstream.

I intended to pay my phone bill. I still hadn't activated online banking because the Priory's firewall prevented patients from installing new software on our devices. But the wi-fi in the library was so slow that after an hour of refreshing the bank's home page, I concluded the bill didn't matter. It had been a placeholder for competence, but now I was competent in other, more tenable ways. The same librarian sat behind the counter as before. I smiled at him. I don't know if he remembered me. I leafed through a paperback. I didn't use the toilet.

Next, I bought groceries. I passed the corner store I had gone to once already and stood outside for a moment, reminiscing about having floundered through the aisles, my fiendish laps punctuated by furious voices, somatic squeezing, and unbearable, insatiable absence. I had been there less than two weeks earlier, yet, walking through the door was like dipping into a bygone era, the spectre of a younger Nicole lingering but benign. The layout was identical. My reaction to it now was deliberate, tempered, and mild. I filled a basket with cereal, chocolate, and candy, all of which I had only ever binged on, and I envisaged going back to the Priory and storing them in my nightstand. *Practice,* I muttered, and the nightstand became a pantry, my bedroom had a kitchen, and I was a non-institutionalized, non-eating-disordered adult who could coexist with food.

This act was time conscious. My purchases had once been associated with bulimia, but inviting them into the present was preparing for a future not dictated by the past. Temporality was linear, at least mostly. This wavered when I got back to the Priory and overheard a patient shouting at his mother, in a one-sided fight over the phone. He was a new arrival. The young man drank; he couldn't leave until he completed twenty-eight-days of the ATP, and he spent his admission telling us his parents had betrayed him. Our similarities were negligible. But when he mused about eventually being homeless, my thoughts diffracted, my edges blurred, and then I aged in reverse. His naivety was too familiar. I yearned to warn him; help him; change him; but I was not this boy. This was not my business. I had gotten tired.

Seventeen

The rest of my hospitalization followed a similar pattern. I retracted when I became enmeshed with someone, and while this was upsetting, it also kept me, me. I can't say for sure if it was moral. "Morality" has competing definitions, and although caring for myself like this barred me from civic participation, "care" necessarily entails prioritizing some outcomes over others. Less cryptically, self-regulation through isolation was a technology of the self: I was "reject[ing] the [w]hole of which the [s]elf is but a part,"[29] and after getting so invested in this whole, and coming to "know" myself as of it, this rejection was disloyal – to my old subject position, to the one I co-constituted, and to those co-constituting theirs with mine. However, I never forget about the others, nor was I abdicating from collective responsibility: I was attempting to stabilize so I could fulfill these responsibilities in perpetuity.

As I write, I'm growing weary. Truthfully, I grew weary some twenty (forty, sixty, one hundred, two hundred) pages (days, weeks, years, lifetimes) ago. Can you tell? I consider now as I did then how to proceed, and now, as then, there is no correct (or "moral") answer. Technically, now the stakes are not as high. A wrong move in storytelling (which I have made several of) is not life or death (technically), whereas a wrong move at the Priory could have killed me or someone else. Imaging this is simple. After all, the literature on deep psychic exploration advises it be done with those who show "reasonable emotional balance" under the supervision of a highly skilled facilitator. While activation of the unconscious may be possible among "seriously mentally ill" people (e.g., me), "more caution and support" is required because "total loss of control" may "extend beyond the framework of the session." In other words, experiential therapy should be just that – therapy – not a weeks-long process one oversees themselves. Stanislov Grof also warns that without a facilitator, loose ends (in the form of "residual emotional and psychosomatic issues that remain unresolved") limit psychic integration.[30] I consider the year after my admission, and I believe this to be true. But, then and now, I have done my best.

To reinforce that what happened in hospital was, in Dr. Herner's words, "not exactly... psychiatric," I will share what happened on my second to last evening. It was dusk, and I was sitting in the gazebo when I heard a commotion near the front. There, patients and a care aide watched a fox limp up the driveway. It was injured, and each of the adjectives I have used to describe my body – emaciated, skeletal, cadaverous – also applied to it. I remembered the cereal I had in my bedside table/pantry and brought two cups' worth outside. I met the fox's eyes and jubilation gave way to sombreness. Starvation manifesting so clearly in another spoke to a gnawing in my belly that had only just awoken. I sprinkled the cereal in a circle. Gingerly, it ate.

This is another memory I would question had I not recorded it. Claims of intimate connection with nature are common, and without the video I still have, I might wonder if I was lying. I did just watch the video, though, and am reminded that "the boundaries between people, animals, and inanimate objects in the environment [were] an illusion"[31] at the Priory. Later, I saw the fox again. I was crouched near the side door, head pounding, stomach churning, other signs of exhaustion more conspicuous by the second. The landing would be rocky. Then the fox emerged from the shrubs, hobbled toward me, and stopped just shy of my outstretched fingers. In that moment and subsequent ones, I was no different from the fox (who was no different from the trees, which are no different from the mountains, which are no different from the soil, or the rocks, and so on). I hoped the fox would be nourished, and because I was the fox (who was the trees, which were the mountains...) I hoped the same for me. By now, the fox has likely died. But I think about it sometimes, and then I look to the trees (and the mountains, and the soil...) and am reminded of my worth.

PART ONE

Eighteen

Before I was discharged, I went out three more times. Each outing was further, more daring, and brought me closer to Vancouver. The first was to a larger town. I ate lunch in a café, and I muted the shocking sights, smells, and sounds with assiduous intent. Specifically, I observed how my abdomen contracted, expanded, and got incrementally fuller, and as I paid the bill, I was aware of and pleased with my ordinariness. Others didn't know I was rehearsing. They also didn't have to. I went to a mall. My child-sized jeans had gotten tight, and I tried on two new pairs, one that fit perfectly and one that sagged on my hips, thighs, and waist. I considered the implications of each and opted for the second, expecting to grow into them. I also brought my passport just to prove I could. Losing it in the airport would have been disastrous.

In retrospect, these and other decisions were remarkably strategic for someone who could have been psychotic. And, as much as I want to describe that which followed in detail, doing so would be redundant. Just note that my micro-acts were cumulatively more important than the sum of their parts. Their true meaning lay in how inspired I felt and together, they were an evidence-base demonstrating I could live life after choosing to. Concurrently, I was self-subjectivizing. This was counter-counter-conduct, and while I know this, a more oppressive fate might have been imposed on me had I not monitored and modified as ardently. Since I can only speculate about this fate, I must assume my extreme effort then (and now) was (and is) worthwhile (though I grew weary some twenty, forty…). Whatever the case, exposition alone would not do justice to how badly sensory input smarted or imbued you, the reader, with the felt sense of having had your reality cranked up. Consider that a good thing.

Before I left, my auditory hallucinations stopped. My brutal honesty did not, but with slower cognition came a longer second between thinking and talking to decide if I should share my mental content. I cared about social norms again, which was less cathartic but necessary to avoid future hospitalizations. The walls also stayed inert, and by my final morning, the previous three weeks felt almost like a dream. When I retrieved my belongings, a nurse leafed through my intake package.

Taped to it was a photograph, and I peered closely, spellbound by a corpse. Skin stretched over cheekbone, mouth agape, my eyes were vacant and otherworldly. I couldn't have been this person. I pocketed the photo (*I cannot afford to forget what has happened here*) and returned to it for months. Then, I let her go.

My departure was emotional. After saying goodbye, I took a taxi to Heathrow airport. I was hours early, and I felt paralyzed by the businesspeople, children, and duty-free stores selling goods that seemed innocuous but weren't. Too restless to sit or stand, I trained my eyes on the floor and walked, slow then fast, with no idea where I was going. Eventually, I got to a corridor. It was dingy and remote, so I followed it to a nondescript white door. Behind it was a multifaith prayer room. Deities sat on a shelf. They wouldn't have meant much normally but, here, they comforted me. Each of us must look for meaning somewhere. I stayed in this room until I boarded the plane. I sat in my seat and, for the first time in days (weeks, years, lifetimes), I closed my eyes and slept.

And, Then…

AND, THEN...

I LANDED IN VANCOUVER ON NOVEMBER 13, 2017. Right away, it was as though all the scary elements of my experience had been left in England. Conversations, decisions, and sleep were easy, and this made life feel easy. I stayed with Mo, as planned, and then on the couches of UBC graduate students and their roommates, until the following February. I also resumed writing, this time without the vacant urgency that possessed me at the Priory. I jotted poetry, it became essays, and before long, I had the first section of what could and would be *The Becoming*. I kept going.

That was three and a half years ago. Much has changed since, including – and especially – the book. I've been immersed in writing for so long now that I'm not even sure what it says anymore. Doubt, I think, is inevitable when a project is all encompassing. I just know I can't read, think about, or look at anything book related for a long, long time.

Concurrently, I'm not sure how I feel about being done. This has been my anchor. For example, I completed the first draft in mid-2018. I still can't explain what happened that year. I got a job, my body stopped working, I left the job, and then, seemingly overnight, I just... fractured. This may be because I could not share my experience. When I tried, I was met with pity or incredulity, and alienation gave way to voices that coalesced into a dual subjectivity distinct from anything before it, including at the Priory. Basically, I was two people. My adult self was present but was subsumed beneath a child whose threat responses were so exaggerated I was barred from social life. Even eye contact and speaking were frightening. I told Meris it felt like I (adult self) was trapped in a glass box begging oblivious passersby to let her out. The box was invisible and all I did was scream, pounding on the glass.

Returning to the book, it distracted me. I deteriorated further once I finished, at which point I had to ask for help. Unfortunately, my ability/ obligation to present "normally" obscured the severity of what was happening. My parents were impatient. Our relationship was tense, and they wondered why I wouldn't just work, practice gratitude, and so on. My roommates were confused. They didn't understand why I couldn't participate in our collective or be near the kitchen knives. And psychiatry prescribed antipsychotic sedatives and mood stabilizers with no discernable effects. Eventually, the embodied impulse to binge, purge, drink, or do something irrevocable was totalizing and severe. I couldn't leave the house. I was afraid to be with people. I was also ashamed, so I refused to apply for government assistance despite not having an income source. Calling myself disabled felt like a betrayal. Finances were an emergency, and finally, I drank. It was that or suicide. I chose harm reduction.

   I went on another, month-long bender that included housing loss, physical and sexual violence, semi-purposeful overdoses, multiple hospitalizations and the degradation that comes with them. It did end, and when it did, I could think clearly again. I believe the drugs corrected my nervous system, so while using had dramatic consequences, I do not regret it. This year also affirmed that "independence" is a myth. I may have started "self-healing" at the Priory, but I needed intensive, live-in support after I got out. Without it, not only could I not make sense of England, trying to, while performing adulthood, was like being a double agent. My depersonalization, derealization, intrusive obsessions, and command psychosis (in biomedical terms) forced me to accept that Madness and disability are permanent ways of being. And now, I imagine disability justice entrenched in our institutions. Reflecting on this has complicated my perspective on autonomy (and time, capitalism, etc.), which is why I have incorporated this perspective into the book. Stanislov Grof's warning about "residual emotional and psychosomatic issues… remain[ing] unresolved" is prescient. In this vein, I am heartened by the work of grassroots Mad coalitions and abolitionists who propose alternatives to carceral interventions. Perhaps those in positions of real power will one day choose to listen.

   In 2019, I brought these considerations with me to rural Alberta. I was bulimic again (and still am) but had decoupled this behaviour from alcohol and drug use. I taught college and was tentatively optimistic about finding a progressive friend group. But amid a busy schedule and a global pandemic, I didn't focus on socializing. Instead, I revised the book. With this next draft, the trend of delineating "what it was like," "what happened," and "what it's like now," as is done in AA, didn't seem appropriate. Traditional memoir obscures the tensions in getting or being "well," and to counter that, I moved away from "raising awareness about" or "de-stigmatizing" serious mental illness. Doing so is honourable but demands serious interrogation of our reliance on psychiatry. As I see it, "awareness" is a nonsense word. Medical sociology, Mad studies, and critical drug studies also make clear that "stigma" is mostly devoid of meaning. That is, we can't discuss de-stigmatization before defining stigma, and as with "addiction," "eating disorders," and "serious mental illness" itself, our attachment to static, a-historic biomedicine precludes transformative dialogue. If nothing else, then, I have sought to make visible how our shared assumptions (about sane/crazy, right/wrong, good/bad, and so on) benefit those who make us sick in the first place. This is not a "recovery narrative." I am not "inspirational." I am one Mad woman. This is my rebuttal.

More recently, I am back in Vancouver. I keep saying I want to leave, and I keep having nowhere else to be. I do have friends – good, loyal friends – and they mean a lot. I am also plagued with existential dread and may have suicided had it not been for the book. Yet I can't accept being enshrined in medical records and my parents' hyperbole. So many of my peers have died without being consulted on how they lived. Their silencing is deafening. Related, earlier drafts contained more detail about my family. However, I stopped speaking to them before moving to Alberta. My last bout of substance use cemented their dangerousness, and my psychic shifts since are nothing short of remarkable. Thus, while my mother is a skillful victim, and I worry about having eliminated important context, revenge has lost its appeal. My parents will always be here. I don't think about them much.

I have also started referring to myself as neurodivergent/autistic. Last year, a practitioner placed me on the spectrum but couldn't say what that means in practice. Many autistic traits overlap with trauma responses, and I have learned to suppress both. Regardless, acquiring one more label does not change my thoughts on labels. I sense that had my parents known how to accommodate my idiosyncrasies, including my eating disorder (which maybe didn't have to become a full-blown eating disorder), and had I not gotten so traumatized, my "serious," *scary* symptoms may not have started later. Or maybe they still would have. There are endless "what-if's," and trying to parse out cause from effect while mired in regret is not much of a life. In addition to a rebuttal, then, this is a conclusion. I have not stopped thinking (if only), but I am prepared to put the diagnostic (and anti-diagnostic) manuals away, at least until I'm not. Now I walk on my toes, flap my arms, and rock back and forth when I want to. That's what really matters.

In terms of your reading of the book, I have offered a roadmap through ideas. Like an introductory course, my conceptual schema is breadth-y, but lacks depth. Writing and thinking this way is pleasurable but not the same as comprehensive theorizing. You are invited to explore further. You are welcome not to. Just don't confuse the two. Also note that superficiality could cause lateral harm. Specifically, Madness, disability, alcoholism, illicit drug use, housing insecurity, and disordered eating are racialized, classed, and gendered. Mine co-occur with privileges, and I have epistemic limitations. For example, I have not shied away from the word "addiction." This is because I am rarely perceived as an "addict," and I can dispel misinformation eloquently, at home, behind the safety of a screen. But drug use (and Madness, disability…) are not homogenous categories. Most Mad, disabled, housing insecure drug users with eating disorders will not end up at Oxford, irrespective of their effort. And, if you think they should, you will have missed the point.

Reconciling my liminality will be a forever process. As I write this, I am thirty-two years old. It has been three and a half years since I started *The Becoming*, six years since I sent the letter, six and a half years since I started working with Meris, and ten years since I sat in my first sociology course and learned about Dr. Bruce Alexander and the Rat Park experiments. For a decade I have learned and unlearned, learned and unlearned, propelled forward by the near-primal conviction that I am so much more than sick and/or bad. I have been sober, and I have been drunk. I have obtained bachelors' and masters' degrees, and I have come to, dazed and incoherent, covered in syringes and cockroaches on piss-stained mattresses in government-funded hotels on Vancouver's Downtown Eastside. I have been a Clarendon scholar, elegant and effervescent, and I have been 50, 60, 70 per cent dead, fortunate to have overdosed in public where other users could find me. I am thirty-two. I live and work in Vancouver. I am not yet certain where I will be when I am thirty-three, but one thing I do know: I am lying dormant, biding time, and growing stronger.

AND, THEN...

I have more to say but will leave it at that. As with every story, this one has been subjective. I have been frank. I have been obtuse. You have not met all of me. I also predict that some of what has seemed salient theoretically and personally may be less so in the future. Finally, I am aware that inevitable critiques of this text will be that it is disjointed and erratic. To this I say, *welcome to my world*. By now, I have lived at the Priory for years. Simultaneously, I am nineteen in a taxi, I am five in my childhood bed, and I am twenty-nine (five, four, three, two, one) as a stranger passes me a hit. As I said to Meris recently, with all these fragments suspended in time and space, I'm not sure what (if anything) is left. And yet, my eyes are heavy, the somatic pain throbs, and breath enters then leaves my lungs.

Inhale.
Exhale.
In.
Out.

My brain is not broken. My body is not broken. My soul is not broken. However, each has been brutally beaten. I am in a perpetual state of mourning for something that never was. And, while there is "truth" in Mad studies, medical sociology, transpersonal psychology, neurobiology, and, yes, psychiatry, I might also just be sad. I'm not sure what I'll do now. Fortunately, I have time.

Acknowledgements

My life is thirty-two years' worth of moments. Together, they form a messy constellation that has mostly been forgotten (or didn't register at all), yet even the most fleeting of these inputs has shaped who and what I am. I can't begin to acknowledge everyone who matters. The few who do stand out have left indelible marks on one or more of the Nicole(s). Without them, I and this book would not exist.

Daniel Oudshoorn. You met me when I was nineteen years old and wasted in every sense of the word. I still remember Christine being excited to introduce us, and I quickly realized that of all the people being paid to care for me, what you offered was different. You have shown me a depth of respect and humanity far beyond what one would reasonably expect to receive, not just during our particular, peculiar interactions, but from anyone, any time. By now, I'm not sure where your voice ends and mine begins. You are brilliant in the textbook sense, which I appreciate, and in more important ways, which has been the distinction between life and death. Thank you for your humour, for making difficult decisions when I haven't wanted you to, and for reminding me, also when I haven't wanted you to, that I am beloved. You taught me to burn bridges – now I know to swim.

Meris Williams. I told you immediately to earn my trust. You did. Your compassion, frankness, and generosity have distinguished you from countless professionals, as has your humility. We both knew that you wouldn't fix me, but unlike the others, you didn't insist you could. Rather, you gave me permission to feel, felt alongside me, and, in so doing, showed me that I may not actually need to be fixed, after all. Thank you for always meeting me where I was, especially when we both wanted to be somewhere – anywhere – else. I still talk to you.

Richard Ingram. Our friendship is sporadic and strange, and I'm not sure how we met. Regardless, I am grateful for it – and you – and whether you know it or not, you have been instrumental in my learning. You introduced me to Mad studies, bought me texts that I wouldn't have otherwise found, and were the first person to read what would eventually be *The Becoming*. I so appreciate your quiet, steady encouragement. Your wisdom is astonishing, and you have been a model of authenticity (whatever that means). I deeply admire you.

Brandon Toews and Andy (Rouchen) Sun. I don't know where I would be without you. At times you have literally carried me, and when the carrying has been figurative, your validation has been relentless. Your consistency and acceptance are unmatched. Thank you for advocating on my behalf, for your willingness to see me, and for maintaining senses of humour about it all. Hopefully the frantic midnight messages can abate for a while.

Mo Ismailzai. I have been honoured to share life with you, even from afar. Sometimes your optimism annoys me, and then I remember that praise doesn't have to be scary. Thank you for showing up in subtle ways with no (or few) questions asked. We may not always understand each other, but you have trusted me to tell you what I need. You see in me what I know is there, and I hope to have reciprocated. I love watching you feel good.

Adam Howe, Max Chewinski, and the 2015 UBC sociology graduate cohort. You were there for me before any of this made sense. Thank you for listening to my ideas, academic and otherwise, for going out of your way to accommodate me, and for not shying away from the messiness. I couldn't have asked for a more welcoming group of colleagues/friends/supporters.

Luciana Ricciutelli, Renée Knapp, and Inanna Publications. Having re-read the draft of the book that you decided to publish, I'm still a bit shocked that you saw its potential. Thank you for responding to my (sometimes too eager) queries and for giving me so much agency. I'm disappointed that I won't get to know Luciana as I would have liked to, and I will forever be grateful for all your hard work amidst so much unpredictability. I am honoured to have been included.

Mary Newberry. Thank you for your helping me get this book over the finish line. Your keen eye has been a blessing.

The thousands of people I have met in homeless centres, psychiatric wards, eating disorder and addiction treatment, detox, drug user networks, supervised consumption sites, back alleys, and SROs. None of you consented to being part of my character development. I do not see you that way. Some of us formed intractable bonds, but much more often we simply collided at the intersections of state and other neglect. In solidarity.

And to my parents – thank you for forcing me to come to my own conclusions about what it means to be good.

NOTES

INTRODUCTION

1. I am paraphrasing the introduction of Amber Dawn's *How Poetry Saved My Life: A Hustler's Memoir* (2013, Vancouver: Arsenal Pulp Press).
2. American Psychiatric Association (2013), *Diagnostic and Statistical Manual of Mental Disorders: DSM-5* (Arlington, VA).
3. Berlant, L. G. (2011), *Cruel Optimism* (Durham: Duke University Press).

PART SIX

1. See Turpel-Lafond, M-E. (2020), *In Plain Sight: Addressing Indigenous-specific Racism and Discrimination in B.C. Health Care*.
2. Alexander, B., Coambs, R. B., & Hadaway, P. F. (1978), The effect of housing and gender on morphine self-administration in rats, *Psychopharamacology*, 5(8): 175–179; Gage, S.H., & Sumnall, H.R. (2018), Rat Park: How a rat paradise changed the narrative of addiction, *Addiction*, 114(5): 917–922.
3. See Williams, P. (2012), *Rethinking Madness: Towards a Paradigm Shift in Our Understanding and Treatment of Psychosis* (San Francisco: Sky's Edge).
4. See for example Smith, D. E. (1978), "K is mentally ill": The anatomy of a factual account, *Sociology*, 12(1): 23–53.
5. See Cerniglia, L., Cimino, S., Tafa, M., Marzilli, E., Ballarotto, G., & Bracaglia, F. (2017), Family profiles in eating disorders: Family functioning and psychopathology, *Psychology Research and Behavior Management*, 10: 305–312.
6. Dej, E. (2016), Psychocentrism and homelessness: The pathologization/responsibilization paradox, *Studies in Social Justice*, 10(1): 117–135.
7. See Nokleby, H. (2012), Comorbid drug use disorders and eating disorders: A review of prevalence studies, *Nordic Studies on Alcohol and Drugs*, 29(3): 303–314; Piran, N., & Gadalla, T. (2007), Eating disorders and substance abuse in Canadian women: A nationally representative sample, *Addiction*, 102(1): 105–113.

8. Goffman, E. (2008), *The Presentation of Self in Everyday Life* (New York: Anchor Books/Random House).
9. See Mandy, W., Chilvers, R., Chowdhury, U., Salter, G., Seigal, A., & Skuse, D. (2012), Sex differences in autism spectrum disorder: Evidence from a large sample of children and adolescents, *Journal of Autism and Developmental Disorders*, 42(7): 1304–1313; Rivet, T. F., & Matson, J. L. (2011), Review of gender differences in core symptomatology in autism spectrum disorders, *Research in Autism Spectrum Disorders*, 5(3): 957–976; Worzynski, K., Ronald, A., Bolton, P., & Happé, F. (2012), How different are girls and boys above and below the diagnostic threshold for autism spectrum disorders? *Journal of the American Academy of Child and Adolescent Psychiatry*, 51(8): 788–797.
10. See Gupta, M. A. (2012), Review of somatic symptoms in post-traumatic stress disorder, *International Review of Psychiatry*, 25(1): 86–99.

PART FIVE

1. See Bourdieu, P. (1986), The forms of capital, in G. Richardson (Ed.), *Handbook of Theory and Research for the Sociology of Education* (Westport, CT: Greenwood Press).
2. For a discussion of the benefits and drawbacks of post-structuralist interview framework, see Grant, A. (2014), Troubling "lived experience": A post-structural critique of mental health nursing qualitative research assumptions, *Journal of Psychiatric and Mental Health Nursing*, 21(6): 544–554; Weedon, C. (1987), *Feminist Practice and Poststructuralist Theory* (Oxford: Blackwell).
3. Luongo, N. (2018), Disappearing in plain sight: An exploratory study of co-occurring eating and substance abuse dis/orders among homeless youth in Vancouver, Canada, *Women's International Forum*, 67(1): 38–44.
4. For a review of the literature on the relationship between eating disorder symptomology and socioeconomic status, see Gard, M. C., & Freeman, C. P. (1996), The dismantling of a myth: A review of eating disorders and socioeconomic status, *International Journal of Eating Disorders*, 20(1): 1–12. For further commentary on rates of eating disorder diagnoses stratified by race/ethnicity in nationally representative, American samples, see Franko, D. L. (2007), Race, ethnicity, and eating disorders: Considerations for DSM-V, *International Journal of Eating Disorders*,

40(S3).

5. See Foucault, M. (2020), *Discipline and Punish: The Birth of the Prison* (New York: S. I. International).

6. Here I am paraphrasing some of the ideas expressed in my master's thesis. The references are as follows: see Gone, J. (2008), Mental health discourses and western mental health proselytization, *Ethos*, 36(3): 310–315; Grant, A. (2014), Troubling "lived experience": A post-structural critique of mental health nursing qualitative research assumptions, *Journal of Psychiatric and Mental Health Nursing*, 21: 544–549; Adams, S., & Pierre, E. (1998), Poststructural feminism in education: An overview, *International Journal of Qualitative Studies in Education*, 13(5): 477–515.

7. See Foucault, M. (2010), *The Archeology of Knowledge and the Discourse on Language* (New York: Vintage Books).

8. See Berk, M. (2013), The DSM-5: Hyperbole, hope, or hypothesis? *BMC Medical*, 11(1): 128–130.

9. Strakowski, S. M. (2014), *Bipolar Disorder* (Oxford American Psychiatry Library, Oxford: Oxford University Press), p. 6.

10. See Read, J., van Os, J., Morrisson, A. P., & Ross, C. A. (2005), Childhood trauma, psychosis, and schizophrenia: A literature review with theoretical and clinical implications, *Acta Psychiatrica Scandinavia*, 112(5): 330–350.

11. See Bentall, R. P., Wickham, S., Shevlin, M., & Varese, F. (2012), Do specific early-life adversities lead to specific symptoms of psychosis? A study from the 2007 The Adult Psychiatric Morbidity Survey, *Schizophrenia Bulletin*, 38(4): 734–740.

12. See Boschloo, L., Vogelzangs, N., Licht, C. M., Vreeburg, S. A., Smit, J. H., Brink, W. V. D., ... Penninx, B. W. (2011), Heavy alcohol use, rather than alcohol dependence, is associated with dysregulation of the hypothalamic-pituitary-adrenal axis and the autonomic nervous system, *Drug and Alcohol Dependence*, 116(1–3): 170–176; Vale, A. (2008), Alcohol withdrawal syndrome, *The Foundation Years*, 4(2): 55–58.

13. See Breese, G. R., Overstreet, D. H., & Knapp, D. J. (2005), Conceptual framework for the etiology of alcoholism: A "kindling"/stress hypothesis, *Psychopharmacology*, 178(4): 367–380; Brown, M. E., Anton, R. F., Malcolm, R., & Ballenger, J. C. (1988), Alcohol detoxification and withdrawal seizures: Clinical support for a kindling hypothesis, *Biological Psychiatry*, 23(5): 507–514.

14. For an historical overview of gender bias in psychiatric nosology, see Ussher J. M. (2013), Diagnosing difficult women and pathologizing

femininity: Gender bias in psychiatric nosology, *Feminism and Psychology,* 23(1): 63–69.
15. See for example Gitlin M. (2016), Lithium side effects and toxicity: Prevalence and management strategies, *International Journal of Bipolar Disorders,* 4(1): 1–10.
16. See Lehmann, P. (2002), *Coming Off Psychiatric Drugs: Successful Withdrawal from Neuroleptics, Antidepressants, Lithium, Carbamzepine and Tranquilizers* (Berlin: Peter Lehmann Publishing).
17. Hari, J. (2015), *Chasing the Scream: The First and Last Days of the War on Drugs* (New York: Bloomsbury). For a perspective from medical sociology on how addiction came to be seen as a medical issue, see Anderson, T., Swan, H., & Lane, D. C. (2010), Institutional fads and the medicalization of drug addiction, *Sociology Compass,* 4(7): 476–494. See also Rosenthal, R. J., & Faris, S. B. (2019), The etymology and early history of "addiction," *Addiction Research & Theory,* 27(5), 437–449. For a post-humanist view on how to theorize loss of control in addiction, see Weinberg, D. (2013), Post-humanism, addiction and the loss of self-control: Reflections on the missing core in addiction science, *International Journal of Drug Policy,* 24(3): 173–181.

PART FOUR

1. Saltzman, L. Y. (2013), It's about time: Reconceptualizing the role of time and loss in trauma, *Psychological Trauma: Theory, Research, Practice, and Policy,* 11(6): 663–670.
2. See Anderson, M. C., & Huddleston, E. (2011), Towards a cognitive and neurobiological model of motivated forgetting, *True and False Recovered Memories Nebraska Symposium on Motivation,* 53–120; Smith, S. M., & Moynan, S. C. (2008), Forgetting and recovering the unforgettable, *Psychological Science,* 19(5): 462–468; Conway, M. A., Anderson, S. J., Larsen, S. F., Donnelly, C. M., McDaniel, M. A., McClelland, A. G. R., … Logie, R. H. (1994), The formation of flashbulb memories, *Memory and Cognition,* 22: 326–343. For a synthesis of the literature on current debates about traumatic memory, see Brewin, C. R. (2016), Coherence, disorganization, and fragmentation in traumatic memory: A response to Rubin et al., *Journal of Abnormal Psychology,* 125(7): 1011–1017.
3. For a critical exploration of the PTSD diagnosis, including the sociocultural-political context in which it emerged and how it become "ubiq-

uitous," see Horowitz, A. V. (2018), *PTSD: A Short History* (Baltimore: Johns Hopkins University Press). For a popular exploration of how the body and mind adapt to traumatic stress, see Bessel A. van der Kolk's *The Body Keeps the Score: Brain, Mind, and Body in the Healing of Trauma* (2014, New York: Viking). For a discussion about how disorientation can positively motivate people to behave differently toward themselves and others, Harbin, A. (2014), Disorientation and the medicalization of struggle, *International Journal of Feminist Approaches to Bioethics*, 7(1): 99–121; Harbin, A. (2012), Bodily disorientation and moral change, *Hypatia: A Journal of Feminist Philosophy*, 27(2): 261–280.

4. For the Minnesota starvation experiment, see Keys, A., Brozek, J., Henschel, A., Mickelson, O., & Taylor, H. L. (1950), *The Biology of Human Starvation* (2 vols.) (Oxford, UK: University of Minnesota Press).

5. See Wabnitz, P., Gast, U., & Catani, C. (2013), Differences in psychopathology between PTSD patients with and without co-occurring dissociative disorders, *European Journal of Psychotraumatology*, 4(1): 21452. See also Nijenhuis, E. R. S., Spinhoven, P., Dyck, R. V., Hart, O. V. D., & Vanderlinden, J. (1998), Degree of somatoform and psychological dissociation in dissociative disorder is correlated with reported trauma, *Journal of Traumatic Stress*, 11(4): 711–730; Sinason, V. (2011), *Attachment, Trauma, and Multiplicity: Working with Dissociative Identity Disorder* (London: Routledge).

Later, I return to dissociation and describe the links between it and neurocognitive impairments in bipolar disorder. The literature cited is as follows: Dorahy, M. J. (2001), Dissociative identity disorder and memory dysfunction: The current state of experimental research and its future directions, *Clinical Psychology Review*, 21(5): 771–795; Braehler, C., Valiquette, L., Holowka, D., Malla, A. K., Joober, R., Ciampi, A., ... King, S. (2013), Childhood trauma and dissociation in first-episode psychosis, chronic schizophrenia, and community controls, *Psychiatry Research*, 210(1): 36–42; Eryilmaz, G., Kesebir, S., Gul, I. G., Ozten, E., & Karamustafalioglu, K. O. (2015), Dissociative experiences in bipolar disorder II: Are they related to childhood trauma and obsessive-compulsive symptoms? *Archives of Clinical Psychiatry*, 42(2): 38–40; Martinez-Aran, A., Torrent, C., Tabares-Seisdedos, R., Salamero, M., Daban, C., Balanza-Martinez, V., Sanchez-Moreno, J., Goikolea, J. M., Benabarre, A., Colom, F., & Vieta, E. (2008), Neurocognitive impairment in bipolar patients with and without history of psychosis, *The Journal of Clinical Psychiatry*, 69(2): 233–239; Glahn, D. C., Bearden, C. E., Cakir, S., Barrett, J. A., Najt, P., Monkul, E. S., Maples, N., Velligan,

D. I., & Soares, J. C. (2006), Differential working memory impairment in bipolar disorder and schizophrenia: Effects of lifetime history of psychosis, *Bipolar Disorders*, 8(2): 117–123.

PART THREE

1. Some of the works drawn from and cited in Parts 3–1, in order of appearance, are as follows: Grof, C., & Grof, S. (2017), Spiritual emergency: The understanding and treatment of transpersonal crises, *International Journal of Transpersonal Studies*, 36(2): 30–43; Viggiano, D. B., & Krippner, S. (2010), The Grof's model of spiritual emergency in retrospect: Has it stood the test of time? *The International Journal of Transpersonal Studies*, 29(1): 118–127; Deikman, A. J. (1971), Bimodal consciousness, *Archives of General Psychiatry*, 25(6): 481; Deikman, A. J. (n.d.), Deautomatization and the mystic experience (available at www.deikman.com); Perry, J. W. (1999), *Trials of the Visionary Mind: Spiritual Emergency and the Renewal Process* (Albany, NY: State University of New York Press); St. Arnaud, K. O., & Cormier, D. C. (2017), Psychosis or spiritual emergency: The potential of developmental psychopathology for differential diagnosis, *International Journal of Transpersonal Studies*, 36(2): 44–59; Bragdon, E. (2006), *A Sourcebook for Helping People with Spiritual Problems*, 2nd ed. (Woodstock, VT: Lightening Up Press); Hardy, A. (1979), *The Spiritual Nature of Man* (Oxford: Oxford University Press); Collins, M. (2008), Spiritual emergency: Transpersonal, personal, and political dimensions, *Psychotherapy and Politics International*, 6(1): 3–16; Grof, S., & Grof, C. (1991), *The Stormy Search for the Self: Understanding and Living with Spiritual Emergency* (Los Angeles: Thorsons); Clarke, I. (Ed.) (2010), *Psychosis and Spirituality: Consolidating the New Paradigm,* 2nd ed. (Chichester, UK: John Wiley); Jung, C. G., & Hull, R. F. C. (2011), *Synchronicity: An Acausal Connecting Principle* (Princeton, NJ: Princeton University Press); Jung, C. G. (1969), *Aion: Researches into the Phenomenology of the Self,* Collected Works of C. G. Jung, vol. 9, Part 2 (Princeton, NJ: Princeton University Press), p. 8 par 14.
2. Moncrieff, J. (2013), *The Bitterest Pill: The Troubling Story of Anti-Psychotic Drugs* (London: Palgrave); Moncrieff, J. (2009), *The Myth of a Chemical Cure: A Critique of Psychiatric Drug Treatment* (New York: Palgrave Macmillan).

3. Laing, R. D. (1967), *The Politics of Experience* (New York: Pantheon Books), p. 76.
4. Rothberg D. (2003), cited in Caplan, M., Hartelius, G., & Rardin, M., Contemporary viewpoints on transpersonal psychology, *Journal of Transpersonal Psychology*, 35(2): 143–162.
5. See for example Deutsch, H. (1942), Some forms of emotional disturbance and their relation to schizophrenia, *The Psychoanalytic Quarterly*, 11(3): 301–321; Zanderson, M., & Parnas, J. (2018), Identity disturbance, feelings emptiness, and the boundaries of the schizophrenic spectrum, *Schizophrenia Bulletin*, 45(1): 106–113.
6. Klein, M. (2017), Notes on some schizoid mechanisms, *The Psychoanalytical Quarterly* 18(1): 122–132. (Original work published 1946).
7. Weber, M. (1930), *The Protestant Work Ethic and the Spirit of Capitalism* (London: Unwin University Books).
8. Jung, C. G., & Campbell, J. (1976), *The Portable Jung* (New York: Penguin Books); Jung, C. G. (1968), Archetypes of the collective unconscious, in H. Read, M. Fordham, G. Adler, & W. McGuire (Eds.), *The Collected Works of C. G. Jung*, trans. R. F. C. Hull, 2nd ed., vol. 9i (Princeton, NJ: Princeton University Press, original work published 1934). See also von Franz, M. L. (2016), Confrontations with the collective unconscious, *Psychological Perspectives,* 59(3): 295–318.
9. Durschlag, H. B. (2016), Severe mental illness: A bridge between neurochemistry and the collective unconscious, *Psychological Perspectives*, 59(1): 30–45.
10. See Coate, M. (1965), *Beyond All Reason* (Philadelphia: Lippincott); Custance, J. (1954), *Adventure into The Unconscious* (London, UK: Christopher Johnson).
11. For neurophysiological work on embodied trauma, see Horowitz, M. J. (1986), Stress-response syndromes: A review of posttraumatic and adjustment disorders, *Hospital and Community Psychiatry*, 37(3): 241–249; van der Kolk, B. A. (1994), The body keeps the score: Memory and the evolving psychobiology of posttraumatic stress, *Harvard Review of Psychiatry*, 1(5): 253–265; Crawford, A. (2010), If "the body keeps the score": Mapping the dissociated body in trauma narrative, intervention, and theory, *University of Toronto Quarterly,* 79(2): 702–219.
12. Lukoff, D. (1988), Transpersonal perspectives on manic psychosis, *The Journal of Transpersonal Psychology*, 20(2): 111–139.
13. See Bateson, G. (1972), *Steps to an Ecology of Mind: Collected Essays in Anthropology, Psychiatry, Evolution, and Epistemology* (San Francisco:

Chandler Publishing Company).

14. See Laing, R. D. (1960), *The Divided Self* (London: Penguin Books); Scott, S., & Thorpe, C. (2006), The sociological imagination of R. D. Laing, *Sociological Theory*, 24(4): 331–352.
15. See Laing, R. D. (2013), Mystification, confusion, and conflict, in Boszormenyi-Nagy, I., & Framo, J. L. (Eds.), *Intensive Family Therapy: Theoretical and Practical Aspects* (Florence: Taylor & Francis).

PART TWO

1. Perry (1999), *Trials of the Visionary Mind*.
2. See for example Derrida, J., Bass, J., & Norris, C. (2002), *Positions* (London: Continuum). See also Foucault, Michel (1980), *The History of Sexuality, Vol. 1: An Introduction*, trans. R. Hurley (New York: Vintage Books); Foucault, Michel (1983), The subject and power, in H. L. Dreyfus and P. Rabinow, *Michel Foucault Beyond Structuralism and Hermeneutics* (Chicago: University of Chicago Press), pp. 366, 393.
3. For a more recent adaptation of Grof's ideas in relation to the subtle body, see Louchakova, O., & Warner, A. S. (2003), Via Kundalini: Psychosomatic excursions in transpersonal psychology, *The Humanistic Psychologist*, 31(2–3): 115–158.
4. Grof, S. (1988), *The Adventure of Self-Discovery: Dimensions of Consciousness and New Perspectives in Psychotherapy and Inner Exploration* (Albany, NY: State University of New York Press), p. 47.
5. Paraphrased from Owens, C., & Dein, S. (2006), Conversion disorder: The modern hysteria, *Advances in Psychiatric Treatment*, 12(2): 152–157. See also Redinger, M. J., Crutchfield, P., Gibb, T. S., Longstreet, P., & Strung, P. (2018), Conversion disorder diagnosis and medically unexplained symptoms, *American Journal of Bioethics*, 18(5): 31–33; Kim, A. (2018), Management of psychogenic nonepileptic seizures, *The American Journal of Psychiatry Residents' Journal*, 2–4; Ali, S., Jabeen, S., Pate, R. J., Shahid, M., Chinala, S., Nathani, M., & Shah, R. (2015), Conversion disorder: Mind versus body: a review, *Innovations in Clinical Neuroscience*, 12(5-6): 27–33.
6. See for example Morrison, P. D., & Murray, R. M. (2009), From real-world events to psychosis: The emerging neuropharmacology of delusions, *Schizophrenia Bulletin*, 35(4): 668–674.

7. See Goffman, E. (1961), *Asylums: Essays on the Condition of the Social Situation in Mental Patients and Other Inmates* (Chicago: Aldine Pub Co).
8. See *The Guardian* (2016, June 2), Inquest finds neglect by The Priory contributed to teen's accidental death; *The Guardian* (2019, May 11). Priory Health Group "put profit above safety" in teenager's death.
9. See for example Conrad, P., & Schneider, J. W. (1992), *Deviance and Medicalization: From Badness to Sickness* (Philadelphia: Temple University Press).
10. See Ka Hon Chu, S. (2014), *Brief to the House of Commons Standing Committee on Justice and Human Rights regarding its study of Bill C-36, the Protection of Communities and Exploited Persons Act* (pp. 1–9); Fritz, K., Heynen, R., Ross, A. M., & van der Meulen, E. (2016), Disability and sex work: Developing affinities through decriminalization, *Disability and Society*, 1, 84–99.
11. See Parsons, T. (1951), *The Social System* (Glencoe, IL: The Free Press). For a modern critique, see for example Varul, M. Z. (2010), Talcott Parsons, the sick role, and chronic illness, *Body and Society*, 16(2): 72–94.
12. See Lemert, E. M. (1951), *Social Pathology: A Systematic Approach to the Theory of Sociopathic Behavior* (New York: McGraw-Hill); Lemert, E. M. (1967), *Human Deviance, Social Problems, and Social Control* (Englewood Cliffs, NJ: Prentice-Hall).
13. See Bradstreet, S. (2006), Harnessing the "lived experience": Formalising peer support approaches to promote recovery, *The Mental Health Review*, 11(2): 33–37; Faulkner, A., & Basset, T. (2012), A long and honourable history, *Journal of Mental Health Training*, 7(2): 53–59; Voronka, J. (2017), Turning Mad knowledge into affective labor: The case of the peer-support worker, *American Quarterly*, 69(2): 333–338; Brown, C., & Stastny, P. (2016), Peer workers in the mental health system: A transformative or collusive experiment?, in J. Russo & A. Sweeney (Eds.), *Searching for a Rose Garden: Challenging Psychiatry, Fostering Mad Studies* (Monmouth: PCCS Books), pp. 183–191.
14. See Davidson, L., O'Connell, M., Tondora, J., Staeheli, M., & Evans, A. (2005), Recovery in serious mental illness: A new wine or just a new bottle? *Professional Psychology: Research and Practice*, 36(5): 480–487; Woods, A., Hart, A., & Spandler, H. (2019), The recovery narrative: Politics and possibilities of a genre, *Culture, Medicine, and Psychiatry*.
15. See Porges, S. (2011), *The Polyvagal Theory: Neurophysiological Foundations of Emotions, Attachment, Communication, and Self-regulation*, Norton Series on Interpersonal Neurobiology (New York: Norton), as cited in

van der Kolk, B. A. (2014), *The Body Keeps the Score: Brain, Mind, and Body in the Healing of Trauma* (New York, NY: Viking), pp. 90, 99.
16. See Acharya, S., & Shukla, S. (2012), Mirror neurons: Enigma of the metaphysical modular brain, *Journal of Natural Science, Biology, and Medicine,* 3(2): 118–124.

PART ONE

1. Hall, E. T. (1983), *The Dance of Life: The Other Dimension of Time* (Garden City, NY: Anchor/Doubleday), pp. 44–58. See also Kaufman-Scarborough, C., & Lindquist, J. D. (1999), Time management and polychronicity: Comparisons, contrasts, and insights for the workplace, *Journal of Managerial Psychology,* 14(3/4): 288–312.
2. Adorno, T. W. (1991), *The Culture Industry: Selected Essays on Mass Culture,* ed. Bernstein, J. (London: Routledge), p. 187. For related content, see Osborne, P. (1995), *The Politics of Time: Modernity and Avant-Garde* (London: Verso).
3. See Foucault, M. (2003), *Society Must Be Defended: Lectures at the College de France, 1975–76* (New York: Picador); Foucault, M., Senellart, M., Ewald, F., & Fontana, A. (2009), *Security, Territory, Population: Lectures at the College de France, 1977–78* (New York, NY: Picador/Palgrave Macmillan); Foucault, Michel (1982), Technologies of the self: Lectures at University of Vermont (Oct.), in *Technologies of the Self* (University of Massachusetts Press, 1988), pp. 16–49; Foucault, M. (1977), *Discipline and Punish: The Birth of the Prison,* trans. Alan Sheridan (New York: Vintage). See also Hancock, B. H. (2018), Michel Foucault and the problematics of power: Theorizing DTCA and medicalized subjectivity, *The Journal of Medicine and Philosophy: A Forum for Bioethics and Philosophy of Medicine,* 43(4): 439–468; Bonnafous-Boucher, M. (2010), The concept of subjectivation: A central issue in governmentality and government of the self, in Binkley, S., & Capetillo, J. (Eds.), *A Foucault for the Twenty-First Century: Governmentality, Biopolitics, and Discipline in the New Millennium* (Newcastle upon Tyne, UK: Cambridge Scholars Publishing), pp. 72–89. For a Foucauldian perspective on time and resistance see Lilja, M. (2018), The politics of time and temporality in Foucault's theorisation of resistance: Ruptures, time lags, and decelerations, *Journal of Political Power,* 11(3): 419–432.

4. Laing (1960), *The Divided Self*, p. 39.
5. Kelly, M. G. E. (2013), Foucault, subjectivity, and technologies of the self, in Falzon, C., O'Learly, T., & Sawicki, J. (Eds.), *A Companion to Foucault*, pp. 510–525.
6. See Giddens, A. (1991), *Modernity and Self-Identity: Self and Society in the Late Modern Age* (Stanford, CA: Stanford University Press), p. 36.
7. See Laing (1960), The Divided Self, pp. 43–47.
8. Laing (1960), *The Divided Self*, p. 58.
9. Grof & Grof (1989), *Spiritual Emergency*, p. x.
10. See Hanisch, C., The Personal Is Political (carolhanisch.org); Hanisch, C. (2015), *The Combahee River Collective Statement* (Library of Congress, Web Archives).
11. See Briskin, A. (2016), *Stirring of Soul in the Workplace* (Sydney, NSW: ReadHowYouWant.com); Jennings, H., Jennings, M-L., & Madge, C. (2012), *Pandemonium, 1660–1886: The Coming of the Machine as Seen by Contemporary Observers* (London: Icon); Semple, J. (2003), *Bentham's Prison: A Study of the Panopticon Penitentiary* (Oxford: Clarendon Press), pp. 3–4; Foucault, M. (2020), *Discipline and Punish: The Birth of the Prison* (New York: S. I. International).
12. Smith, D. (1978), "K is mentally ill": 23–53.
13. Paraphrased from Deveaux, M. (1994), Feminism and empowerment: A critical reading of Foucault, *Feminist Studies*, 20, No. 2, *Women's Agency: Empowerment and the Limits of Resistance*, 223–247.
14. See Rinaldi, J., LaMarre, A., & Rice, C. (2016), Recovering bodies: The production of the recoverable subject in eating disorder treatment regimes, in J. Coffey, S. Budgeon, & H. Cahill (Eds.), *Learning Bodies: The Body in Youth and Childhood Studies* (Singapore: Springer), pp. 157–172; Lester, R. J. (1997), The (dis)embodied self in anorexia nervosa, *Social Science & Medicine*, 44(4): 479–489; Lock, A., Epston, D., Maisel, R., & Faria, N. de. (2005), Resisting anorexia/bulimia: Foucauldian perspectives in narrative therapy, *British Journal of Guidance & Counselling*, 33(3): 315–332. See also, for example, Dell'Osso, L., Abelli, M., Carpita, B., Pino, S., Castellini, G., Carmassi, C., & Ricca, V. (2016), Historical evolution of the concept of anorexia nervosa and relationships with orthorexia nervosa, autism, and obsessive-compulsive spectrum, *Neuropsychiatric Disease and Treatment*, 12, 1651–1660.
15. Perry (1999), *Trials of the Visionary Mind*, pp. 135–136.
16. Hancock, B. H. (2018), Michel Foucault and the problematics of power: Theorizing DTCA and medicalized subjectivity, *The Journal of Medicine*

      and Philosophy: A Forum for Bioethics and Philosophy of Medicine, 43(4): 439–468.
17. LeFrançois, B., Beresford, P., & Russo, J. (2016), Editorial: Destination Mad studies, *Intersectionalities: A Global Journal of Social Work Analysis, Research, Policy, and Practice*, 5(3).
18. Perry (1999), *Trials of the Visionary Mind*, p. 133.
19. Grof (1988), *The Adventure of Self-Discovery*, p. 259.
20. Laing (1960), *The Divided Self* (p. 41).
21. See McLuhan, M., Fiore, Q., & Agel, J. (1967), *The Medium Is the Massage: An Inventory of Effects* (New York: Random House). See also McLuhan, M. (1967, March 19), McLuhan: Now the medium is the massage, *New York Times* (timesmachine.nytimes.com).
22. Laing (1960), *The Divided Self* (p. 61).
23. Adorno (1991), *The Culture Industry*, p. 188.
24. Cooley, C. H. (1902), *Human Nature and the Social Order* (New York: Scribner's), pp. 183–184.
25. Grof, S. (1988), *The Adventure of Self-Discovery*, pp. 45–47.
26. See Mills, C. W. (2000), *The Sociological Imagination*. (Oxford: Oxford University Press), p. 6.
27. See Jung. C. G. (1971), Psychological types, in *The Collected Works of C. G. Jung*, vol. 6 (Princeton, NJ: Princeton University Press); Jung, C. G. (1969), Psychology and religion: West and east, in *The Collected Works of C. G. Jung*, vol. 11; Jung, C. G. (1966), Two essays on analytic psychology, in *The Collected Works of C. G. Jung*. vol. 7, p. 112.
28. Lilja, M. (2018), The politics of time and temporality in Foucault's theorisation of resistance: ruptures, time-lags and decelerations, *Journal of Political Power*, (3): 419–32; Foucault, M. (1990), *The History of Sexuality, Vol. 1: An Introduction*.
29. Gamez, P. (2018), Did Foucault do ethics? The "ethical turn," neoliberalism, and the problem of truth, *Journal of French and Francophone Philosophy*, XXVI(1): 107–33.
30. Grof, S. (1988), *The Adventure of Self-Discovery*, pp. 251, 252, 253. Goretzki, M. (2007), *The Differentiation of Psychosis and Spiritual Emergency* (Unpublished Doctoral Dissertation: University of Adelaide), p. 44.
31. Grof, S. (1988), *The Adventure of Self-Discovery*.

Photo credit: Veronica Cho

Nicole Luongo is a writer and educator living on the unceded territories of the xʷməθkʷəy̓əm (Musqueam), Sḵwx̱wú7mesh (Squamish), and səlilil̓wətaʔɬ (Tsleil-Waututh) Nations (colonially "Vancouver"). She holds bachelor's and master's degrees in sociology from the University of British Columbia and approximately 1/60 of a PhD from the University of Oxford. Her paid and unpaid work has been informed by experiential knowledge and is situated at the intersections of Madness, disability, drug policy, and housing justice. She is figuring out what she likes.